THE UK EQUITY GAP

To Mum and Dad

The UK Equity Gap
The Failure of Government Policy Since 1945

CHRIS LONSDALE
The University of Birmingham

Ashgate
Aldershot • Brookfield USA • Singapore • Sydney

© Chris Lonsdale 1997

All rights reserved. No part of this publication may be reproduced, stored in a retrieval system, or transmitted in any form or by any means, electronic, mechanical, photocopying, recording, or otherwise without the prior permission of the publisher.

Published by
Ashgate Publishing Limited
Gower House
Croft Road
Aldershot
Hants GU11 3HR
England

Ashgate Publishing Company
Old Post Road
Brookfield
Vermont 05036
USA

British Library Cataloguing in Publication Data
Lonsdale, Chris
   The UK equity gap : the failure of government policy since 1945
   1. Business enterprises - Great Britain - Finance 2. Venture capital -
   -Great Britain 3. Great Britain - Economic policy - 1945-
   I.Title
   338.6'041'0941'09045

Library of Congress Cataloging-in-Publication Data
Lonsdale, Chris.
   The UK equity gap : the failure of government policy since 1945 / Chris Lonsdale.
      p.   cm.
   Includes bibliographical references and index.
   ISBN 1-85521 865 8 (hardcover)
   1. Great Britain–Economic policy–1945– 2. Equity–Great Britain–History. I. Title.
   HC256.5.L63   1997
   338.941'009'045–dc21   97-23058
                                                                 CIP

ISBN 1 85521 865 8

Printed in Great Britain by The Ipswich Book Company, Suffolk.

Contents

List of Tables   *vii*
List of Abbreviations   *xi*
Preface   *xiii*

PART I: GOVERNMENT AND THE UK EQUITY GAP

1   The Financial Sector and Relative Economic Decline in the UK   3

2   Government and the UK Equity Gap Since 1945   33

PART II: THE COMPARATIVE PERFORMANCE OF GOVERNMENT POLICIES TO BRIDGE THE EQUITY GAP

3   Labour's National Enterprise Board   87

4   The Conservatives and the UK Institutional Venture Capital Industry   123

5   The Conservatives' Business Expansion Scheme   157

6   Further Evidence on Government Policy to Bridge the Equity Gap   171

PART III: CONCLUSION

7   Conclusion   187

Appendices   209
Bibliography   219
Index   235

List of Tables

1.1	Growth of GDP 1962 to 1972	7
1.2	Percentage Shares of the Value of World Manufacturing Exports 1950 to 1979	8
1.3	International Growth Comparison 1980 to 1989	8
1.4	UK Balance of Payments Current Account 1983 to 1990	9
1.5	UK Share of Research and Development Spending in Europe	10
1.6	Expenditure Per Head on Civil Research and Development 1983	10
1.7	Percentage of GDP on Research and Development Expenditure 1985	11
1.8	Gross Fixed Investment as a Percentage of GDP 1960 to 1989	11
1.9	Dividend Pay-outs in the UK and Germany 1982 to 1988	13
1.10	Non-residential Gross Fixed Capital Formation 1961 to 1979	18
1.11	Fixed Investment as a Share of GDP 1988 to 1993	19
1.12	Real Rates of Return in Manufacturing 1960 to 1979	20
1.13	Continuum of Conceptually Differentiated Policy Positions in the Area of the Equity Gap	26
2.1	ICFC/3i Outstanding Investment 1951 to 1993	43
2.2	WDA Equity Investments Under £250,000 1976 to 1979	64
2.3	WDA Investment Levels 1979 to 1990	67
2.4	Electra Risk Capital ERC I Portfolio	71
2.5	Government Sponsored Business Introduction Services	76
3.1	Cost of the Purchase of NEB Investments 1976 to 1991	89
3.2	Number of NEB Initial Investments Made Under and Over £200,000	90
3.3	NEB Investment Thresholds	91
3.4	Return on Capital Employed by NEB 1976 to 1980	93
3.5	NEB Performance Against the Cost of Government Borrowing 1981 to 1990	93
3.6	NEB's Profit and Loss on Disposal of Investments 1978 to 1991	94
3.7	Adjustments to the NEB's Disposal Record	95

3.8	NEB Investments Under £500,000 - Disposal Outcomes	96
3.9	NEB Investments of £200,000 or Less - Disposal Outcomes	97
3.10	Outcomes of Four of the Investments Transferred to Grosvenor Development Capital in 1981	98
3.11	Celltech's Performance 1981 to 1992	112
3.12	The Withdrawal of the NEB from Celltech	113
3.13	1994 Projection of Growth in the UK Biotechnology Industry	115
4.1	Total Aggregate Investment of BVCA Members 1979 to 1994	129
4.2	Average Size of UK Investments 1984 to 1994	130
4.3	Average Size of UK Investments - By Stage 1984 to 1994	130
4.4	UK Investment by Financing Stage - % of Amounts Invested 1984 to 1994	131
4.5	UK Investment by Financing Stage - Amounts Invested 1984 to 1994	132
4.6	UK Investment by Region - % of Amounts Invested 1985 to 1994	134
4.7	Investment Activity by Region 1993	135
4.8	UK Venture Capital Industry Performance by Year: 1994 Survey	137
4.9	UK Venture Capital Industry Performance by Investment Specialisation: 1994 Survey	138
4.10	UK Venture Capital Industry Performance by Investment Specialisation: 1995 Survey	138
4.11	UK Venture Capital Industry Upper Half and Upper Quarter Performance by Investment Stage: 1995 Survey	139
4.12	UK Venture Capital Industry Lower Quartile, Median, and Upper Quartile Performance by Investment Stage: 1995 Survey	140
4.13	Candover: Profits After Tax 1984 to 1992	142
4.14	Informal Investment Performance: Aggregate Evidence 1988 to 1994	148
5.1	Investment Raised Under the BES 1983/84 to 1993/94	158
5.2	BES Investments by Economic Sector 1983/84 to 1985/86	160
5.3	Amounts Invested Through the BES 1988/89 to 1993/94	160
5.4	Average Investment Sizes of BES Funds 1983/84	161
5.5	Average Investment per Company Under Three Methods of BES Investment 1983/84 to 1987/88	163
5.6	Finance Raised by Investment Size 1988/89 to 1993/94	163
5.7	BES Investment by Investment Stage 1983/84 to 1993/94	164

5.8	1992 Value of BES Investments Made Between 1983/84 and 1987/88	166
5.9	BES Results from Guaranteed Schemes: Annual Tax-free Return per £1 Share	167
6.1	Scottish Development Agency Return on Capital Employed 1977 to 1991	172
6.2	WDA Annual Rate of Return on Investment 1980 to 1990	174
6.3	Current Client Base of the Government Sponsored BIS	176
6.4	Number of Investment Matches Facilitated by the Government Sponsored BIS	177
6.5	Venture Capital Trusts Launched in 1996	181
7.1	Alternative Fiscal Intervention Schemes and their Effects	198

List of Abbreviations

AMA	Association of Metropolitan Authorities
BES	Business Expansion Scheme
BIS	Business Introduction Services
BL	British Leyland
BSS	Business Start-up Scheme
BTG	British Technology Group
BVCA	British Venture Capital Association
CBI	Confederation of British Industry
DoI	Department of Industry
DTI	Department of Trade and Industry
EIS	Enterprise Investment Scheme
ICFC	Industrial and Commercial Finance Corporation
IMF	International Monetary Fund
IRR	Internal Rate of Return
MBI	Management Buy-In
MBO	Management Buy-Out
NEB	National Enterprise Board
NRDC	National Research Development Corporation
OECD	Organisation of Economic Co-operation and Development
SDA	Scottish Development Agency
SDF	Scottish Development Finance
SE	Scottish Enterprise
SME	Small to Medium Size Enterprise
TEC	Training and Enterprise Council
USM	Unlisted Securities Market
VCR	Venture Capital Report
VCT	Venture Capital Trust scheme
WDA	Welsh Development Agency

Preface

A great deal has been written about the existence of an equity gap in the UK in the 1990s, not least because of the abolition of the Business Expansion Scheme, the launch of the Enterprise Investment Scheme and the Venture Capital Trusts, and the development of the informal venture capital market. Furthermore, two years ago the Labour Party embraced the issue by announcing its intention to create a small business development bank should it be elected to government. The small business pages of the daily newspapers have regularly focused on the issue, as have the myriad of business journals in circulation. Whilst this attention is clearly to be welcomed, I have always retained the feeling that the new policy initiatives, future plans and the reams of business comment have not been based upon a systematic assessment of what has occured in this area in the past. In this study I have sought to provide just such an assessment.

Broadly speaking, there are three main contributions I have sought to make in this study, which charts the activity of government since the Second World War. Firstly, I have brought together the range of initiatives governments have put forward in this area and put them within a framework which allows a systematic assessment to be made. The framework I have used encompasses the alternative ways in which the state can intervene in the running of the economy. The policy approaches I have identified are direct state intervention, fiscal intervention, non-financial intervention and laissez-faire. When applied to this particular economic issue a number of characteristics of policy can be assigned to each position, characteristics which can be identified in the policies enacted in the real world. This allows the *policy approaches* to be assessed as well as the individual policies, an important attribute as individual policies often fail, not because the principle behind the policy was flawed, but because of its execution. The manner in which a policy is implemented is often the consequence of the conflicting interests of those in the policy process, a process which often takes the policy away from its original objectives, or introduces loopholes which cause unintended consequences. The intention in this study is to get beyond such distorting factors and understand the potential utility of the various approaches.

The second contribution of the study is an assessment of the four policy approaches. This is achieved through an analysis of the performance of the various policies enacted by governments over the past twenty years. The analysis, however, focuses upon the policies as policy approaches and assesses the influence of factors which are particular to them. In the case of fiscal intervention, for example, there are four cases which contribute to a conclusion about its potential to bridge the equity gap. The evidence presented on policy in the study has been restricted to the past twenty years or so, partly because it is in this period that the majority of the initiatives have been enacted, but mainly because of the need to gain access to information. The analysis primarily includes the National Enterprise Board, the Scottish Development Agency (now replaced by Scottish Enterprise), the Business Expansion Scheme, the Government's sponsorship of five Business Introduction Services, and the Government's laissez-faire approach to the UK institutional venture capital industry, although other policies are touched upon. In undertaking this assessment I have used three criteria: the effectiveness of the policies in raising finance; the effectiveness of the policies in targeting that finance at the equity gap; and the financial performance of the investments made / promoted by the policies. The use of these criteria allow the policies to be assessed with a greater degree of accuracy and objectivity than would otherwise be the case. The assessment has involved the bringing together of much of the statistical data available on venture capital in the UK. The presentation of this data is another aspect of the study which readers may find useful. The third and final contribution of the study comes in the form of a series of recommendations which I believe logically follow from the assessment of the various policy approaches. These recommendations, I believe, would improve the availability of equity finance for small firms without causing any significant disruption to the established interests. Indeed, the recommendations constitute evolution rather than revolution.

Whilst I believe this study will be of interest to those involved in venture capital it is important to understand that this is primarily a political analysis. I have noticed that many books on venture capital are largely descriptive about the industry and written by venture capitalists, financial consultants or specialist business writers. I am none of these. Consequently, I have no doubt I will have made a number of technical errors about the conduct of venture capitalists or the meaning of certain aspects of law. For this I apologise. Yet, despite this suspicion, I do believe that my assessment of policy is as accurate as the nature of my investigations permit, and that the recommendations would represent an improvement in the way policy has been designed over the past twenty years or so. It is on this I wish this policy study to be judged. Furthermore, as this is a political analysis I have made a number of points I would expect to be contested by many readers. They are offered in the spirit of academic debate.

Before the study proceeds there are a few other points which need to be made. Firstly, being a political scientist I recognise that there are distinctions drawn in the discipline between the terms *state* and *government*. I have decided not engage in that debate and these two terms and the term *public sector* are used interchangably in this study. Secondly, I have in this study assumed a relationship between start-up and early stage investments and investments below £400,000. I recognise that it is not always the case that such investments are below £400,000, but given the averages reported by the British Venture Capital Association it would appear that the relationship is strong. Thirdly, my understanding of the term equity capital is informed by the definition provided by the British Venture Capital Association. In this study it refers to *the means of financing a company whereby the investor acquires an agreed proportion of the share capital in return for providing the requisite funding*.

Finally, I would like to express my sincere gratitude to the many people who have co-operated in the writing of this book - the willingness of people to help me over the years has been overwhelming. I would like to thank the many venture capitalists and business introduction service executives who have spared the time to speak to me, sometimes at considerable length. I would also like to thank the former National Enterprise Board employees and board members who took the time to see me. I am especially grateful to Rusi Kathoke, Tim Addison and Stewart Block for digging out a large amount of information on the National Enterprise Board which I would otherwise have been unable to obtain, and to Lord Ryder, Sir Leslie Murphy and Lord Scanlon for providing me with an insight into the thinking at the very top! I am also particularly indebted to Colin Mason, Richard Harrison, Scottish Enterprise, the Welsh Development Agency, the EIS Association, the consistently helpful British Venture Capital Association, Lucius Cary, Claude Brownlow, Gerard Fairtlough and Derek Harris. Finally, I am grateful to Simon Lee for discussing with me many of the issues contained in this book, to Andrew Cox for supervising me during my days as a PhD student, and to my father, Martin Lonsdale, for undertaking the unenviable task of proof-reading.

Note: Crown copyright is reproduced with the permission of the Controller of Her Majesty's Stationary Office.

PART I

GOVERNMENT AND THE UK EQUITY GAP

1 The Financial Sector and Relative Economic Decline in the UK

The Definition of an Equity Gap

The term 'equity gap', at the most basic level, refers to a shortage in the availability of equity capital, a deficiency of supply in relation to demand. The concept first came to prominence in the UK in 1931 when a gap was identified by the Macmillan Committee on Finance and Industry. It commented: 'It has been represented to us that great difficulty is experienced by the smaller and medium-sized businesses in raising the capital which they may from time to time require, even when the security they offer is perfectly sound.'[1] The Committee identified a gap for equity requirements of £200,000 or below. Over sixty years later this is equivalent to about £5 million. Few argue that a gap exists up to this level in the 1990s; indeed, there is overwhelming evidence that the institutional venture capital industry caters well for this type of investment, and that equity sources are well backed up by other sources of finance. Instead, the current understanding of the term is that it is a shortage in the supply of equity finance for investments under £400,000. This shortage is believed to be more acute for businesses in their early-stages. It would be wrong, however, to say there is a consensus on the issue. Many political and economic actors deny the existence of an equity gap in the UK, whilst others argue over the extent of the problem. There is also disagreement over the further issue of how important the problem is for the economy as a whole.

The many disagreements over the equity gap centre around the question of viability. Venture capitalists (and indeed all financiers) will only invest if they feel a proposition is viable. Yet the definition of viability to venture capitalists and small businesses is nearly always different. This is because to venture capitalists viability is not simply defined in terms of the ability of companies to produce a return, but is also defined by the *level* of that return. The levels of return required by a venture capitalist may exclude even profitable companies with apparently promising prospects. A venture capitalist may decide that the growth prospects for a company, although expected to materialise, are not likely to reach their required levels; the business is, therefore, not worthy of finance. These required levels are often set by the needs of those who invest in the venture capitalists themselves, that is the investment institutions in the City, as the venture capitalists will be looking to raise funds from them in the future.

Under these circumstances, observers, including government, need to decide from whose perspective they wish to judge the existence of an equity gap. The view stated here is that government, at least, should look at the issue from the point of view of small business, as it surely has a responsibility for supporting potentially profitable businesses. An economy cannot afford a section of its profitable business sector to be denied finance simply because of the requirements of the financial sector. Once this decision has been made the definition of the UK equity gap can be finalised thus: *the shortage in the availability of equity capital in amounts of less than £400,000 to businesses with a reasonable prospect of profitability.* This definition is somewhat vague, but given that it rules out the perspective of the financial sector, it provides a basis upon which government policy towards the gap can be built.

A further requirement for policy-making is an understanding of the factors causing the existence of the equity gap. A number of these can be identified, the first being the aforementioned differences in the perception of acceptable returns. This divergence between venture capitalists and small business is made greater by the fact that venture capital investors accept that a proportion of their portfolio will fail and lose them money. Consequently, those which are successful are expected to be sufficiently profitable to compensate for the failures - venture capitalists need to aim high. A second factor is the transaction cost effect on venture capital investment. Transaction costs are, quite simply, 'the costs of consumption over and above the purchase price'.[2] Market failure, and the contribution that makes to the equity gap, occurs when transaction costs become significant both in absolute terms and, of great relevance to the equity gap, as a proportion of the actual investment cost. It is this aspect which makes transaction costs so much more significant for small investments than for larger ones. Venture capitalists all agree that the costs of investigating, writing up the contract and monitoring investments - the transaction costs - do not increase in line with the size of the investment. The costs of making a £4 million investment are nowhere near ten times the cost of making a £400,000 one. These proportionally higher transaction costs have a serious impact upon the potential profitability of many small investments and increase the number of small companies which, in the view of the venture capitalist, are 'not viable'.

A third factor which causes the existence of an equity gap is the aforementioned higher risk of liquidation. In the early days of venture capital in the UK, many funds were set up to make extremely ambitious start-up and early-stage investments. Many of these funds lost a great deal of money as they underestimated the risks which were involved in this type of investment. It has now been accepted that as a general rule, start-up and early-stage investments, the type which are often made in amounts less than £400,000, are inherently higher risk than later-stage investments. This is because later-stage companies usually have a number of established products and a customer base, whilst start-up and early-stage companies are usually relying on projections and occasionally prototypes or draft plans. It is not the case that individual early-stage investments will not produce as high a return as later-stage investments, many in fact produce very large returns, but rather that due to the higher risk over an entire portfolio the returns are expected to be lower. With early-stage companies it is often very difficult to predict what the demand for a product might be when it does not yet exist, and on many occasions the venture capitalist gains the impression that the business people he/she is dealing with are being over-optimistic in their projections anyway.

This situation is confirmed by a former British Venture Capital Association (BVCA) Chairman, Ronald Cohen, who also introduces a fourth factor. He commented: 'In the early eighties, venture capitalists were keen to accept high levels of business and financial risk. But towards the middle of the decade, there was a general shift away from business risk. This was partly a result of burnt fingers from start-up investments in the early eighties but also because of a move towards the quicker returns to be made from backing [management buy-outs (MBO)] and exiting in a rising market.'[3] This fourth factor is indeed the ability of the investor to exit. One of the fears of the venture capitalist is that he/she will be unable to sell its stake in a small firm. This fear was alleviated somewhat by the creation of the Unlisted Securities Market, now replaced by the Alternative Investment Market, but particularly in the case of early-stage investments fears still exist. It is these four factors, therefore, a government must consider when it is framing its policy initiatives.

Gordon Murray believes that, in fact, two equity gaps can be identified in the UK. Arguing that the institutional venture capital industry is divided between those which offer later-stage finance and those which offer earlier-stage finance, Murray believes that there is potential for the two types to complement each other in the provision of equity to earlier-stage companies. The seed or early-stage capital provider would support the firm in its earlier-stages; then once it had reached a certain maturity the later-stage financiers would move in. From his research, however, Murray found that this was not happening to any significant extent. Murray believes that this has led to a situation where there are two gaps. He explains: 'There is the initial difficulty of raising sufficient third party equity to start the business, including the testing of novel ideas. Once the firm has established the feasibility of the concept and started initial production and sales, it faces a second equity gap in finding the finance for commercial expansion, once the resources of the early-stage investor are exhausted.'[4] According to Murray, as far as the first gap is concerned, the situation over seed capital has become such that 'the popularity of the term 'seed capital' is rapidly diminishing. Several respondents [in the venture capital industry] noted that this term is invariably associated with small, very risky, and frequently unsuccessful investment.'[5]

There are, therefore, many perfectly respectable reasons why an equity gap exists in the UK. Indeed, given the significant adverse transaction cost effect on small equity issues, it would be surprising if there were not some sort of recognisable gap. Why free marketeers and people in the financial sector should argue so vehemently to the contrary is on the face of it difficult to understand. Yet if one looks deeper, the real reason is clearly visible: it has been political. Ever since the Macmillan report in 1931 the identification of a gap has been associated with a greater role for the state in the financial sector. As is revealed in chapter two the Treasury, the Bank of England and the financial sector have been fighting against such a role since that time, with the creation of the Industrial and Commercial Finance Corporation (ICFC) in the 1940s being one attempt to remove the issue off the agenda. These efforts have been well rewarded as the state has largely been kept out of the financial sector to this day.

Although identifying an equity gap is relatively straightforward, once a definition has been settled upon, quantifying it is much more difficult because of problems with measurement. The main problem is that it is impossible to scientifically quantify the costs of non-investment as it cannot be conclusively proved that a firm would have been more profitable, or indeed stayed in business, had a certain amount of finance been invested. Yet government, despite this problem, can act to help the situation by taking certain measures, assessing their impact by gauging the credibility of the claims of those which are still not satisfied with the levels of equity finance on offer. The gap will never be fully closed, but it can be narrowed without knowing its exact size. At present, an assessment of the credibility of small business complaints on this issue would suggest that an equity gap is still a significant problem for the economy.

The Wider Context of the Equity Gap Debate

The debate over the existence of an equity gap for small business is, of course, set in the context of a relatively declining UK economy. While the British economy is thought to have gone into relative decline some time around 1870, when it began to be challenged by the United States and Germany, its status as a leading economy in the world only began to be undermined after the Second World War. This decline was shielded from the great British public by the ever-increasing living standards permitted by the post-war boom, which lasted until the early 1970s. Yet by the 1950s there was a growing realisation in many quarters that the country was being outperformed by other advanced nations, and that government policies were merely managing, not reversing decline.

The relative decline, so long disguised, became more obvious in the 1970s when the country suffered from stagflation and chronic industrial unrest. By 1976 the state of the economy was such that the British Government was forced to go cap-in-hand to the International Monetary Fund. Statistically the decline was undeniable. Tables 1.1 and 1.2 illustrate the UK's lacklustre performance in two areas. Any number of other tables could be produced which would tell the same story.

Table 1.1 Growth of GDP 1962 to 1972 (Annual Average %)

West Germany	3.6
Japan	9.2
United States	3.0
United Kingdom	2.2

Source: Adapted from A.Gamble, *Britain in Decline*, London, Macmillan, 1994, p16.

Table 1.2 Percentage Shares of the Value of World Manufacturing Exports 1950 to 1979

	1950	1960	1970	1979
UK	25.5	16.5	10.8	9.7
West Germany	7.3	19.1	19.8	20.8
Japan	3.4	6.9	11.7	13.6
USA	27.3	21.6	18.5	15.9

Source: Adapted from A.Gamble, *Britain in Decline*, London, Macmillan, 1994, p17.

There has perhaps been a more vigorous dispute about the performance of the UK economy since 1979 when the first Thatcher Government was elected. At the time of the third Thatcher election victory in 1987, the people of Britain, not to mention the economists amongst them, could have been forgiven for thinking that the Government really had wrought an economic miracle. Growth was high, strikes were low, inflation gave the impression of being under control, and the country's confidence was high, boosted by the UK's rediscovered high international standing. Yet within three years Mrs Thatcher had gone and the economy was entering what turned out to be the longest recession since the 1930s. Once again the talk was of decline. Many argue that the Thatcher years did not see a fundamental reversal of the UK's relative economic decline.

Table 1.3 International Growth Comparison 1980 to 1989 (Annual Average %)

UK	2.2
Germany	2.0
Japan	4.2
USA	2.6
OECD	2.8

Source: Adapted from C.Johnson, *The Economy Under Mrs Thatcher 1979-1990*, London, Penguin, 1991, p266.

The vigorous growth of the second half of the 1980s is now viewed sceptically, because it merely led to an unnecessarily long recession. Overall, the growth rate of the UK was very ordinary in the 1980s, below the OECD average, although not below all of the UK's main competitors. Manufacturing industry was affected badly by the first Thatcher recession of 1980 to 1981, and this had consequences for the UK's trade position later in the decade. The 'judge and jury' of economic performance, inflation, also cast an unfavourable verdict on the period, with the index moving up by 70% during the decade, as against 56% for OECD countries as a whole. By the start of the 1990s the state of the UK economy looked all too familiar.

Table 1.4 UK Balance of Payments Current Account 1983 to 1990 (£bn)

1983	3.8	**1987**	-4.3
1984	1.8	**1988**	-15.5
1985	2.7	**1989**	-19.9
1986	0.0	**1990**	-13.8

Source: Adapted from C. Johnson, *The Economy Under Mrs Thatcher 1979-1990*, London, Penguin, 1991, p310.

Current debate about the UK economy focuses upon the Conservative Party's claim that the recession of the early 1990s was painful but necessary, and that due to 'market reforms' the UK is now better equipped than its European competitors to survive the globalisation of trade. A recent report by an Institute of Public Policy Research commission, however, suggests that traditional weaknesses in the economy remain and that the country should not become too triumphalist.

Some commentators believe that a major factor in the UK's relative economic decline has been the operation of the financial sector. The financial sector is said to have been short-term in its focus and reluctant to invest in British business. This is a contentious view and one that is disputed by the financial sector's many supporters. The following three sections discuss the main features of this debate.

Criticism of the Performance of the UK Financial Sector

Will Hutton commented in 1994: 'There is no single villain in the destructive relationship between British finance and industry; it is the operation of the whole that is the problem ... The City is at once the single biggest economic problem facing the country and its most powerful vested interest group. There is no possibility of long-run economic success without its reform.'[6] This comment is typical of a body of thought critical of the financial system. Adherents to this view contend that the operation of the financial system causes problems like the equity gap, and severely disadvantages the UK relative to its competitors which, it is argued, have more accommodating financial arrangements. There are two broad criticisms of the financial sector. The first is that business, mainly small business, cannot gain access to the finance it needs, with the result being that its development is constrained. The second is that even when business is successful in acquiring finance, the terms on which it is provided are designed more for the convenience and profitability of the investor than for that of the recipient. This again is said to result in business being constrained.

Table 1.5 UK Share of Research and Development Spending in Europe (%)

1967	27
1982	17

Source: Adapted from D. Clutterbuck and S. Crainer, *The Decline and Rise of British Industry*, London, WH Allen, 1988, p169.

Many statistics have been produced to support the argument that there has not been sufficient industrial investment in the UK. A common area to point to is the UK's record on research and development. Tables 1.5 to 1.7 all show the UK to have been outperformed in this respect.

Table 1.6 Expenditure Per Head on Civil Research and Development 1983 (£)

United States	76
West Germany	73
Japan	60
United Kingdom	47

Source: Adapted from D. Clutterbuck and S. Crainer, *The Decline and Rise of British Industry*, London, WH Allen, 1988, p168.

Table 1.7 Percentage of GDP on Research and Development Expenditure 1985

United Kingdom	1.7
France	1.8
United States	1.9
West Germany	2.5

Source: Adapted from G. Brown, *Where There is Greed ... Margaret Thatcher and the Betrayal of Britain's Future*, Edinburgh, Mainstream, 1989, p45.

Table 1.8 Gross Fixed Investment as a Percentage of GDP 1960 to 1989

	1960-1973	1974-1979	1980-1984	1985-1989
Germany	24.9	20.8	21.1	19.6
France	23.5	23.4	21.2	19.3
United Kingdom	18.3	19.3	16.8	17.9
Europe	23.2	22.2	20.5	19.4

Source: Adapted from G. Brown, *Where There is Greed ... Margaret Thatcher and the Betrayal of Britain's Future*, Edinburgh, Mainstream, 1989, p37.

Statistics for overall investment in the economy are also presented by the sector's critics. The UK lagged behind its major competitors in terms of gross fixed investment for thirty years in the 1960s, 1970s and 1980s, as can be seen in table 1.8. Harold Lever and George Edwards believe that some of the responsibility for the poor performance of the UK in industrial investment can be explained by the operations of the financial sector. They argue:

> Pension funds and insurance companies ... invest those savings mainly in financing the government or in buying existing investments on the stock market and property ... but very little of these funds goes to support new investment ... The banks collect most of the rest of the nations savings and are by far the greatest source of those investment funds which business and industry must have to supplement their retained profits ... however, a large proportion of their funds goes to finance consumption ... only a dangerously small fraction of the totals of past and present savings goes to finance investment.[7]

They notice a contrast with other leading industrial nations: 'The facts are that the French, Germans and Japanese financial institutions lend a much greater proportion of the funds they collect to business and industry than the great British institutions.'[8] Twelve years later, in 1992, Edwards saw no reason to have changed his views. He still insisted that:

> In France, Germany, and Japan banking's main task is to provide credit to industry, and this is the main source of the manufacturing superiority of these economies. These investment credits exceed the value of the original source of the savings impetus, through the credit creation mechanism. And they are expansionary - that is they add more to output than they add to inflation ... [this] means that Britain, the US and other consumer credit, stock market dominated economies can never create the same levels of investment (and investment growth) as the Asian and European bank-dominated investment credit economies.[9]

The argument against the City goes beyond this quantitative measure, however, with the key to the failings of the City lying in the terms on which finance is provided. The best known aspect of this criticism is the alleged 'short-termism' of the UK's financial institutions. The charge of short-termism is aimed at both the banks and the stock market. The banks are said to be reluctant to lend long-term, especially to small businesses. This, it is argued, promotes a climate of uncertainty with companies never sure whether their loans or overdrafts will be renewed. Whilst some of the banks' apologists argue that to look at the length of loans is misleading as a high proportion are renewed as a matter of course, critics dismiss this as demonstrating a lack of understanding about how business works. They argue that the crucial point is that the business manager cannot be sure whether or not the loan will be renewed, and therefore cannot plan the future of the business with any certainty. Will Hutton believes that short-termism is a very serious problem for the UK, and emphasises the point by comparing UK banking practice with that of Germany: '[The National Westminster Bank between 1985 and 1990] trebled its UK lending, and of the £31 billion increase more than half was for loans of less than a year in duration. Deutsche Bank meanwhile extends more than half its loans for four years or longer.'[10] The basis on which the banks lend is also said to be a hindrance to business. This quote from an anonymous British businessman is said to be typical: '...every banker we have approached is only willing to lend against last year's balance sheet, not next year's cash flow...'.

Those who operate in the stock market are also said to be guilty of short-termism in that they are alleged to place a greater value on profits and dividends today than investment and the promise of greater profits in the future. Evidence for this view is said to be found in the statistics for dividend payments, which show UK companies paying out far more of their profits in dividends than is the case in other industrialised countries. A comparison of dividend payments in the UK and Germany in the 1980s (see table 1.9) illustrates the point.

Table 1.9 Dividend Pay-outs in the UK and Germany 1982 to 1988 (% of profits)

	UK	Germany
1982	26	15
1984	24	11
1986	31	12
1987	39	14
1988	34	18

Source: Adapted from W. Hutton, 'Short changed by short-termism', *The Guardian*, 20 June 1990.

Criticism of the stock market is nothing new. In 1938 Harold Macmillan wrote of his concern over the judgement of those who made the crucial decisions about the future of industrial companies:

[It is] said by Mr Keynes ... and by critics of the existing financial order ... that these vitally important decisions are not governed by "the genuine expectations of professional entrepreneurs", but by "the average expectations of those who work in the stock exchange". To illustrate how ignorant and ill-advised the stock exchange estimates of what the future business prospects may be, Mr Keynes tells us that day-to-day fluctuations of an ephemeral and non-significant character tend to have an altogether excessive and even absurd influence on the market.[11]

The concept of short-termism is still very popular with politicians today. Paddy Ashdown, for example, recently put his weight behind the concerns:

> Britain's economy is notoriously obsessed with short-term gains at the expense of long-term success - 'casino-capitalism' as it has been aptly dubbed ... the result of this pressure on companies is to discourage innovation and long-term planning ... This starves the future by choking off investment in the essentials for a successful industrial strategy ... It helps explain why so many British success stories are companies which have low capital requirements.[12]

Will Hutton's approach to the issue has been very much affected by an incident which occurred while he was working as a stockbroker at Phillips and Drew. It concerned the closure of the BSA motor cycle plant in Birmingham in 1974. He believes it was just another example of the City's myopia:

> It was when I watched the evening news and I saw what was actually happening in Birmingham, where the company was actually closing, where men and women were being laid off work, that I realised how fundamentally frivolous the City had been about BSA. Was there any thought of mobilising a rescue package, was there any sense in which the holders of equity in this company would mobilise banking support, investment support and restructure the company. None.[13]

Those commentators who criticise the financial sector are not without their supporters in industry. A 1994 Coopers and Lybrand survey of businesses turning over between £8 million and £500 million found that 79% of those interviewed believed that short-termism in the City was a factor contributing to the decline of British industry.[14]

Explanations for the Problematic Relationship Between Finance and Industry

The basis of many arguments critical of the financial sector is historical. The development of the UK financial sector differed from the development of those in other leading economies in that it was not created to finance industry. Finance in the UK pre-dates manufacturing industry. This historical fact is deemed by many to have been crucial in the development of the relationship between finance and industry. Perhaps the best known exponent of this analysis is Geoffrey Ingham. He explains: 'There is now general agreement that early industrialisation in Britain in the eighteenth and early nineteenth centuries took place largely independently of the formal institutions of the monetary systems ... [C]apital requirements of industry were relatively meagre ... investment capital flowed elsewhere ... into foreign loans, British government securities and the provision of credit for international trade.'[15] Ingham's view is backed up by the more journalistic Will Hutton, and Anthony Hopwood, from the London School of Economics. Hopwood comments:

> In continental Europe the major financial institutions developed in the context of facilitating industrial development and that was certainly the case in Germany, the Netherlands and France. So right from the beginning these institutions had to have a close relationship to industry. In Britain the financial institutions were established before industrial development, for state financing and financing the Empire, and for much of the period of British industrial development in the nineteenth century had a very loose relationship with the financing of industry.[16]

Ingham argues that as the financial sector did not develop to service industry, it developed practices and attitudes that were detrimental to its later development. However, he disagrees with the argument that the most detrimental practice of the City was its large scale investment overseas. Writers such as Hilferding argued that 'finance' was simply exported overseas, with the significance being that it meant that from its establishment the City of London was not dependent on the continued prosperity of the UK economy, which later led to a certain indifference to the UK's manufacturing industry. Ingham's own view is that the largest part of non-industrial capital was, in fact, directed into international commercial activity, including insurance, currency dealing and commodity broking. It was *this* factor that meant that British money capital was not dependent on the domestic economy. Ingham sees the general attitude of the financial sector reflected in the operation of the stock market:

> A crucial determinant of the British pattern of industrial financing is, I believe, to be found in the operation of the London stock exchange and, in particular, the institutionalisation of a strong secondary market for already issued shares ... The volume and velocity of transactions as measured by *turnover* provides a rough indicator of the extent to which stock markets are concerned with the relatively autonomous commercial activities of trading in securities (as opposed to the flotation of new issues) ... Turnover on the London exchange is considerably higher than elsewhere, and reflects the dominance of the secondary market.[17]

The dominance of the secondary market, he believes, can undermine industry. He explains: 'If, as seems likely, the long-term productive potential of companies is neglected, it is because the financial intermediaries who operate the secondary market do not depend directly on the performance of any particular company for their profits.'[18] Andrew Glyn and Bob Sutcliffe take a Marxist perspective and argue that the division in the structure of British capitalism is attributable to two factors. The first is that there was an even pace in the development of international industrial capitalism in the nineteenth century. They argue:

> The appearance of the division between industry and finance coincided with the accentuation of foreign competition for British industry. To face this competition vast new investments in modern industrial plant had to be financed; that would have required in Britain the same integration of industry and finance as existed in Germany, France and America. This did not happen and the alternative structural change in capitalism which did take place was that financial capital decided to look outwards and invest abroad.[19]

Glyn and Sutcliffe's second factor was the fundamental contradiction between capital and labour. They wrote: 'The banks and the City did not want to involve themselves directly in domestic industry because they evidently expected larger - or at least more secure profits outside England. And it is very likely that one of the underlying reasons for this was the realisation that the growing strength of the working class would make the profitability of industrial investment at home increasingly precarious.'[20]

A third explanation given for the problems between finance and industry is the existence of a fundamental economic conflict of interest between the two fractions of capital. Financial institutions believe that their best interests lie in keeping their money relatively liquid so that they can take advantage of a more profitable opportunity should it arise. Therefore, much investment in industry is committed only in the short-term. The conflict of interest arises because for manufacturing industry the time scale of returns on investment is much longer-term. Returns in manufacturing come from designing a better product that will sell in the market, or from developing a more efficient method of production. For example, the benefits of investment in the aerospace industry can take over fifteen years to be realised, as was the case with the Rolls Royce RB-211 engine. Thus, a conflict of interest, with the banks criticised for providing loans that are damagingly short-term, and institutional investors criticised for showing too little commitment to companies and pressing for too high a level of dividends.

A fourth explanation for the alleged deficiencies in the provision of finance to industry is one which focuses on cultural factors. At the centre of many such theories lies a belief that Britain has an 'anti-manufacturing culture'. Explanations for the cause of this culture are many, but most of them assert that in the UK involvement in manufacturing industry lacks the prestige that other occupations enjoy, and indeed that which industrialists enjoy in other countries. This lack of prestige has consequences for the relationship between finance and industry, with perhaps the most serious effect being that it causes the financial system to lack knowledge of industry, particularly in high technology areas. A spokesman for British Steel giving evidence at a Parliamentary inquiry into innovation said: 'Many analysts have little knowledge of the basic technologies involved and, therefore, cannot apply any critical analyses to what they see and are told.'[21] This view was backed up in the same report when it was revealed that 'the Prudential has only one engineer on its analytical team.'[22] The distance between the financier and the industrialist in this respect can weaken what might already be a short-term and arms-length relationship.

Arguments in Defence of the Financial System

The case against the financial system certainly appears to be a strong one, yet in actual fact its proponents have had little success in advancing it. This is partly because it is impossible to prove beyond doubt many of the arguments they put forward - as was mentioned earlier it is impossible to quantify the costs of non-investment. In addition, those who defend the financial system in their relationship with industry include powerful groups; indeed, this section will include comments from the Conservative Government, the Bank of England, the CBI, and the Institute of Directors. These groups dismiss both the view that the financial sector operates in a way which is inimical to the interests of industry and that which states that the financial sector is responsible for the relative economic decline that has been experienced during the twentieth century.

This is not to say that the financial system's defence is wholly dependent on the influence of its proponents; a number of persuasive arguments have been constructed. The arguments are usually underpinned by a strong belief in the superiority of market forces in bringing about optimum economic outcomes, and also by a belief that the financial system should be able to regulate itself. Harold Rose provides a structure as to how a defence of the financial system can be built. He begins by arguing that criticisms of the financial sector rest on two central assumptions. Firstly, that the UK's poor economic performance has been *mainly* due to a too low level of investment and, secondly, that this too low level of investment has been due to the UK's financial system. He contends that 'if *either* of these two propositions is untrue, the criticism of British financial operations becomes a question of less weighty significance.'[23] Rose then provides evidence that refutes the critics' case. He makes four counter-propositions. The first is that if one takes away the performance of Japan, the UK's investment performance has not been significantly worse than its other competitors, certainly not 'so far below ... as to render plausible the contention that our main economic weakness has been insufficient investment.'[24] Rose provides figures to illustrate his contention.

Table 1.10 Non-residential Gross Fixed Capital Formation 1961 to 1979

	Total as a % of GDP		Plant & Machinery as a % of GDP	
	1961-1970	1971-1979	1961-1970	1971-1979
Germany	17.7	16.0	9.5	8.9
Japan	27.1	24.9	-	11.5
UK	14.7	15.2	8.7	9.5
USA	13.7	13.2	6.9	7.1

Source: Adapted from H. Rose, 'Britain's financial system and economic performance: old charges renewed', *Barclay's Review*, May 1982, p29.

In 1996, the Institute of Directors provided more recent evidence supporting this view. The Institute presented figures showing that if housing investment is taken out of the calculations the UK sits comfortably in the middle of international investment comparisons.

Rose's second point is that economists disagree over the extent to which national differences in growth and productivity are explained by levels of investment. He argues that what most economists do agree on is that the very large differences in national output per capita are too large to be attributable to one single factor. He contends that unquantifiable factors such as innovation, efficiency, and 'culture' are likely to be more significant factors. Rose's third contention is that Britain appears to require more investment than other industrial countries to obtain the same increase in output, and that this cannot possibly be blamed on the financial system. He explains:

> Investment has been less productive in Britain than in other countries. Whether one blames this on poor management, union restrictive practices or government policy, one fact predominates. It is that ... the profitability of industrial investment in Britain has tended to be relatively low and has become desperately so in recent years ... What is needed to generate higher investment and growth is an improvement in the rate of return, one far greater than [could come from] any improvement in the cost of finance that might possibly be obtained by changing Britain's financial system.[25]

Table 1.11 Fixed Investment as a Share of GDP 1988 to 1993 (%)

	Total	Non-residential
USA	16.9	12.8
Japan	30.5	24.8
Germany	20.2	14.6
France	20.5	15.2
Italy	19.4	14.2
UK	17.9	14.2
Sweden	19.1	13.8

Source: Adapted from Institute of Directors, *Short-termism and The State We're In*, London, IoD, 1996, p16.

Table 1.12 emphasises this. Rose's final point is that financial systems are adaptive. He claims that

> financial systems tend to be adaptive, a reflection of industrial and commercial conditions rather than a major cause of them. If other factors favour economic growth, "finance" is unlikely to be a constraint, least of all in a relatively small country like Britain with access to the international capital markets. The converse is equally true: if management is inefficient, or labour practices restrictive, or government policy too short-sighted, no change in the supply or pattern of finance is likely to alter the outcome.[26]

Table 1.12 Real Rates of Return in Manufacturing 1960 to 1979

Averages	UK	USA	Germany	Japan
1960-1962	15	27	29	n/a
1963-1967	14	36	21	n/a
1968-1971	11	26	22	n/a
1972-1975	8	21	16	18
1976-1979	6	22	17	15

Source: Adapted from H. Rose, 'Britain's financial system and economic performance: old charges renewed', *Barclay's Review*, May 1982, p29.

Rose is backed up in his defence of the financial system by the CBI and the Bank of England. The CBI's view on the issue is subject to change. This occurs on many issues, and is something to be expected from an organisation which represents such a wide body of interests. In 1987, however, they came out very clearly on one side reporting that they did not perceive a problem with the supply of finance to industry: 'The Task Force found no evidence to link the attitudes of the City directly to the long-term decline of the nation's manufacturing sector - nor to its resurgence in recent years.'[27] The Task Force, in fact, saw the issue very differently: 'It has been companies that have not been giving sufficient weight to long-term development. This has not, in any way, been due to pressures from the City.'[28] The Bank of England has also made many statements in defence of the system; this one made in 1980 is typical of their backing:

> It is clear that the system of company finance ... has shown considerable resilience in a time of great pressures. Some sources of finance have receded in importance - most notably the market for fixed-interest securities - but new methods of finance, closely attuned to the tax system and to companies' needs, have taken their place. It is, of course, not possible to judge from aggregate statistics whether or not companies have felt themselves constrained by the availability of external finance, but the rapid expansion of new forms of finance does suggest healthy competition among suppliers of funds.[29]

Defenders of the financial system have also countered the more specific criticisms levelled against it. One of the criticisms is that the stock market is short-termist in its attitude towards industry. One of the features of this alleged short-termism has been the relatively high number of corporate take-overs. Critics of the system argue that a low commitment 'take-over culture' has been created where company managements dare not cut the dividend, even during years of low or non-existent profits, for fear of a hostile take-over bid. This, it is argued, has a damaging effect on the company as the management is forced to cut in other areas - often investment in capital and research and development. A recent report by the Institute of Directors was the latest to refute this scenario. The Institute argued that there is little evidence to support the view that institutional fund managers exert pressures for short-term returns. It is admitted that there may be too many take-overs, but it is suggested that it is not short-termism *per se* that leads directors to act in ways which are inimical to the long-term health of the company; it is the *belief* that they are under short-term pressures to produce high dividends.[30] The Conservative Government also dismissed the accusation of short-termism in its contribution to the 1991 House of Lords Select Committee Report on Innovation. It was insisted that 'the possibility of take-overs provides a spur to management ... we should not place the primary blame on the openness of our capital market.'[31]

A second target of the financial system's critics is the banking sector. The banks are criticised for not making a greater commitment to industry; they are accused of remaining at arm's length. Defenders of the system are particularly irritated by studies that compare the UK banking sector with that of other industrialised countries. The example that is most often used is that of Germany, which, it is claimed, has a banking system that makes a longer term commitment to industry. Defenders of the UK financial system reject this view on two counts. Firstly, they refute criticism of banking practices in the UK, but also they argue that the favourable reputation of the German financial system is something of a myth. In an attempt to confirm this, a paper was commissioned by the 3i European Enterprise Centre at the Cranfield School of Management. In the paper Stephen Clements conducted a survey which looked to separate the attitudes of German small to medium sized enterprise (SME) managers towards their banks from their actual behaviour in response to their dealings with them. His contention was that what the businessmen said about their banks was not reflected in their actions. Clements admits that if one merely looks at the attitudes of SME managers towards their banks, i.e. what they say about them, then indeed 'these are all attitudes that might be contrasted with the situation in the UK.'[32] The findings in short were: 'Most (74%) view the bank as a partner. Most (87%) think the bank is helpful. Most (90%) view their relationship with the bank as good or excellent. Most (73%) think the bank has a good or excellent understanding of their business. Most (81%) knew how bank charges were calculated and most (77%) thought they were reasonable. All, without exception, thought the bank would stand by them if they were in short-term difficulties.'[33] So even German businessmen themselves contribute to the myth. What they said in the survey is consistent with the claims made by British commentators about the German banking system. Indeed, no doubt Clement believes that this is the kind of evidence, i.e. anecdotal, from which many of the said commentators derive their views. Clement, however, then brings in the second part of his evidence, that of the businessmen's actions. The summary of this was that

> most (65%) would only seek advice from the bank as necessary, and 19% would not seek it at all. Contact with the bank seemed informal with only 53% of them sending annual accounts (92% of owner managed firms) and only 26% sending them business plans and budgets ... Firms were convinced that the banks were primarily concerned with the security of their investment and the long term health of the business was very much a secondary concern ... Over half the surveyed companies had changed their banks at some time.[34]

Clements concludes that his findings support the views of Jeremy Edwards and Klaus Fisher that 'the relationship between banks and business is more loosely defined than is commonly supposed.'[35]

Defenders of the financial system also contend that its critics do not take into account the levels of inflation the economy has suffered when criticising the levels of investment in the post-war period. Inflation, it is argued, was one of the main reasons why investment was lower in the 1960s and 1970s than might have been hoped for. Because of the unstable economic environment investors were not confident they would be able to realise an adequate return and therefore held back. Yet the financial sector should not be criticised for what was merely prudence. After all, a large amount of the money invested belongs to the public, and is given to the financial institutions on trust. In the more settled environment of the mid-1980s investment levels increased sharply, demonstrating that the financial sector is perfectly willing to invest in British industry, as long as the conditions are right. It is concluded that on this evidence attempts to increase investment should focus on the defeat of inflation rather than on reform of the financial institutions.

The financial system's supporters go further than merely defending the system, however. Armed with their certainty about the virtues of free-market principles, they look upon the UK financial system as a model for other countries. Dimitri Vittas gives an example of this: 'If the problems of the potential conflicts of interest, and the potential abuse of privileged information can be effectively overcome, without unduly undermining the efficiency of operations of the newly emerging financial conglomerates, the UK system could have a real chance of becoming the prototype financial system that most other countries might wish to imitate.'

Those who have defended the financial system in its relationship with industry have been successful in warding off any attempts at fundamental reform. Harold Rose put forward two propositions which needed to be true if it was to be claimed that a serious problem existed with the financial system. Firstly, that a lack of investment was the main reason for the UK's economic underperformance, and secondly, that the financial sector was to blame for the low levels. Defenders of the system contend that both these propositions are false. British economic underperformance is not mainly due to a lack of investment, nor has the financial system been responsible for any shortcomings. As one commentator notes, their attitude continues to be that 'the critics are well intentioned but misguided [and] it is rough justice that the City should have to put up with such ill-informed criticisms.'[36]

The financial sector has also had to defend itself against a specific argument that it does not serve the small business community. Dimitri Vittas has been one who has sought to counter such arguments. He comments: 'All the major commercial banks in the UK are now competing for small business with a widening range of specifically tailored financial products and advisory services.' In line with Harold Rose and the Bank of England, Vittas again uses the defence that the market will constantly adapt to new demands placed upon it. Indeed, it has been argued that far from there being an equity gap in the UK for small business, the real problem is that too much money is chasing too few deals - the problem is demand not supply. Ewan Macpherson, chief executive of 3i, is an advocate of this view: 'The problem is not so much overall lack of capital as lack of demand. If small companies are held back for want of long term capital, the reason sometimes seems to be that they are unaware that such capital exists - or that they are reluctant to use it. Directors of family businesses, for instance, may refuse to dilute their equity.'[37] Robert Drummond, former chairman of the BVCA, argued in 1992 that it was not only the lack of demand that made the equity gap thesis false, it was the lack of quality demand. Venture capitalists can only make their money from companies which have the desire to grow. This allowed him to comment that 'venture capitalists are agents of change; they are not interested in backing "lifestyle" companies where the owners are only interested in what they can get out of the business, not how they can expand it and grow. Nor are the venture capitalists interested in companies that lack management ability and are not prepared to do anything about it.'[38]

Rodney Clark, a leading writer on the venture capital industry both in the UK and abroad, made a slightly different point. He argued in the late 1980s that any shortages of equity for small and early-stage deals were merely cyclical. Industries have trends, he argued, and this should not be mistaken for a structural problem in the market. He believed that a recovery in the supply of such finance would take place for two reasons. Firstly, many investments that were made in the early days of the industry, and now required development capital, would soon have gone through the investment cycle. This would be followed by an increase in early-stage deals. Secondly, there was also an issue of fashion. In the late 1980s MBO had become popular in the industry. The economic climate meant that there were many opportunities and the industry had taken advantage. Clark believed, and he claimed that his view was backed up by the industry itself, that early-stage deals would once again become popular when there were not so many MBO opportunities. Clark also claimed that the later-stage deals the industry was making were actually beneficial for the prospects of an increase in the provision of early-stage finance. MBO, in particular, build up the reserves of venture capitalists, making it possible for them to take advantage of an early-stage deal when it came along. It must be said, however, that this thesis has not being borne out by events in the 1990s.

Alternative Approaches to the Problem of the Equity Gap

There is nothing that has been written on the relationship between finance and industry that suggests that the debate will be resolved. For every convincing statistic provided to defend the financial sector there is another that can be used to indict it. As has been stressed it can never be conclusively proved that there is a substantial equity gap. It cannot be said for certain that if a company had received x amount of finance it would have grown by y percent. Opinions on the subject often come down to belief. Those who believe that free markets provide optimum economic outcomes tend to dismiss problems such as the equity gap. Those who are more suspicious or, of course, outright hostile to the free operation of markets, tend to sympathise with problems like the equity gap. This study is written on the basis that, while the financial system satisfies most small business needs, there is an equity gap for small business in the UK for requirements of less than

£400,000. It is also believed that this is a significant problem for the economy as many promising small businesses are being stifled by the lack of equity available to them. The lack of equity finance at this level may well be among the reasons why the UK's 'Mittelstand' is one of the economy's weakest areas. The study also proceeds from the view that government needs to become more involved in this issue than is currently the case.

The Labour Party and the Conservative Party's philosophical positions on the role of the state in the economy have been reflected in the policies that the parties have formulated as solutions to the problem of the equity gap. For example, the 1974-1979 Labour Government decided that a direct interventionist approach needed to be taken. Labour believed that the market had failed over a long period of time to direct equity finance to deserving small and medium sized businesses. Therefore, they set up a state institution to have as one of its roles the provision of finance to such companies: the National Enterprise Board. It began its operations in November 1975, and in a 10 year period invested equity in over 150 companies.

On the other hand, the Conservative Government elected in 1979 had very different ideas about how the equity gap should be bridged. The Conservatives believed that a state institution was unnecessary, if only the market was allowed to function freely. The party believed that there were plenty of investors willing to commit their capital to all types of investment opportunities, but that they would only do so in a stable economic environment and when they were allowed to keep the rewards of their risk-taking. Accordingly they made a conscious choice to allow the then emerging institutional venture capital market to develop naturally, without state interference - a policy of laissez-faire. In terms of the equity gap, early-stage investments and those under £400,000, this has continued to date with the government yet to interfere directly in the operations of the institutional venture capital industry to effect an increase in its investment at that level. Yet there are other ways in which government can intervene to try to bridge the equity gap and, indeed, other policy types have been implemented in the post-war period. Indeed, this study proceeds on the assumption that there are four conceptually differentiated positions in the area of the equity gap: direct state intervention; fiscal intervention; non-financial intervention; and laissez-faire. These are discussed below.

Table 1.13 Continuum of Conceptually Differentiated Policy Positions in the Area of the Equity Gap

⟵―――――――――――――――――――――――――⟶

| Direct State Intervention | Fiscal Intervention | Non-financial Intervention | Laissez-faire |

Direct state intervention

The most interventionist approach the state can take to the problem of the equity gap is actually to become involved in the making of investments itself. Indeed, the precise definition of the term direct state intervention in this context is *the direct provision of equity finance by the state*. That the state should act in such a manner implies a lack of faith in the ability of market forces to solve the problem of the gap. A policy of direct state intervention usually takes the form of a state institution which is set up as an semi-autonomous body. The institution will normally have a board made up of 'non-political' figures, but who are appointed by the relevant Secretary of State. In the case of the Industrial Reorganisation Corporation (IRC), a Labour policy of direct state intervention aimed at a different perceived industrial problem, the first managing director was a Mr R Grierson, who was at the time an executive director with SG Warburg. Usually, much rhetoric about the independence of the institution is heard from both politicians and the members of the institution itself. The ability of the institution to act independently, however, is usually constrained by the fact that the government is the institution's paymaster. In any case, it is unlikely that a government would appoint someone who did not sympathise with its policy objectives. The NEB was a further example of a policy of direct state intervention. Part of its remit was devoted to targeting finance at a perceived equity gap for small business. It is the main case study by which this approach to the problem of the equity gap will be assessed. The evidence from this case study will be supplemented, however, by evidence on the venture capital role of the Welsh Development Agency (WDA) and the equivalent body in Scotland.

Fiscal intervention

The second position the state can take to the equity gap is to initiate a policy of fiscal intervention. Fiscal intervention is defined as *a policy where the state uses fiscal incentives to promote a particular outcome*. The policy is very widely used in the economy to achieve economic and political objectives. Companies receiving tax allowances to encourage internal investment spending is an example of fiscal intervention as is the creation of tax exempt special savings accounts or TESSAs to encourage personal saving. In this context the outcome of fiscal intervention, is hoped to be the elimination of the equity gap. To this end, the policy seeks to encourage investment in the perceived range of this gap. It seeks to do this by simultaneously restricting investment within certain limits (the size of the investment and the type of company) and by offering tax relief as an incentive. The use of this approach again suggests a view that the market, without intervention from the state, is unable to solve the problem of the gap. It is a lesser critique of the ability of the market, however, as the policy involves, in the actual investments promoted, the use of private capital. The motivation for such a policy is the belief that investments in the range of the equity gap are of above average risk, and thus less likely to be made without an incentive. A policy of fiscal intervention may be operated by the public or private sector; it depends on the exact nature of the scheme. The policies which have been aimed at the problem of the equity gap thus far, however, have been run by the private sector. It is the contention of this study that the Business Expansion Scheme (BES) was an example of fiscal intervention. This policy is thus the focus for an assessment of this approach. Three other policies, the Business Start-up Scheme (BSS), the Enterprise Investment Scheme (EIS) and the Venture Capital Trust scheme (VCT), also fall into this category and their performance is considered as well.

Non-Financial intervention

Non-financial intervention is a very broad category of state action. It can be defined as *state action of a non-financial nature that is aimed directly at promoting a particular outcome*, again, in this case the desired outcome being the elimination of the equity gap. This is quite a vague definition which needs further explanation. Governments make decisions that do not involve the provision of finance or fiscal incentives every day, so a meaningful definition cannot just be a catch-all for these actions - actions that may touch many policy areas simultaneously. Therefore, when the term non-financial intervention is used, it means an act of intervention that not only produces a desired outcome, but also *directly* aims to produce such an outcome. In this context then, it means a policy intervention designed specifically to alleviate the equity gap. A second point is that the policy does not aim any finance at the actual investments in question; they still take place under normal market conditions. Indeed, the major distinction between a policy of non-financial intervention and the previous two positions is that although there is the recognition of a gap, there is not the recognition that it is caused by the relative unattractiveness of such investments. The motivation that usually leads to a policy of non-financial intervention is a belief that there are practical problems in the market - often over information - which lead to the shortfall in investment.

The example that is highlighted in this study is the setting up by government of a number of business introduction services (BIS) for the facilitation of informal venture capital investment. These are agencies that seek to bring together potential investors and investees - a kind of dating agency. The public sector BIS are mainly run by Training and Enterprise Councils (TEC), and were set up on the premise that there existed a large number of people who were looking to invest in small businesses but were unaware of any opportunities to do so. The problem was one of information, not risk. BIS have not in all cases been set up by the state, and indeed the pioneer, Lucius Cary of Venture Capital Report, was from the private sector. Nevertheless, there were very few up until the 1990s and, as a result, the government intervention had a significant impact in the area. Consequently, they are worth considering as a particular state approach to the equity gap problem.

Laissez-Faire

The final position that is considered in this study is the laissez-faire stance. For an economy to be run on such principles is an ideal. However, within a particular policy area it is possible for a largely laissez-faire approach to be taken. It can be defined as *an approach to the equity gap that involves no direct policy initiatives designed to stimulate that particular type of investment.* The motivation for such a policy is the belief that unimpeded market forces provide the best solution to economic problems. Many have argued that this view is appropriate to the problem of the equity gap, although there are not so many who believe this at present. The Conservative

Party, when elected in 1979, argued that the reason why there were a number of finance gaps was that market forces had been perverted by an over-interfering state, and that if the state retreated from the scene matters would correct themselves. Again, a central distinction of this position against the other positions is the view taken of the attractiveness of investments in the range of the equity gap. The laissez-faire position rejects the view of the first two positions which state that investments in that range are commercially unattractive. On this there is agreement with the approach of non-financial intervention. However, a laissez-faire view also disagrees with that position over the need for the state to be involved even in a non-financial manner. It is the contention of this study that the state has taken a largely laissez-faire stance towards the institutional venture capital market, in respect of the problem of the equity gap. There has been no attempt to channel any of the market's resources into the range of the equity gap through an interventionist policy. Consequently, the performance of that market in addressing the problem of the gap is assessed as an outcome of a laissez-faire policy.

A Brief Note on Direct State Intervention

It is necessary to briefly clarify the use of the term *direct state intervention* in this study. Direct state intervention on a continuum of solutions to the equity gap is not the same as that which is used on a continuum, for example, showing alternative ways of running the whole economy. If it is suggested that a policy of direct state intervention is necessary to bridge the equity gap, this is not a recommendation for the abolition of private ownership and a movement of the economy towards a socialist model. This is because what is being looked at in this study is an equity *gap*, a criticism that states that *not all* of small business's financing needs are catered for, not that *none* of their financing needs are being catered for. None of the positions on the continuum set out above, therefore, are arguing for the abolition of private enterprise. It is accepted in this study that the private sector will finance most of the needs of business, and even most of the needs of small business. The contested point is over how the unsatisfied needs are to be met - whether a solution is likely to come through a greater adherence to uninhibited market forces, or whether the answer lies the other way with a certain degree of state intervention. This intervention, or indeed non-intervention, can then be one of the four types outlined above.

There are many who do not accept this constraining of the debate, and instead believe that the equity gap is just another problem caused by the flawed nature of capitalism. Marxists have a much more fundamental critique of the system than is presented in this study and believe that there needs to be a fundamental shift in the ownership of the economy. Specific to this study, Marxists believe, in broad terms, that if the state had control over investment decisions there would be a much more efficient allocation of resources, with problems like the equity gap disappearing. The decision of the study to disregard this position needs to be justified, and can be in two ways. Firstly, it is the contention of this study that the extent of the problem of the equity gap is not sufficient to warrant any fundamental shift in the ownership and control of the economy. The very fact that a *gap* is being investigated in this study implies, correctly, that other financing needs are being met, and history seems to provide little evidence that centralised control of investment decisions leads to a better distribution of resources than the situation that is under discussion in this study.

This first point of defence is supplemented by the argument that a substantial shift in the ownership of the economy is not possible anyway, as there would be structural constraints on any state that might try to carry out such a policy in a capitalist society. This view can be justified by simply referring to one of the policies featured in this study, the NEB. There were many reasons why the NEB never took the radical shape the left had originally planned for it. David Marsh and Gareth Lockesley believe that the structural power of capital was a crucial factor.[39] They comment that this power

> establishes the framework within which the Government, and indeed all the interest groups, function. The Government has autonomy but that autonomy is constrained by certain imperatives of the capitalist system. The Government depends on sustaining the process of capital accumulation, thus attempting to keep up the profitability of the private sector, retain financial confidence and reduce inflation. Such aims serve the interests of capital and may be pursued by Government independent of the representations made by individual companies, financial institutions, or peak organisations.[40]

Aims of the Study

The role of this study is to test the relative effectiveness of the alternative policy approaches established in this chapter using evidence from the post-war period. This serves two purposes. Firstly, it allows a judgement to be made on the policies pursued by the two main parties over this period. It will be seen that none of the policies has been particularly successful, although this has been for different reasons. Secondly, it permits an understanding of the potential of the four policy approaches to address the problem of the gap in the future, which is important given that new policies are being formulated in this area with ever greater frequency. The assessment of the evidence on the post-war period is presented in chapters three to six. In these chapters the policy approaches are judged against three criteria. Firstly, the effectiveness of the approaches in raising finance is measured. Secondly, the effectiveness of the approaches in targeting that finance at the equity gap is assessed. Thirdly, the performance of the approaches in promoting or undertaking profitable investments in the range of the equity gap is also assessed. In the next chapter, however, the range of policies implemented during the post-war period are set in historical context.

Notes

[1] *Report of the Committee on Finance and Industry*, London, HMSO, Cmnd 3897, 1931, p173.
[2] Geroski, P, 'Meaning of market failure', *Financial Times Mastering Management 18*, 8 March 1996, p13.
[3] Cohen, R, 'Venture capital is crucial to recovery', *The Observer*, 18 October 1992, pB2.
[4] Murray, G, 'The second equity gap', *UK Venture Capital Journal*, January 1993, p23.
[5] *Ibid.*, p28.
[6] Hutton, W, 'The Treasury wakes up to our real problems', *The Guardian*, 10 March 1994, p17.
[7] Lever, H and Edwards, G, 'How to bank on Britain', *The Sunday Times*, 9 November 1980, p16.
[8] *Ibid.*
[9] Edwards, G, 'British banks do not give credit where it is due', *The Guardian*, 10 February 1992, p11.
[10] Hutton, W, 'The long and short of investment', *The Guardian*, 17 May 1991, p8.
[11] Macmillan, H, *The Middle Way*, London, Macmillan, 1938, p254.
[12] Ashdown, P, *Citizen's Britain*, London, Fourth Estate, 1989, p103.
[13] Hutton, W, on *The John Bull Business*, BBCtv, 1992.
[14] Coopers and Lybrand, *Made in the UK: The Middle Market Survey - Executive Summary*, London, Coopers and Lybrand, 1994, p3.
[15] Ingham, G, *Capitalism Divided: The City and Industry in British Social Development*, London, Macmillan, 1984, p65.
[16] Hopwood, A, on *The John Bull Business*, BBCtv, 1992.

[17] Ingham, *op.cit.*, p67; p69.
[18] Ingham, *op.cit.*, p70.
[19] Glyn, A and Sutcliffe, B, 'The Rivalry of Financial and Industrial Capital', in Coates, D and Hillard, J (ed) *The Economic Decline of Modern Britain: The Debate Between Left and Right*, Brighton, Wheatsheaf, 1986, p246.
[20] *Ibid.*
[21] House of Lords Select Committee, *Report on Innovation in Manufacturing Industry*, London, HMSO, 1991, p16.
[22] *Ibid.*
[23] Rose, H, 'Britain's Financial System and Economic Performance: Old Charges Renewed', *Barclays Review*, May 1982, p28.
[24] *Ibid.*
[25] *Ibid.*, pp29-30.
[26] *Ibid.*, p30.
[27] Clutterbuck, D and Crainer, S, *The Decline and Rise of British Industry*, London, WH Allen, 1988, p319.
[28] *Ibid.*, p322.
[29] Bank of England, 'Financing British Industry', *Bank of England Quarterly Bulletin*, September 1980, p323.
[30] Institute of Directors, *Short-termism and The State We're In*, London, IoD, 1996.
[31] Government response to the *House of Lords Select Committee Report on Innovation in Manufacturing Industry*, June 1991, p8.
[32] Clements, S, *The Relationship Between German SMEs and Their Banks*, Cranfield, 3i European Enterprise Centre, 1992, p1.
[33] *Ibid.*
[34] *Ibid.*
[35] *Ibid.*, p6.
[36] Hutton, W, 'The long and short of investment', *op.cit.*
[37] Ewan Macpherson, 'Will the bait be tasty enough?', *Financial Times*, 10 May 1994, p12.
[38] Drummond, R, 'Overcoming an image problem', *Investors Chronicle, Survey: Venture Capital and Europe*, 9 October 1992, p15.
[39] Marsh, D and Lockesley, G, 'Capital in Britain: Its structural power and influence over policy', *West European Politics*, Vol 6, No 2, 1983, pp36-60.
[40] Marsh and Lockesley, *op.cit.*, pp37-38.

2 Government and the UK Equity Gap Since 1945

In response to the continuing complaints about the existence of an equity gap, governments in the post-war period have implemented a number of policies. This chapter sets these policies in historical perspective. It is important to note, however, that it only deals with those policies which have been implemented *directly* to address the problem of the gap. Many general economic policies and tax changes have taken place over the past 50 years, but these are not considered, not least as it can be argued that such measures do not, and indeed cannot, address the factors behind the existence of an equity gap. General economic policies do not, for example, have any impact on the fact that later stage investments are perceived as lower risk than early stage investments. It is also not the case that a bouyant economic environment necessarily affects the existence of a gap. Figures presented later in the study on venture capital investment in the late 1980s bear testimony to this. This chapter also reveals the attitude of the financial sector towards the idea of the existence of an equity gap and towards the intervention of the state. It can be seen that the financial sector has consistently and largely successfully resisted state intervention in the financial sector, partly through direct pressure and partly due to its structural position in the economy.

Macmillan Committee Report on Finance and Industry

As was mentioned in the previous chapter, the starting point for the study is the 1931 report of the Macmillan Committee on Finance and Industry. This Committee was appointed with the broad brief of inquiring into 'banking, finance, and credit, paying regard to the factors both internal and international which govern their operation, and to make recommendations calculated to enable these agencies to promote the development of trade and commerce and the employment of labour.'[1] The report is mainly remembered, however, for paragraph 404 where the Committee identified the existence of the much contested 'equity gap'. The Committee reported:

It has been represented to us that great difficulty is experienced by the smaller and medium-sized businesses in raising the capital which they may from time to time require, even when the security offered is perfectly sound. To provide adequate machinery for raising long-dated capital in amounts not sufficiently large for a public issue, i.e. amounts ranging from small sums up to say £200,000 or more, always presents difficulties. The expense of a public issue is too great in proportion to the capital raised, and therefore it is difficult to interest the ordinary investor by the usual method.[2]

As an answer to this problem the Committee recommended the creation of a new institution 'to devote itself particularly to these smaller industrial and commercial issues ... We see no reason why with proper management, and provided British industry in general is profitable, such a concern should not succeed.'[3] The significance of this finding should not be underestimated. For the first time it was being established by a significant and respected body that the financial sector was failing a key sector in the economy, and moreover that a new institution should be placed into the financial sector to deal with the problem. Simultaneously this was a challenge to the authority of the financial institutions and a sanction to the emerging interventionist ideas of many political figures.

Government and the Structure of Finance in the UK in the Post-war Period

There is no doubt that the financial sector perceived the Macmillan report as a threat to their freedom from government interference. Indeed, although the report led to the creation of ICFC, it is revealed in this chapter that this was merely a calculated attempt by the Treasury and the Bank of England to avoid a more serious form of political intervention. In this task the financial sector has been generally successful over the post-war period. For example, just in the area that concerns this study, ICFC, now 3i, has become just another financial institution whilst the other political initiatives since 1945 have either been disbanded or operate only at the margins. The financial sector has comfortably avoided its nightmare scenario of a powerful state backed industrial finance institution challenging its position and practices.

The latest 'threat' to the financial sector came in 1994 when Stephen Dorrell, then Financial Secretary, announced that the Treasury would be investigating whether 'our financial structures encourage the development of successful entrepreneurial activity'.[4] In particular, there was concern over difficulties in raising capital for hi-tech start-ups and the high level of dividends companies were paying out to their shareholders. The mentioning of the word 'dividend', however, led to a huge protest from the City, and a memorable contribution from Lord Hanson, who accused Mr Dorrell of sounding like a 'socialist'. As a result the investigation was quietly dropped and shortly afterwards Mr Dorrell moved on from the Treasury. From ICFC to the very latest developments, the financial sector has been successful at resisting government intervention in its affairs despite strong evidence that the effect has been the damaging of productive industry. To have been able to maintain this resistance has required considerable influence in the political system. A number of commentators have identified the sources of this influence.

Explanations for the dominance of finance

Many of the explanations for the continued dominance of the financial sector focus on the Bank of England. In institutional terms the Bank is clearly an asset to the financial sector. Frank Longstreth argues that 'the position of finance has been preserved through its penetration of key state bureaucracies, its ability to control important levers of power. The Bank of England is the linchpin of this presence, its traditional autonomy confirmed rather than eliminated by the Nationalisation Act of 1945. The Bank's position of authority is the locus of financial interests in the state.'[5] The traditional autonomy of the Bank is a key element as this autonomy from the state has been used to pursue the interests of finance. The Bank is the government's banker but has been able to pursue the interests of finance through its position on economic committees and the like. The manning of the Bank is also a significant factor in the support it gives to the financial sector. Traditionally the Bank has appointed its Governor from the financial sector; Robin Leigh-Pemberton from the National Westminster Bank is a recent example. It is argued that with such people at the helm of the Bank it is inevitable that it will promote the interests of finance. Sir Leslie O'Brien, the Governor in 1970, brought both the institutional and personal factors together when he said that the Bank was 'an arm of Government in the City ... [with an] understanding of the legitimate interests and needs of City institutions... I am not, then the representative of the City but I do represent City interests where I think it is right and proper to do so ... I am a discriminating advocate.'[6] Longstreth concludes that the City has been 'in the privileged position of having its "discriminating advocate" at the heart of the state apparatus where economic policy is formulated.'[7] It is a position not enjoyed by manufacturing industry and is, thus, of huge advantage to the financial sector. This institutional source of power, however, is said to be backed up by even more powerful forces. Forces that come from finance's structural power.

Theories of the structural power of capital are criticised for many reasons, one of which being that they do not take into account the divisions *within* capitalism. As a consequence, there are further theories which state that finance capital has structural power *over* industrial capital. The first structural advantage that finance has over industry is the urgency of financial crises. Industrial crises unfold over a much greater period of time than financial crises. One could argue that the effect of the 1979-1981 Thatcher economic policies on manufacturing industry was absolutely catastrophic for the economy, yet it was an effect that unwound over a number of years; there was no short period in which the situation was deemed to need 'emergency' attention. There have been numerous occasions, however, when a financial crisis has been the only matter on which a government has been able to concentrate. Financial crises often present themselves as a matter of the government's life and death. The recent exchange rate mechanism crisis can be seen as an example of this. Throughout August 1992 the government struggled to keep up the level of the pound. By the beginning of September the struggle was becoming increasingly desperate and the latest progress was headline news every day. Economic policy at that time was being framed in order to deal with the demands of a financial crisis rather than the needs of the productive sector. As Will Hutton noted at the time: 'Here we are two years into the recession with a growing threat of an interest rate rise hanging over a chronically depressed economy. A slump is emerging as a very real possibility.'[8]

The ability of financial crises to dominate a government's economic policy is perhaps most famously associated with the 1964-1970 Labour Government. Frank Longstreth concluded: 'Labour was faced with [...a financial] crisis almost immediately upon forming a government in 1964, and the initial response to this, the decision not to devalue, set the parameters for Labour's policy, or the lack of it, over the next six years.'[9] Furthermore, the precipitation of a financial crisis need not be a reaction to economic circumstances. Particularly of relevance to a Labour Government is the ability of the financial sector to precipitate a crisis in reaction to policy. Any fundamental shift in the balance of public policy towards industry would be initiated in this knowledge. Another element of finance's structural power is ideological. The financial sector is said to have been aided in defending its interests because such a defence has been perceived as a defence of the national interest. Michael Lisle-Williams concludes:

> Such a defence has been legitimised by an ideology associating the national interest with British creditworthiness abroad, private control of financial institutions, and strong sterling. Its consequences have been that objectives related to the exchange rate, balance of payments, level of inflation, and money supply have taken precedence over the quantity and quality of capital stock, manpower and output in manufacturing, and over more general social goals.[10]

Longstreth concurs on this point: 'The City has ... largely set the parameters of economic policy and its interests have generally predominated since the late nineteenth century. Its dominance has been so complete that its position has often been taken as the quintessence of responsible financial policy.'[11] Whether these theories accurately identify and quantify the influence of the financial sector is open to question. What is clear, however, is that government policies implemented in the post-war period in an attempt to solve the problem of the equity gap have not challenged the primacy of that sector. The range of initiatives which have been implemented are nevertheless worthy of consideration from two points of view. Firstly, the policies have been major initiatives involving the outlay of a considerable amount of public money. It is right that their contribution to the economy be accurately measured. Secondly, evidence on these the policies provide an understanding of the relative efficacy of alternative government approaches to the equity gap - the main task of this study.

Government Policies in the Post-war Period

The Macmillan Commitee report did precipitate some response in the years up to the Second World War, although it can be best described as half-hearted. The private sector made some attempt at creating new institutions. Between 1934 and 1935 three institutions of note were established; Charterhouse Industrial Development Co, Credit for Industry, and Leadenhall Securities Incorporation. The industrial finance problem for small and medium sized businesses at that time was illustrated by the example of Credit for Industry. This company offered long-term credit, for up to 20 years, in sums of between £100 and £50,000 on what were said to be slightly more favourable terms than the norm.[12] The company received a large amount of applications, but its tough criteria of requiring firms to have been profitable for the previous three to six years meant that only a few were financed. Indeed, after five years its loans, less repayments, amounted to only £384, 909.[13] The response of the financial sector to the Macmillan report, therefore, was slight. Indeed, Richard Coopey argued that their most significant move in this area was the creation of the Securities Management Trust which occured prior to the report in 1929. The response of government was also muted, not least because of the non-interventionist ethos which existed in the Treasury. Indeed, it was only during the Second World War that ideas about the active use of the state in economic regeneration became established and influenced this issue. The war effort had been organised through state planning and the Labour Party believed that planning would be required after the war if Britain was not to return to the dire economic and social circumstances of the 1920s and 1930s. In this context the Labour Party began to press for greater action over the equity gap. They were to face stubborn resistance as the Bank of England, the Treasury, and the financial system set their faces against change.

1945: Industrial and Commercial Finance Corporation

The first significant attempt by the state to bridge the equity gap was the formation of ICFC in 1945. Whilst ICFC was a private sector body funded mainly by the clearing banks there is no doubt that its formation was due to political intervention, particularly from the Labour Party. Indeed, it is the case that the eventual nature of the body was the result of negotiations and manoeuvring by a number of interests, including the Treasury and the Board of Trade. Two points about ICFC are particularly relevant for this study. Firstly, the clearing banks, who were to be ICFC's shareholders, were greatly reluctant to become involved, with one of the banks continuing in its efforts to undermine the institution for some time after it had begun its operations. Secondly, many of those involved in the creation of ICFC, including the Treasury and the yet to be nationalised Bank of England, saw the institution as a way of resisting any direct intervention in the financial sector by the state. These characteristics of two of the most important actors in the industrial and financial arena explain much that has occured over the past 50 years in relation to state intervention and the equity gap. Furthermore, the story of the creation of ICFC gives a fascinating insight into the workings of the political process.

Given the essentially ideological battles that were fought over ICFC it was not surprising that its early years were uneasy, yet it survived and is now a major, if not greatly known, financial institution. The institution has undergone a number of restructurings over the past 50 years including a merger in 1973 when it became known as Finance for Industry, and a complete makeover in 1983 when it began operating under the title Investors in Industry, abbreviated to the more familiar 3i. 3i currently boasts a portfolio of 3,400 investments and managed funds of £2.7 billion, and in 1994 experienced a further change when it was floated on the stock market.

The Treasury and the Bank of England hoped that the limited pre-war reaction of the financial sector to the Macmillan report would satisfy the political clamour for something to be done about the alleged equity gap. This was not the case, however, and by the time thoughts had turned to life after the war a strong case had been advanced in favour of significant intervention by the state in the economy. In particular there was a determination amongst many in the political system that certain interests, especially financial, would not be allowed to return the country to the pre-war norms as had been the case after the First World War. This was a determination shared by Labour politicians, who were significant players in the formulation of the reconstruction plans.

The initial plans for ICFC were formulated in the Committee on Post-War Employment (CPWE), which was set up in July 1943. Coopey and Clarke, in their recent history of ICFC/3i, play down the influence of Labour figures, both on this committee and on the creation of ICFC in general.[14] The Labour Party had originally drawn up proposals for a National Investment Bank which was to be an institution to 'approve, and increasingly perhaps initiate, all new capital issues'.[15] However, this body had weak support amongst the party's leadership and was dropped as an immediate aim. Labour's influence on the CPWE was limited to the Board of Trade's representatives who in reaction proposed a compromise measure - a private sector investing body. Whilst conceding defeat over a state initiative, the Board of Trade wanted to have considerable influence over the new private sector body, including some input over commercial decisions. Their lack of influence on the Committee was demonstrated when even this restricted ambition was defeated. Although the Board of Trade clearly did lack influence on the committee, the fact remained that some sort of small business investment institution had been placed on the agenda. That its methods of operation were decided by other players should not obscure this fact.

It is nevertheless true, as Coopey and Clarke note, that the real influence over the nature of the eventual institution lay with the Treasury and the Bank of England.[16] The Bank of England went even further than the Treasury in their opposition to a new institution. Not only did they oppose a state institution, they also opposed any new developments in the private sector. They eventually consented to a body of the nature of ICFC, but their support was simply based upon the view that in the prevailing political atmosphere an institution needed to be formed in the private sector to avoid the far worse fate of the state intervening directly in industrial financing. To this end the Bank began to seek the support of the City institutions that would be involved. When approaching the important City players the Bank made no secret of its motives, as can be seen in Governor Montagu Norman's communication with a senior official in the Midland Bank. He stated that the proposals for ICFC had 'the blessing of Whitehall and nothing short of it has [its blessing] ... [M]y purpose is to satisfy Whitehall: to keep them out of the Banking business and free of malevolence towards the bankers - which at the moment are stakes worth playing for.'[17] The Deputy Governor Otto Niemeyer went even further, admitting privately: 'As you know I don't believe much in this body and hope (and expect) that they won't do much'[18] Indeed, the Bank saw its role as 'overcoming reluctance in the City while calming a degree of over-enthusisasm in Whitehall'.[19]

The 'over-enthusiasm in Whitehall' extended to the Treasury, as the ministry and the Bank of England were not by any means in total accord. The Treasury, whilst opposing the ambitions of the Board of Trade to have influence over the Corporation's commercial freedom, nevertheless wished it to have close relations with government, and in particular act in a way which would complement the government's regional policy. This the Bank opposed fundamentally as it would again affect the Corporation's ability to act in a strictly commercial manner. On the issue the Bank of England would carry the day. Two of the main pillars of finance and industry in the UK, therefore, were unequivocal in their opposition to any sort of state intervention in industrial financing. There was grudging support, for wider political reasons, of a private sector institution (or institutions as it turned out), but even the Treasury's somewhat contradictory wish for that institution to incorporate some of the government's regional aims into its brief was rejected. The minimum possible was to be done in the hope that it would allow the financial sector to weather the storm of what was clearly felt to be tiresome and ill-conceived interference by political interests. Nevertheless, this minimum was still a significant advance given the state of industrial financing at the time.

The Bank of England's lack of enthusiasm for any sort of development was, not surprisingly, matched by the clearing banks who had been allocated responsibility for funding ICFC. As was mentioned above, the Bank warned the clearing banks that if they did not acquiesce in the creation of ICFC they may be punished by far more interventionist action by government. It was even suggested that a Labour government might attempt to nationalise the banking sector. As Coopey and Clarke comment, apart from their obvious general wish not to be cajoled into certain actions by government and the Bank of England, the clearing banks had two specific reasons for opposing their involvement in funding ICFC. Firstly, the banks did not wish to tie up their resources in a long-term, and to them, politically inspired corporation. Financial institutions in the UK have traditionally prefered to keep their advances liquid. Secondly, the rationale of the Corporation offended banking logic. The Corporation was designed to provide finance for what were perceived to be higher risk investments, yet it was being suggested that these companies should receive the finance on preferential terms. The bank's conventional response to higher risk is higher rates of interest; thus a fundamental conflict of philosophy existed.

Despite opposing the development in principle, a number of the banking chiefs agreed with the Bank of England's pragmatic line that this institution was needed to avoid direct intervention by the state. This group, however, did not include Charles Lidbury of the Westminster, who was the most trenchant hardliner. His opposition continued after ICFC opened its doors and he refused to co-operate in educating local managers about the Corporation's existence and role. The result of this was that in the first six months of ICFC's operations investment resulting from introductions by Westminster amounted to one £5,000 investment, the smallest amount ICFC would consider.[20] His opposition was not successful in preventing ICFC's formation, however, as at a meeting held in May 1944 between the Bank of England and the clearing banks plans for the Corporation were finally agreed in principle. These were finalised in the following October and a date was set for the commencement of ICFC's activities.

Coopey and Clarke in their history of ICFC appear anxious, for whatever reason, to play down the political element in its origins. They argue that ICFC was not influenced directly by Labour Party policy makers, although they accept that ideas about using the state to solve economic problems, promoted by Labour at that time, was an important 'negative' factor, as it produced a fear of substantial state intervention in the financial sector. Yet this factor was surely the *most* important reason for the creation of ICFC. Without the political pressure no institution would ever have been set up. The evidence for this comes in Coopey and Clarke's own account of the views of those they believe were the key actors: the Bank of England, the Treasury and the clearing banks. It is inconceivable that they would have acted to form ICFC if there had not been political pressure; after all there was little or no belief in these quarters that any significant problem existed over the financing of small firms.

ICFC eventually came into existence in July 1945. It was initially provided with £15 million in share capital and was given the power to borrow up to a further £30 milllion. The aim of ICFC was 'to provide credit by means of loans or the subscription of loan or share capital or otherwise for industrial and commercial business or enterprises in Great Britain, particularly in cases where the existing facilities provided by banking institutions and the Stock Exchanges are not readily or easily available.'[21] ICFC was empowered to invest between £5,000 and £200,000 in a single company, a range in line with the gap identified in the Macmillan report. The chairman of ICFC was to be appointed by the Bank of England, with other directors being chosen by the Corporation's shareholders, the clearing banks. Having been formed in difficult circumstances ICFC encountered a serious threat to its survival within three years of trading. There was great pressure on the Corporation in its early years to invest its funds quickly so as to show the financial community that it was a permanent institution. This led to a number of investments being made which contained a high element of risk. Within a few years a number of these companies had come to grief, losing ICFC considerable amounts of money, £600,000 between 1947 and 1949.[22] This was what the banks hoped and expected to happen, and they used the failed investments to press their case to either withdraw from their commitment or have it reduced.

The banks were not successful in this, however, and the Corporation's fortunes improved as did those of the economy as a whole. The Corporation had learned valuable lessons about the costs of hurried and ill-considered investment, and had learned about the importance of organised after-investment monitoring. Yet this period demonstrated the continued opposition and unhelpful attitudes of the banks. Whether their opposition was born of a genuine belief that such an institution was unnecessary and doomed to failure, or whether there was also an element of pique at the suggestion that they were not doing their jobs properly (which is implicitly what ICFC's very existence was saying) it is hard to believe that such an episode could have happened in any other European country. Further problems were experienced by ICFC in the 1950s when they became caught up in the credit squeeze. Yet by this stage ICFC had established its practices and begun to build up its reputation. Indeed, the Corporation's presence on the financial scene was not seriously threatened again. During the 1960s and 1970s it steadily built up its commitments, with rapid growth occuring in the 1980s.[23] In 1994 the organisation, by then restructured under the name of 3i, was floated on the stock exchange, since when the original shareholders, the banks, have begun to offload their stakes.[24] In June 1995 21% of 3i's stock was sold by the banks and the Bank of England. This sale realised a profit of £176 million.[25] Perhaps the intolerable burden of supporting ICFC had been worthwhile after all.

Table 2.1 ICFC/3i Outstanding Investment 1951 to 1993 (£m)

1951	20.25	**1975**	246.90
1955	28.62	**1980**	378.31
1960	38.37	**1985**	1603.78
1965	66.42	**1990**	2348.22
1970	152.11	**1993**	2428.24

Source: Adapted from R. Coopey and D. Clarke, *3i: Fifty Years of Investing in Industry*, Oxford, Oxford University Press, 1995, pp403-406.

ICFC, now 3i, has not been without its critics. Many argue that the organisation has been too conservative in its lending practices, a tendency which has ensured it has not provided a solution to the problem of the gap. Yet Donald Clarke argues that it is government that must be held accountable for any shortcomings in ICFC/3i's performance. He argues that if only government had given the organisation the same guarantees that were given to Germany's KfW, it could have raised greater amounts on the market and have provided industry with more of the industrial finance it needed. Nevertheless, the story of ICFC/3i is a fascinating case study of the relationship between the state, finance, and industry in the UK. Much that has happened since the war in relation to the equity gap could have been predicted from an understanding of the origins of ICFC. What was particularly striking was the view of the banks that their attempt to protect the status quo was not 'political', an accusation that they regularly aimed at others. Yet it can be argued that the protection of a free market is just as much a political act as the advancing of a form of intervention, as it is the act of defending sectional interests. Indeed, given the circumstances the UK faced after the Second World War, it could certainly be said to have been so in this case. The banks also revealed their commitment to short-termist banking practices, wishing for advances to industry to remain 'self-liquidating' and 'readily realisable'. Indeed, their characterisation of any other practice was disdainful. It was merely lending to 'the incompetent, the thriftless and the indolent, to say nothing of the unbusinesslike inventor, who are sadly apt to lose other people's money as well as their own'.[26]

1948: National Research Development Corporation

One of the main concerns for Britain in the post-war period was its apparant inability to develop innovations. British scientists had a fine reputation as inventors, but many inventions were developed by organisations overseas or not at all. In order to remedy this situation the Labour Government set up the National Research Development Corporation (NRDC) in 1948. The provision of finance for the development of scientific breakthroughs was only a small part of the NRDC's activities, yet it was an important part. The very nature of innovative projects meant that investing finance was high risk, and most investors, particularly the City institutions, came to the conclusion that they were better served investing their capital elsewhere. The role of the NRDC was to 'seek out promising inventions from both the Government-funded sector and from private sources, and, where appropriate, to launch these on their way to successful exploitation.'[27] The NRDC's criteria for investment was wide. They stated that the Corporation would 'consider participation in the funding of any venture involving technological innovation, so long as the venture is deemed by the Corporation to be in the public interest and can demonstrate a reasonable prospect of commercial success.'[28] Harold Wilson who, as President of the Board of Trade, took the original legislation through the House of Commons, commented in 1974 on the value of the Corporation's activities:

> NRDC has been willing to provide practical assistance in developing a sound idea in the form of direct financial support or suitable arrangements for production under licence. This remains an important role, but in recent years even the largest companies in this country have felt the need for, and in many

cases obtained, the financial support of the Corporation for projects involving considerable elements of risk and uncertainty.[29]

In terms of its functions the NRDC largely stayed the same during the post-war period, with its financing role remaining important. Evidence of this was seen in 1980 when the Corporation set up a £2 million fund to enable it to increase its investment in small business and start-up situations.[30] The fund offered finance in amounts ranging from £10,000 to £60,000, which could be in the form of equity, preference shares, or loans. There were changes, however, during the Thatcher years, as the Government, suspicious of the need for public financing bodies, sought to diminish the financing role. As will be discussed later in the chapter, the NRDC was merged with the NEB in 1981 to form the British Technology Group (BTG), and in 1983 it was decided that this organisation would concentrate on the technology transfer role of the NRDC. The most significant event, however, occurred in 1985 when the Government finally ended the Corporation's right of first refusal for inventions arising in universities and publically-funded research bodies. This required the Corporation to evolve into a more competitive body that was able to attract business rather than expect it as of right.

The NRDC while in public hands encountered no shortage of criticism. One of the main complaints was that it was too bureaucratic and slow to react to new developments. According to a former employee with the NEB, the 1981 merger revealed the undynamic nature of the Corporation. She argued that the NRDC could not adapt to new developments, something which was most graphically exposed during the making of the investment in Celltech, the biotechnology company, an investment discussed later in the chapter. Other criticisms have focused upon the record of the NRDC, with many arguing that it has been based upon a few very successful inventions, while its general performance has been uninspiring. These criticisms no longer concern studies of public sector financing bodies as on 31st March 1992 the privatisation of BTG (the NRDC and NEB elements had been dropped by then) was completed.

1950s and 1960s: A reliance on existing institutions

In 1959 the Radcliffe Committee, which had been set up to assess the workings of the monetary system, reported that 'with certain modifications ... the existing institutions can look after the ordinary requirements of small businesses for capital'.[31] Predictably, the most serious problems still existing were for small innovative companies. The fact that their borrowing requirements were large in proportion to their existing capital structure and that their business was of a higher risk than normal, were obstacles to the raising of investment capital. It was reported that the problem might be helped if a loan guarantee scheme be set up. The Committee's general belief that small business was adequately catered for by existing arrangements was reflected in government policy in the 1950s and 1960s. The Conservative Party of the 1950s agreed with the views expressed by the Committee, and in any case, had no desire to upset the financial sector. Meanwhile, the Labour Party, elected to government in 1964, was more concerned with creating the Department of Economic Affairs and its National Plan, and on providing an instrument for restructuring big business, which it did in 1966 with the formation of the IRC. The IRC was designed to promote industrial efficiency and profitability by assisting the reorganisation and development of appropriate industries. The justification for the IRC was that production units in the UK were too small to be competitive in world markets. It was given £150 million to help it carry out its task and promoted developments such as the merger of GEC and Associated Electrical Industries.

The Heath Government, elected in 1970, constituted a shift to the right, and it was primarily concerned with removing the state from economic life rather than intervening any further. To this end it disbanded the IRC. When its U-turn came in 1972, it was more concerned with companies like Rolls Royce than smaller companies, although it did pass the 1972 Regional Selective Assistance Act which has been a substantial source of government help to business. Labour's defeat in 1970, however, convinced the left of the party that holding power was futile unless they were willing to ignore the established rules of the game. They argued that government had to be radical and, if it was to improve the lives of the working people, take control of the commanding heights of profitable industry. It was in this atmosphere that the next major initiative was formed.

1975: National Enterprise Board

The initial plans for the NEB, the most significant attempt yet at creating a state investment institution, were far removed from the eventual roles it fulfilled. Tony Benn and his supporters from the left of the party were the original creators of the Board. The left had big plans for the Board, seeing it not merely to complement capitalism, as traditionally most Labour economic and industrial policies aimed to do, but to replace it in a conscious attempt to redirect wealth and power in Britain towards the working class. The plan for the Board was to involve the effective confiscation of the top 25 (at least) industrial companies in the UK. Through ownership of leading companies in key industrial sectors the left were convinced they could control those sectors, and thus assume a significant grip on the operation of the economy. The group rationalised that 'firms in any given sector are strongly influenced by the investment planning, plant building, and pricing policies of their most feared competitor ... Fear of losing their share of the market can be a more effective stimulus than the wise words of government.'[32] That the policy was to be a significant break with the way the economy had been run in the past was considered a selling point. The Group proclaimed:

> The experience of Labour Governments has made it increasingly evident that even the most comprehensive measures of social and fiscal reform can only succeed in blunting the hard edges of a capitalist economy, and cannot achieve any fundamental change in the power relationships which dominate our society ... if the causes of inequality are to be attacked at their roots, structural change is necessary. The main element in that structural change can only be the transfer of economic wealth and power from a small economic oligarchy to the people.[33]

However, Benn and his supporters faced considerable opposition from the right and the centre of the party which held most of the senior posts in the Shadow Cabinet. Harold Wilson, who had little time for either Benn or his plans, refused to accept that the Board should be given the power of compulsory acquisition and insisted on its ommission from the 1974 General Election manifesto. This point Wilson believed was the crucial element, as its explicit absence from the policy meant that the Conservatives faced a more difficult task in attacking the policy on the hustings. Wilson also felt that the omission of the compulsory element would reassure business itself, and prevent Labour having to come into office with the private sector in complete panic. On the other hand Wilson understood the need for unity and allowed Benn to include much of his policy in the manifesto. As a result the policy still contained, by post-war standards, a radical agenda.

Wilson was confident, however, that once in government he would be able to dilute the policy still further, a tactic which culminated in Benn himself being removed from the Department of Industry in June 1975. In February 1975, before his removal, Benn went to the House of Commons to present the NEB to an expectant nation. The main features were that the Board was to have 'an initial tranche of £700 million with the power to increase this amount, if Parliament approves, to £1,000 million.'[34] The announcement also confirmed that 'the National Enterprise Board will have no compulsory powers of acquisition. The White Paper set out the Government's specific nationalisation proposals, which will be dealt with by the normal legislative process separate from the National Enterprise Board.'[35] Wilson commented some years later, following his resignation as Prime Minister: '[C]ontrary to the revolutionary hopes which surrounded the NEB when it was conceived in opposition days, Eric Varley's department ... ensured that it would not operate like a rogue elephant. It had to operate within the existing rules governing the provision of industrial finance.'[36] In any case, Wilson had no choice but to neuter the policy. The effect on business confidence of an NEB acting with compulsory powers could well have been significant, and like all governments operating within a capitalist system, the Labour Government was dependent on business for its own performance and popularity. The policy, therefore, evolved into a familiar social democratic instrument and was able to offer a friendly face to the business world when it finally opened its doors on 20th November 1975.

Investment under Labour

In the following March draft guidelines for the NEB were published. They were confirmation that Wilson had been able to tone down the operations of the NEB, and where there was still ambiguity the presence of Varley was a relative comfort to business, given their mistrust of Benn. *The Economist* observed that 'the NEB's guidelines favour the bosses'[37] The journal considered that the draft guidelines for the Board were 'like the curate's egg, good in parts ... the best way to run Britain's new National Enterprise Board will be to allow it to be enterprising; the worst way will be to treat it as the emergency department of the national lame duck and job preservation clinic. The draft guidelines for the NEB ... presage a bit of both. Lord Ryder [NEB Chairman] will do well indeed if it is the enterprise bit that wins.'[38] Eric Varley and Lord Ryder wanted the NEB to be a complement to the financial sector, not a competitor. Ryder even hoped that once the NEB had established itself it would get involved in joint deals with City financiers, deals that the private sector would not initiate on its own.[39] Out of the ambiguity of the early months of the NEB a number of clear roles emerged. The first was its role as a holding company for the state's equity shareholdings. The Board took responsibility for British Leyland (BL), Rolls Royce, Herbert, Dunford and Elliott, Brown Boveri Kent, Ferranti, and the

Cambridge Instrument Company - the so-called lame ducks. A second role was responsibility for industrial reorganisation, similar to that of the IRC of the 1960s. Ryder in his Chairman's statement said that the NEB would be involved in 'promoting the rationalisation or restructuring of firms or groups within particular sectors of industry.'[40] Thirdly, the NEB was expected to regenerate the regions. To this end regional Boards were set up in the North-East and North-West.

Finally, the NEB was to provide industrial finance for small and medium sized companies. This is the role that concerns this study and is the one which is judged in chapter three. The investment was to be in the form of both equity capital and loans and was to be aimed at the perceived 'gap' for funding at the lower end of the investment market. At this time there was a very limited venture capital presence in the UK - the Board was not treading on any toes in this role. It is open to question whether these four roles should have been taken on by the same institution. It was not that they were necessarily conflictual, but that they blurred what it was that the NEB was hoping to achieve, and in the case of managing the state lame ducks brought the NEB a great deal of adverse publicity. This is a point Lord Ryder recognises in retrospect: 'There is no doubt that the role damaged the reputation of the NEB. Companies were frightened of getting involved with the NEB, not least because they were worried about being labelled a lame duck themselves.'[41] Despite the many problems the NEB faced it was still able to make five investments in 1976 and was followed by a further 22 in 1977. *The Economist* reporting on the NEB's first year said: 'After a stormy birth when some free-marketeers saw the NEB as a weapon to undo capitalism, it has managed to get by with relatively little controversy.'[42] However, in the remaining years of Labour rule this was not always so. In increasing their portfolio to 65 by the 1979 election, the NEB ran into a number of issues that concerned its position as a state venture capitalist.

One issue that often arises in connection with state industrial policies is the creation of unfair competition. The NEB was accused of this in relation to its activities in the tanning industry. The Board set up a new company, British Tanners Products (BTP), out of the beleaguered Barrow Hepburn Group, with the NEB taking half the equity. Barrow Hepburn's competitors were up in arms arguing that not only did the Board's intervention mean that they were facing subsidised competition (in an industry already suffering from over-capacity) but that the deal struck with the NEB was absurdly generous. Having alienated many of its supporters (and those who were agnostic) with its involvement with BTP, it was important for the Board that the investment was a success; it was not, and lost it £5.56 million.[43] A further issue is whether the state should compete against private companies for business. The Labour Government had made the decision that the NEB would act as a complement to the private sector rather than as a competitor, yet they were prepared to countenance certain investments that contradicted this dictum. One such investment was the 1977 decision to compete against Trafalgar House for the Fairey Group. The City was reported to be 'howling with indignation: the lame duck hospital had the effrontery to take on the private sector at its own game.'[44] The Board had to make some investments like this, however, if it was ever to produce a return near to the 15-20% demanded by 1981. This controversial investment was more successful than that of BTP, and the Board returned the company to the private sector three years later at a profit of £3.81 million.[45]

There were also doubts over the Board's attempt to create a strong British presence in computers and microelectronics. The Board created three new companies: Insac, a software company; Inmos, a micro circuits manufacturer; and Nexos, an office technology company. The results of this policy were mixed as two of the companies lost the Board a great deal of money. Insac lost the Board £6.86 million when it was passed on to the private sector in 1982, whilst Nexos lost £34 million and was dismantled in the same year. The criticism aimed at Nexos was that, while the concept was basically sound, there was little evidence that there was sufficient demand for the eventual products. Furthermore, it was argued that insufficient finance was made available to develop it properly; ten times the finance provided was really required. Inmos, however, was more successful and was bought by Thorn-EMI in 1984 for £95 million, a profit for the NEB of £29.6 million.[46] The Board's overall performance in this sector is still seen by many though as unsatisfactory.

The Labour period was dominated by the Board's involvement with BL. Michael Edwardes, the successful South African businessman, was hired in 1977 in an attempt to turn around the overweight and loss-making giant. Yet by 1979 *The Economist* was able to comment: 'The main problem for BL is simple: it cannot generate enough investment cash to prevent its competitors driving it off the road ... BL still make too many cars in too many factories with too many workers. Little has changed after five years [of Labour Government] and after the expenditure of £775 million of taxpayers' money.'[47] Keith Joseph, the first Conservative Industry Secretary, found the problem equally as taxing. Joseph's department prepared a paper for Cabinet which argued that Edwardes should be granted his wish for a further £900 million. Joseph was so unhappy about this that he finally ended up arguing against his own paper. In 1981 BL was eventually transferred out of the NEB and brought back to the Industry Department, but this was too late for the NEB. The company had drained the Board of its time and its finance - and, crucially, lost the Board much of its remaining credibility. It was, perhaps, partly due to the Board's heavy involvement with BL that its small business role was relatively neglected. Between 1975 and 1979 the NEB made 22 investments under £200,000. These were in a wide range of industries extending from sports equipment to medical engineering. This level of investment, however, was not enough to have any effect on the gap

During these years the NEB constantly faced the accusation that its investment record was very unsuccessful. As was mentioned earlier, any institution which had to take on BL, Alfred Herbert, and Rolls Royce was bound to be open to criticism. The NEB was also attacked for overly adventurous investments like BTP. On top of this the Board was also vulnerable over the steady stream of smaller, less controversial investments that lost it money. Instances always seemed to be available that could be seized upon by critics. There were a number of reasons for this. Firstly, the NEB was acting as a venture capitalist. This was a form of investment that few understood in the 1970s. As a result every investment that lost money carried with it political implications, despite the fact that loss-making investments are part of the nature of venture capital and are treated as such by venture capitalists in the private sector. Secondly, the NEB's regional role had led to the Board's regional offices making investments which probably had too much of a political aspect to them. There was strong pressure to save and create jobs in the regions and some investments were spectacularly unsuccessful. Thirdly, the fact that the NEB was operating in a weak economy did not help either.

The large number of unsuccessful investments allowed hostile commentators and MPs to reel off lists of failure. Michael Grylls, an arch-opponent of the NEB, came to debates on the Board armed with, to him, irrefutable evidence of the Board's folly:

> The NEB went into Thwaites and Reed ... That was highly unsuccessful. It lost £300,000 when it was taken over, and is still, I believe losing large sums of money. Nobody else in the clock-making business wanted this company ... We had another loss - Hivent, in Washington New Town ... into which the NEB put £54,000 some weeks ago. That company has already gone bust. This is the sort of thing that the NEB is doing and it is costing £7 million a year.[48]

In a book that Grylls wrote with John Redwood, they described the NEB as having 'put money into a motley collection of smallish companies.'[49] The Government, of course, put up a staunch defence of the Board's investment activities. This defence involved a mixture of exaggeration about the successes the NEB did have, explanations, or indeed amnesia about the investments that went wrong, and optimistic speculation about recent investments. There was hype, as well, about the significance of the Board in the economy, something demonstrated by Varley when he said that 'it has now been in operation for little over three years and it is already impossible to imagine the British industrial scene without it.'[50] Gerald Kaufman described it as 'an indispensable feature of the industrial landscape.'[51] He accounted for the failure rate by arguing that

> the NEB acts an industrial doctor, seeking to cure the ills of companies - often small companies - which have management or cash problems but which have potential worth exploiting if these problems can be cured. Sometimes they cannot be cured, and the critics of the Board in the debate today have seized on these. But it would be a very strange doctor who accepted patients only if they offered a written guarantee that they would recover.[52]

With the Labour Government in desperate trouble by late 1978, Leslie Murphy, the second NEB chairman, had to consider the prospect of having to operate under a Conservative Government, albeit one that had moderated its stance from an initial intention to abolish the Board altogether. Yet the situation that was to face the Conservatives when they came into office was made more difficult following the increase in the financial limit that was granted by the 1979 Industry Act. The £700 million (and the £300 million option) which the NEB had been given in the 1975 Act was increased to a level of £4,500 million, although much of this was earmarked for BL. The problem that awaited the Conservatives was how they were going to extricate themselves from the commitments that had been made by Labour. The Tory line had already moved to accepting that the Board should remain 'to run its existing portfolio, with the instruction that it should, with due care for the public interest, sell its assets when it can.'[53] BL and Rolls Royce had, of course, caused problems for previous governments, but there were also other problems with companies such as Inmos that required further investment. The scene was set for a clash between the desire of the party, especially the right-wing, for the destruction of the Board, and the reality of the Board's ongoing commitments.

Investment under the Conservatives

In May 1979 the Labour Party duly lost the General Election, propelling the Conservatives into power. Sir Keith Joseph had been careful to dampen down expectations of an early solution to the ideological problem the NEB posed for the party, and when he made his Commons statement on the Board's future he disappointed the right of his party by setting out five roles. First, the NEB would keep the lame ducks in its portfolio, as long as there was a prospect of a return to profitability. Second, the NEB would be allowed to take over further struggling companies, but only if there were temporary problems. Third, the NEB was to sell off its portfolio as soon as possible. Fourth, the NEB would be permitted to continue managing the high-tech companies in its portfolio, and invest in further high-tech companies, if a private sector partner could be found. Finally, the NEB was to continue, as part of the Government's regional policy, an industrial investment role in the North and North-West. The final two roles, in particular, meant that the Board would continue to invest in the range of the equity gap. Indeed, in the case of the high technology investment role, *The Economist* argued that 'explicitly, Sir Keith is admitting something that he has always denied - that there is a hole in the financial system for channelling risk capital in this direction.'[54]

Sir Keith justified his guidelines by arguing: 'We favour the encouragement of private initiative and enterprise, not the promotion of public ownership. But it will take time to restore the full vitality of the private sector.'[55] He continued this line of argument during the second reading of the Industry Bill in November: 'In our view, it is not sensible to maltreat savings and capital, blame them as a result for failing to do all they could be expected to do, and then set up a public agency to fill the gaps. There should be no need for public sector investment finance in manufacturing industry provided that savings and enterprise are sensibly treated.'[56] Whether Joseph's policy was a backdown or a planned and politically astute gradual rundown of the NEB is a matter of dispute. What cannot be denied is that numerically, if not in overall value, over half of the NEB's investments were made after the Conservatives were elected, and that does not include the investments that were made by the subsidiary, Oakwood Loan Finance Limited.

Joseph's most immediate problem was Rolls Royce. He eventually took Rolls Royce back into the Department of Industry, partly because relations between the NEB and Rolls Royce had deteriorated badly over the previous twelve months. This deterioration encompassed the relationship between Sir Leslie Murphy and Sir Kenneth Keith, the chairman of Rolls Royce. In response to the transfer, the existing NEB board members resigned, and a new board was selected, hand-picked by the Secretary of State, or rather by Sir Peter Carey, his Permanent Secretary, on his behalf.[57] Many felt that the change in the composition of the board at this time was important, as there was the suspicion that they were chosen to enact Government policy rather than to exploit their independent position.

At the end of a turbulent year, therefore, Joseph had a new Board of his own choosing, new guidelines ensconced in the 1980 Industry Act, and new rules on the NEB's financial limits. Some sort of pattern was emerging in the Government's policy towards the NEB. It had lost Rolls Royce, and shortly afterwards lost BL. In addition it had begun disposing of its other investments and it was constrained in making new investments. Over the next five years, however, the NEB was more active than many had expected. As was mentioned earlier, in terms of the number of investments, the NEB made most of them under Conservative rule. In the time up to the 1983 election the NEB was to demonstrate that even though the tide of ideas was clearly against it, there was life after Labour.

After this troubled year the NEB settled down to its new roles. In the Chairman's report of 1980, Frederick Wood, the Board's fifth chairman (Arthur Knight had retired on health grounds and John King had also had a brief spell before moving to British Airways) expressed his hope that 'the NEB can ... now concentrate on its tasks of promoting advanced technology, investment in the English regions, and acting as a source of assistance to small firms.'[58] Although this was how the NEB was to operate during these years, in 1981 there was further structural change. With an ever increasing amount of attention being paid by the NEB to advanced technology it was decided that the Board should develop closer links with the NRDC. The two boards entered into discussions and on 20th July 1981 were reorganised under the banner of the BTG. The two bodies remained separate legal entities but their staff and activities were merged.

On the face of it the merger appeared an obvious move. As the Chairman noted: 'It is generally admitted that the United Kingdom's record in commercial exploitation of its inventive genius has never, since the Second World War, matched up to the quality of the inventions themselves. We hope that, by combining the technical expertise of the NRDC with the commercial flair of the NEB, the BTG will be able, in conjunction with private sector finance, to help improve on this record.'[59] After only six months the

Chairman was reporting that 'the effect on both organisations has, I believe, been beneficial. The NEB has gained from the technical expertise and experience of the NRDC's staff, while the NRDC has been able to tap the financial skills of the NEB. The result has been to enhance the performance of both organisations.'[60]

This corporate version of the merger seems incontestable. There were other views, however. *The Economist* interpreted it in political terms: 'The Thatcher Government's solution [to the unpopularity of the NEB within the party] has been to bring the two groups together ... The low key, practical services the NRDC provides will continue, the more unrealistic ambitions of the NEB will disappear.'[61] Caroline Vaughan, a former employee of the NEB, believes that the merger, whether intentionally or not, hastened the end of the NEB. Not only was the NRDC going to become dominant within BTG, but she felt that the two institutions did not, as Freddie Wood claimed, complement each other at all. She commented: 'The Government found initially that it could not kill the NEB, but it eventually found the answer with the BTG merger. That killed it. The NRDC was not at all dynamic like the NEB. Take Celltech for example, that could not have come out of the NRDC. They could not cope with the birth of Celltech, it was totally antithetical to their views.'[62]

Indeed, the accounts of the founding of Celltech, a biotechnology company formed in 1980, tell of an NRDC that was unimaginative and pre-occupied with protecting its position. Gerard Fairtlough, a former NEB employee and a founder of Celltech, notes that 'at that time the NRDC had a monopoly in the exploitation of discoveries made in the course of work supported by the Research Councils and they viewed Celltech as the thin edge of a wedge that might break it up.'[63] This tension in the relationship is also noted by Mark Dodgson who wrote: 'By 1980 the NRDC was facing criticism from a variety of sources and for a variety of reasons, including being over-bureaucratic, unimaginative, and unable to pick winners.'[64] To Dodgson the merger of NRDC and NEB was not by any means a logical move, of which the Celltech problem was but one example.

Before and after the formation of BTG, the NEB's operations between 1980 and 1983 were in three main areas: divestment, high technology and small companies. The divestment requirement had been set out by Joseph from the time of his first policy statement back in July 1979. An initial requirement was that £100 million was to be raised in the financial year 1979-80, although this was rescinded on the grounds that it would have put the NEB in a weak bargaining position. However, the process of divestment went ahead apace. The larger companies in the Board's portfolio were some of the early disposals. ICL, Ferranti and Fairey were all sold in the first year at a handsome profit. The NEB also conceded defeat over Herbert, losing nearly £60 million from its liquidation, although it must be remembered that this was not an NEB-initiated investment. Many of the smaller ventures were also sold off, with Automation and Technical Services, Computer and Systems Engineering, and Systems Designers International being amongst those realised at a profit.

It was also decided that eight of the NEB's smaller investments would be transferred to a wholly-owned subsidiary called Grosvenor Development Capital. This was set up in March 1981. In the following February three institutional investors, Equity Capital for Industry, the British Rail Pension Fund, and County Bank (which was the representative for a number of other investors) acquired 71.5% of Grosvenor's equity. This provided Grosvenor with £7 million for further investment.[65] This move, which seemed fairly insignificant, brought the Government some criticism, as well as showing the lack of seriousness with which the Government viewed the public sector as a source of investment finance. Andy Curry was one who highlighted the issue. He commented: 'The move is in line with the BTG's statutory duty - imposed upon them by the Conservative Government - to sell off their investments when they become profitable. What this means is that while BTG sustain all the losses on their [Grosvenor's] unsuccessful attempts to start high technology companies, they see only 29% of the return on the successful ones.'[66] The NEB was getting the worst of both worlds.

Perhaps the most interesting investments at this time were the NEB's high technology ventures. In line with the new guidelines the NEB entered into a joint venture in July 1980 to create a new biotechnology company, the previously-mentioned Celltech Ltd. The NEB hoped that it would 'secure a major place for the United Kingdom in the commercialisation of developments in biotechnology.'[67] The NEB took 44% of the equity in this joint venture, the other 56% being shared amongst four private sector investors. The investment was considered important as there were 'serious concerns about the state of British biotechnology ... the US phenomenon of scientists and venture capitalists joining to exploit the potential of the new biotechnology ... seemed to be almost wholly absent in Britain.'[68] The investment seemed to be tailor-made to show that the NEB was still needed, even if only to galvanise the private sector. Over the next two years the NEB invetsed in three further biotechnology companies, Dytes Ltd, Speywood Laboratories Ltd and IQ (Bio) Ltd. The NEB was also involved in other high technology areas. Computer-aided design and machine-vision were two and, of course, there was the ongoing commitment to Inmos.

The NEB's commitment to small firms was also emphasised by the setting up in 1981 of Oakwood Loan Finance Ltd. This body was created to provide loans of up to £50,000 to small companies. In 1982, 29 offers of finance were made involving £1.15 million.[69] Overall the company made about 70 investments. Although Oakland was for some a last resort, it was more common for the finance to be used by companies to improve their gearing. The NEB also continued to make equity investments in small firms, and again with varying degrees of success. One investment that proved a great success was Epichem Ltd. This company was a manufacturer of silane gas which was used in the manufacture of microprocessors. The company had not been able to attract any interest from the private sector, not least because the gas was very unstable which made the investment risky.

Despite the fact that the NEB had been placed within BTG and had been active in disposing of its investments, there was still pressure on the Government to reduce the role of the NEB still further. By 1983 the economy was out of recession and this led the Government to believe that the private sector would be willing and able to deal with the type of investments the NEB was still active in making. As a result the reprieve that the NEB obtained after the 1979 election was about to be revealed as merely a stay of execution.

The eventual rundown of the NEB

On 30th September 1983 Cecil Parkinson announced that BTG was to have a new role. In actual fact what it amounted to was a reduction in the Group's numerous activities, with those that were associated with the NEB being dropped. This left the Group with responsibility for carrying out the technology transfer functions that the NRDC had brought to the merger. BTG's new role was designed 'to ensure that maximum advantage is taken of the commercial potential of successful UK research and development.'[70] The role was said to include 'maintaining contact with research work; evaluating the marketability of new ideas; helping their development and protection with patents; helping potential investors find research work worth investing in, and if no other funds could be found, supporting start-up companies based on worthwhile research.'[71] The NEB remained in name but most of the staff were either moved to the technology transfer operations or left the organisation altogether. The NEB's role was now to run down its portfolio. It had taken four years but the NEB had finally been put out of its misery. By 1990 the NEB portfolio contained just one item, the Oakwood Loan Finance company which remained until it could run down its own activities. The disposals were achieved through three methods: selling to the private sector; transferring investments to Oakwood to dispose of; and transferring investments to the NRDC. In 1990 the final industrial investment was relinquished. In this the NEB had the last word as the investment in the company, the Aregon Group Ltd, was realised at a profit of £1.17 million.[72]

In the 1980s the NEB was an institution out of its time, politically at least. It had not helped itself with some of the investments that it had made and the 'lame ducks' tarnished its image before it had even opened its doors for business. It is doubtful, however, that anything would have saved it in a decade where the Government looked to the private sector for solutions. Under the circumstances the NEB probably hung on for as long as could be expected. As has already been noted, BTG was privatised in 1992, with ironically one of the investors being Grosvenor Venture Managers which was originally the NEB's own Grosvenor Development Capital. Benn's dream had come to nought.

Regional Development Agencies

The NEB was not the only state investment institution set up by the 1974 to 1979 Labour Government. In reaction to increasing concern over the effect of Britain's relative economic decline on the country's regions, the SDA and the WDA were established. The agencies were to have a number of roles, one of which was the investment of equity and loan capital in small business. The two agencies for a long time operated in a similar manner, facilitating inward investment, building factories, providing business advice and investing capital. By the mid-1990s their attitudes towards acting as a state venture capitalist had diverged somewhat. The WDA has downgraded significantly its venture capital investment operations, whereas the SDA, now known as Scottish Enterprise (SE), has undergone a recent expansion.

1975: Scottish Development Agency

The SDA began its operations in December 1975 with the very broad set of objectives of furthering the development of the economy, of creating and safeguarding employment, and of improving the environment.[73] To these ends the Agency was endowed with a number of powers, including the ability to 'invest in industry and to create new companies'.[74] Mindful of the suspicions of many in the financial community about the ability of public sector bodies to invest competently, the Government set the Industrial Investment Guidelines to require the agency 'to secure an appropriate rate of return'.[75] The SDA provided loans as well as equity capital, sometimes as part of a mixed package. The loans were often offered at below market rates. For example, it was announced in 1978 that the Agency's small business division was offering loans for businesses in country areas at 3% under the market rate.[76] The Agency's level of lending activity at this time was indicated by figures for 1975 to 1978 which revealed that over 300 loans had been made involving the investment of £1 million.[77]

The Agency was also active in its venture capital role, although this was not merely directed at small business, as the £1.5 million investment in Henry Balantyne and Sons Ltd, a woollens manufacturer demonstrated. There were, however, a number of venture capital investments in the range of the equity gap. For example, in 1977 the Agency invested £95,000 in Highland Metals Limited, a galvanising company, which had many of the region's oil-related businesses amongst its customers. In 1977 it also invested £135,000 in the form of an equity and loan package in Triadynamics (Machines and Patents) Limited, a specialist industrial components developer. The finance was aimed at increasing the firm's rate of output, which was insufficient to allow the firm to operate profitably. In this instance the investment was not successful and a receiver had to be appointed in 1978. In 1979 the agency invested £99,000 in Stanley Mills (Scotland) Ltd, a small textile firm. This finance was in the form of an equity and loan package, with the SDA holding 16% of the voting rights. The Agency reported in 1981 that the finance had allowed the firm to be purchased from a larger group and had paid for additional equipment. These developments had seen the firm move into profit and create new jobs.[78] As with the NEB, the SDA had no powers of compulsory purchase and merely looked to invest in companies which had 'a promising future, but which may not easily attract private investment.'[79] By 1979 the SDA had invested in about 20 such companies, costing the agency about £20 million.[80] This has to be set in the context of the UK not having, at that time, a recognisible venture capital industry. The BVCA estimates that in 1979 private sector venture capitalists only invested about £20 million in the whole of the UK.

In May 1979 the Conservatives were elected to office, with an agenda which, as has already been discussed, did not include the promotion of state venture capital. Yet as the 1980 to 1982 recession hit Scotland particularly hard, the Government did not abolish the role, perhaps for fear of alienating the Scottish people still further. Instead, the role was amended to bring it more in line with the Government's political views. The first way in which this manifested itself was in the downgrading of the role in relation to the other activities of the Agency. Indeed, by 1987 the Agency seemed most concerned to sing the praises of the 'enterprise culture' which according to the Government was 'flourishing' in Scotland.

Although downgraded somewhat, the Agency's venture capital arm still made an important contribution to the Scottish economy in the 1980s, as an independent report highlighted in 1987. The results of this report enabled the Agency to comment: 'On the strength of the findings of independent consultants, the Agency Review concluded that the Agency's investment function has made a worthwhile and cost-effective contribution to the Scottish economy and stated that it was instrumental in fostering the development of entrepreneurship in areas and industries where it was badly needed.'[81] It was ironic that at the same time as the Government was winding up the NEB, deeming it an unnecessary relic of mistaken socialism, state venture capital in Scotland was busily fostering entrepreneurship and, no doubt, the aforementioned enterprise culture. According to the independent report not only had the investment role been cost-effective but it was also of some significance for the regional economy. It estimated that over the period 1981 to 1985 the companies which received finance from the SDA generated additional gross output of £275 million, both through the extra private investment the Agency's funds attracted and through the increase in output. 10,400 jobs were said to have been created as a result, in a cost-effective manner.[82] The role, therefore, remained a significant one but no longer enjoyed the top billing as it had done at the beginning of the decade.

A second change to the SDA's investment role was the new policy on disposals. On coming into office the Government announced that it wished bodies like the SDA to return its equity holdings to the private sector as soon as was practicable. This policy was put into immediate effect in January 1980 when 51% of the SDA's equity stake in Braidwood, a plastics moulding company, was sold to Intercobra Ltd, a larger plastics group.[83] Because of this policy it is very difficult to assess accurately the performance of the SDA's investment as those companies which were successful were most likely to find their way back into the private sector before the Agency was able to reap the full benefit for its balance sheet. This situation, and the fact that investment by the agency was inevitably affected by the recession of the early 1980s, arguably the result of the Conservative monetarist experiment, meant that the record of this state venture capital institution, set up by Labour, was very much shaped by Conservative policies (with the same being true for the NEB and the WDA). It also meant that the Agency was prevented from building up a large portfolio.

A third change to the SDA's investment role concerned the practice of the Agency using their public sector capital to leverage in private finance. This practice was adopted on direct instructions from central government. In reaction the Agency developed relationships with a number of the leading financial institutions including ICFC, Midland Bank Industrial Finance, The Royal Bank of Scotland, and the Clydesdale Bank. In 1982 the Agency was able to boast that its £5.8 million investment in the previous 12 months had attracted a further £40.7 million from the private sector.[84] By 1987 the Agency's capital was being met 13.4 times by the private sector. The SDA commented: 'Syndication of financing has now become the norm in the venture capital field; this is a feature that is welcomed by the Agency as the sharing of risk frequently leads to more appropriate funding packages and to a greater number of propositions being financed.'[85] The model investment during the Conservative period was exemplified by the £400,000 equity and loan package invested in August 1980 in Future Technology Systems Ltd, a newly formed electronics company. The public sector funds provided by the SDA were part of a joint public-private package. The Scottish Northern Investment Trust and the Norwich Union Life Insurance Society both invested £250,000 in a package that was in total worth over £1 million.[86] The government clearly would have prefered a situation where public sector venture capital was not necessary at all; however, they at least felt they had made some progress by insisting on investments of this composition.

During this time there was also evidence of co-operation with the NRDC. The investment in GR International Electronics Ltd was made jointly with the Corporation. The SDA invested £50,000 in ordinary and preference shares and a further £150,000 in the form of a secured loan. The capital was used to finance the development of a new computer-assisted instrument to detect microbiological growth, and at a difficult time for business GRI gained new orders for its range of products from the Post Office, British Rail, and the Open University.[87] Some of the small venture capital investments were less successful. For example, Perm-U-Board (UK) Ltd, a £90,000 recipient of Agency finance, went into liquidation in 1980, only 18 months after the investment. Cutbacks in local authority spending were blamed for the demise of this manufacturer of insulating wall boards.[88]

The 1987 report showing the success of the Agency's venture capital investment ensured, despite the ideological climate which saw off the NEB, that the role survived into the 1990s. In the 1996-97 BVCA directory, SE, the body which replaced the SDA, reported that it had invested £52 million to date, and that its current portfolio size was 110. To emphasise their continuing role, SE announced in 1996 that a new fund was to be formed, one which was to include both public and private money.[89] The fund has been called, appropriately enough, the Scottish Equity Partnership and has £25 million available to small businesses requiring less than £500,000. The finance arm of SE, Scottish Development Finance (SDF), is managing the fund which will make investments in a wide range of industries and in all equity forms. The involvement of SE with private sector venture capitalists in the UK is emphasised: 'Over the years we have built up an extensive network of co-investors from within the UK venture capital industry. SDF can help you to attract additional investment from them either now, or at a later stage in the development of your company.'[90] State venture capital, albeit of a 1990s style, is still alive, in Scotland at least.

1976: Welsh Development Agency

The WDA was established on the first day of 1976. It had a similar brief to that of the SDA, and was also given the powers 'to provide financial or other assistance to industry [and] create new companies'.[91] Like the SDA it was required 'to secure an appropriate rate of return on its investment activities.'[92] In many cases the Agency provided loans, but much of the time it bought up equity capital. The WDA's investment covered all sizes of business, including those hampered by the existence of an equity gap. In March 1977 the WDA revealed that its strategy for Wales was to focus upon manufacturing, which it believed was the 'key to prosperity'. Consequently, much of its investment capital went to this sector of the economy. Early examples included Inglefield Power Engineering, a manufacturer of pressure vessels and Channel Sound and Vision, a manufacturer of microphones. The Agency also showed itself willing to take majority shareholdings in small companies. One such company was JE Williams Automatic Revenue Controls Ltd. The agency took a 60% stake in the company as part of a £72,000 equity and loan agreement, later increased to £155,000. The government was keen to state that the investment had led to the creation of 40 new jobs.[93]

By the end of the 1978-1979 financial year the WDA had invested in 159 companies. This had cost the agency £13.7 million, with £1.6 million of that investment going to small businesses.[94] The agency reported that 3000 jobs were expected to have been created as a result of their investment, and that many existing jobs had been made more secure. The early results of their investment were also recorded:

> The Agency's investment policy is dictated by the need to generate economic activity in Wales. By the very nature of this remit the WDA has to be prepared to be more venturesome in its investments than orthodox sources of funding, while still ensuring that it remains on course to meet the target rate of return. Inevitably there have been some failures. At the end of the year there were six investments against which it had been necessary to make provision for capital losses ... The total provision was £329,000 against investments amounting in sum to £540,000, and represents approximately 2.5% of the net investment portfolio.[95]

Equity investments under £250,000 made by the WDA in the financial years 1976 to 1979 are shown in table 2.2. The WDA, like the SDA, was affected in 1979 by the election of a Conservative Government. The Agency's investment role was relegated in importance and the rules guiding its investment were amended. It was commented in 1981: 'The Government now regards the Agency's investment role as complementary to other functions. The Agency has a duty to dispose of investments as soon as practicable and it is required to refrain from making an investment if private sector funds can be found to be available.'[96] In addition, the Agency's discretion over investment was reduced. Government approval was now required for investments over £1 million, whereas it had previously been £2 million.

As with the SDA, these policy changes make it very difficult to assess accurately the record of the WDA in its investment activities and, indeed, the official formula for judging the WDA's investment performance was redrawn as a result. Yet, despite these policy changes, the WDA continued to invest during the 1980s to the extent that by the end of the decade the agency had a portfolio of 962 companies. Furthermore, during the 1980s the Agency launched three new venture capital initiatives which actually raised the profile of its investment role, and indeed made it the leading venture capital institution in Wales.

Table 2.2 WDA Equity Investments Under £250,000 1976 to 1979

	Total Investment	Share Capital	% of Voting Rights Held
Argenthall Ltd	£250,000	£40,000	40.0
A&E Circuits Ltd	£232,000	£95,000	41.3
DB Plastics Ltd	£230,000	£60,000	48.0
Alf Parkman	£220,000	£23,125	20.5
HG Tubes Ltd	£210,000	£35,000	28.0
Wettern Electric Ltd	£171,000	£21,000	30.0
Wheway Watson (Holdings)	£168,000	£168,000	5.9
JE Williams ARC Ltd	£155,000	£24,000	60.0

Source: Adapted from *WDA Annual Report*, 1978 and 1979.

Prior to this and in response to the Conservative guidelines, the WDA redoubled their efforts in developing links with the major banking institutions. In 1979 they agreed with the high street banks to operate jointly a loan guarantee scheme for firms which required finance up to £50,000. The scheme involved the WDA carrying out feasability studies into firms and, where appropriate, providing guarantees.[97] The WDA, although clearly interested in gaining Government approval through projects like this, by no means lost confidence in the worth of their existing activities, and this was no more so than in the venture capital role. To confirm this the WDA set up a new venture capital fund in 1982 called Hafren Investment Finance Ltd. Hafren invested mainly equity capital in small businesses in amounts ranging from £10,000 to £100,000 - very much part of the equity gap. One of the reasons why the new subsidiary was able to do this was that it offered 'a readily identifiable package of investments in a fairly standardised form, together with a simplified procedure for application and assessment.'[98]

The decision to make the service 'user-friendly' was taken in the knowledge that, as was explained in the opening chapter, one of the main reasons why the equity gap exists is because of the transaction cost-effect. This is where the costs of making the investment - the investigation costs, the cost of drawing up the contract, and the monitoring costs - are too large as a proportion of the amount invested for it to be economic. It was hoped the standard procedures would overcome this problem. In its first year of business Hafren invested £608,000 in 13 businesses. Ten of these businesses were attracted to Wales by the offer of these funds. The companies backed by Hafren included manufacturers of closed-circuit cameras, satellite antennae, and children's inflatables.[99] The second year saw its total investment reach £1 million, its capitalisation increase to £1.5 million, and its upper investment limit increase to £200,000. The level of demand for its finance was such that in 1984 the marketing of the fund was reduced temporarily.

This venture capital fund was augmented in 1983 by a seed capital fund for even smaller requirements. Seed capital funding was very difficult to acquire in the 1980s in the UK; even in 1988, a boom year for the economy, it was only *recorded* as £1.9 million. The role of the fund was 'to enable business entrepreneurs in Wales to get promising projects off the drawing-board and into commercial production.' The fund was to 'help at the critical time when individual investors or fledgling enterprises need finance to develop initial designs into working prototypes to show they can be turned into successful products.'[100] The finance on offer ranged from £2,000 to £20,000.

In 1984 the WDA produced a corporate plan for the years up to 1990. This reaffirmed the Agency's commitment to help bridge the equity gap in Wales. The Agency pledged itself to

> identify particular funding gaps in which Agency finance can be used to attract additional private funds and thereby enable new projects to go ahead in Wales; develop links with the City, with other funding sources and with universities, using WINtech and the Agency's seed capital and venture capital resources; [and] use the investment role in conjunction with the other Agency programmes, in particular business development and special projects where this might offer an opportunity to bring forward private sector participation.[101]

To these ends the Agency set up another venture capital body in 1984, the Welsh Venture Capital Fund. A pool of £5.6 million was raised for investment which was to be aimed at 'new projects and growth businesses in Wales'.[102] On announcing the new fund the Agency stated its view about the importance of a vibrant venture capital sector for economic growth and the WDA's role in promoting such a sector:

> The venture capital business in the UK is young but one which has a significant role to play in the economic resurgence in Wales. The WDA, as one of the major sources of venture capital in the Principality, has been called upon not only to provide funds for new and expanding businesses but also to act as a catalyst to mobilise additional investment by venture capitalists from outside Wales. It is often difficult for City institutions to perceive all the

nuances of investment opportunities in parts of the country with which they are not familiar, and the WDA's detailed knowledge of local business conditions ... and its reputation as a knowledgable investor are important influences in persuading outside investors to do business.[103]

The fund was subscribed to by a mixture of institutions. Half of the money came from City firms, with the other half coming from a range of bodies in Wales, including the Church of Wales, and county council pension funds. The WDA itself put up £1.2 million of public money and the overall fund was managed by a newly formed company jointly owned by the WDA. The fund was empowered to invest in amounts upto £500,000 in 'unquoted companies ranging from "greenfield" start-ups to established enterprises.'[104] The WDA was in no doubt about the significance of this development: 'The creation of the Welsh Venture Capital Fund was a first step by the WDA towards developing a distinct, local financial sector within Wales able to offer a competitive range of funding packages.'[105] The Agency also believed that the fund allowed it to offer the business community flexibility. Many funding needs were said to be catered for: 'The WDA, in its readiness to invest in amounts as little as £10,000 fills a clear gap at the lower end of the venture capital market. At the other end of the scale the Agency is able to invest funds in packages as large as £1 million, and by deploying its own funds it is able to attract additional private sector funds and thus expand the amount of funds available to Welsh business.' Indeed, in the financial year 1984-85 the WDA increased its overall investment portfolio from £17.3 million to £22.5 million.[106]

The WDA was innovative and pro-active in its approach to venture capital, and its investment in general. Although there was a concious, and enthusiastic attempt to involve the private sector, and a policy which required constant disposals, the WDA was very much an active state venture capitalist during the Conservative years of the 1980s. Furthermore, there was not a hint of apology about their involvement in such activities. The WDA firmly believed that their intervention as investor and catalyst was crucial if venture capital was to become established in Wales, and given what was available before they had some justification for this view. The investment of the WDA continued apace for the rest of the decade, as table 2.3 reveals.

Table 2.3 WDA Investment Levels 1979 to 1990 (£m)

1979-80	4.2	1985-86	7.4
1980-81	0.9	1986-87	5.2
1981-82	2.6	1987-88	8.4
1982-83	9.8	1988-89	8.5
1983-84	13.0	1989-90	9.6
1984-85	13.0		

Source: Adapted from *WDA Annual Report,* 1979-1990.

Over the decade the WDA had its fair share of success and failure. One of the worst failures was its investment in Dragon Data Ltd in 1982. This £535,000 investment was given great publicity at the time, as it was believed that Dragon's '32' home computer was 'one of the most successful products to be launched on the domestic market over the last 12 months.'[107]

The investment was syndicated between the WDA and private sector institutions, including the ill-fated venture capital fund Prutec, which invested fully £8 million in Dragon. In 1985 Dragon went into liquidation, to a large extent taking Prutec with them.[108] The WDA, which had already made provisions the year before, had to accept its own quite substantial loss. On the other hand in 1983 the WDA enjoyed two substantial returns on investment. The first profit was made on Bio-Isolates (Holdings) of Swansea. An investment of £100,000 had been made in this company in 1979 when the firm began a pilot production plant which extracted pure protein from cheese whey. When the WDA relinquished their final stake in Bio-Isolates in December 1983 the total proceeds amounted to £1,085,960, a total rate of return of over 1000%.[109] In the November of the same year the WDA's shareholdings in Myson Group plc was also sold. In this case the original £600,000 had appreciated to £1,128,000.[110]

There is no question that the venture capital role of the WDA has been downgraded in the 1990s. The view of the WDA is that this downgrading was not due to direct political intervention. Whilst there is no reason to doubt this viewpoint, it is unquestionably the case that in the 1990s in the UK, in general, an atmosphere existed which favoured less intervention by government and, where it did intervene, initiatives which did not involve the picking of winners. Nevertheless, in 1996 the WDA were still operating on a number of fronts and still believed that a genuine gap existed. They have a small budget available for loans of up to £100,000, which is used in genuine risk situations. Indeed, the Agency takes a sales royalty in certain circumstances. Secondly, they operate a fund called the Technology Growth Fund, which aims to promote the growth of small technology based firms. The method of financing usually involves the Agency offering a joint package of a loan, secured on the firm's intellectual property, and an equity participation. The limit for investments under this fund is £150,000. The Agency has also been involved in offering convertible loans in recent months.

A further initiative is also due to be launched in 1997. The WDA are currently involved in negotiations to set up a new venture capital fund in conjunction with the private sector. This fund will focus mainly upon small high technology firms, although it will have the discretionary powers to consider other small firms should compelling cases arise. A majority of the finance will be provided by the private sector. In addition to this the WDA is involved in setting up a Business Angel Network for Wales. A study was undertaken by the Cardiff Business School, which reported a number of observations. Firstly, it was stated that business angel activity in Wales was poorly organised, and as a result the current number of active angels was only a fifth of the potential number. Secondly, the demand for, and supply of, angel investment was likely to be in amounts of about £50,000. Thirdly, a network would need to provide about 100 such opportunities to satisfy investor demands. Consequently, a 'network operated at arms length but accountable to the WDA' has been recommended, which would also involve four regional intermediaries. The expected output of the network has been stated as a pool of 200 to 250 investors by year three; 100 investment opportunities per annum; £1 million of investment each year, leveraging in a further £3 million of other finance for the firms involved; and up to 260 jobs created each year.[111]

Finally, the WDA has commissioned a study into the potential of small firms to generate more working capital from their own resources. Many venture capitalists comment that small firms come to them for finance when if one looked closely at the finances and resources of the business, finance could be raised without the need for access to external sources. It is envisaged that the Agency would offer advice on how small firms could leverage their internal resources to the maximum advantage.

Election of the Conservative Government 1979: A movement towards laissez-faire

As has been seen in the accounts of the NEB, the SDA and WDA, the Conservative Government, whilst being largely in favour of letting free enterprise solve economic problems, felt it necessary to allow these institutions continue functioning. In the case of the NEB the policy was to allow the Board to continue investing in small high technology ventures in the short-term while the incentives for private investment were restored. The other activities were dropped as the Board was gradually wound down. The regional development agencies were a slightly different case as the need for regional assistance had been accepted throughout the post-war period. The roles of the SDA and WDA were accordingly amended rather than abolished, with the investment role considered to be marginal in any case. As was noted in the account of the NEB, Sir Keith Joseph was totally committed to the encouragement of private enterprise and he argued that the financial sector was capable of providing all the opportunities that a sound company needed for securing venture capital.'[112]

As a result the Government adopted a laissez-faire attitude to the development of the institutional venture capital industry in the UK. There have been no direct measures to encourage the industry to invest in the range of the equity gap, nor, of course, has there been any attempt at compulsion. On the face of it this policy would appear to have been dramatically successful and a vindication of Joseph's belief in the availability of venture capital and the ability of the private sector to provide solutions to economic problems. Yet in terms of bridging the equity gap there have been many criticisms of the industry, with many claiming that it has made no impression on the problem at all. This fact was obviously clear to Government, as by 1981 they had implemented a policy to increase the amount of *informal* venture capital invested in small business. The BSS, launched in Geoffrey Howe's infamous "monetarist" budget, was a policy of fiscal intervention, yet the Government did not alter its laissez-faire position on institutional venture capital and the performance of this policy is analysed in chapter four.

The 1981 Budget: Concessions to the Limitations of Market Forces

There is no doubt that in 1981 the Government was still fully committed to its belief in the primacy of market forces and the dangers of state intervention. This was the Budget in which Sir Geoffrey Howe cast aside all warnings about the 'folly' of his monetarist beliefs and pressed ahead with further fiscal contraction. The Government continued to assert that the role of government was to create the conditions in which enterprise could flourish. Yet, as Joseph's 1979 statement on the NEB had shown, ideological purity is a luxury for those charged with the responsibilities of office. The Government compromised on the NEB in 1979, and did the same in 1981 when it created the Loan Guarantee Scheme (LGS) and the BSS. The LGS was set up as 'raising finance is a major problem for small firms and ... it can be a serious limitation to the growth or start-up of a business'[113] The LGS was to alleviate this situation by providing financial institutions with guarantees on their advances to small business. The policy in the 1981 Budget which dealt directly with the equity gap, however, was the BSS.

1981: Business Start-up Scheme

The BSS was a tax incentive scheme designed to make investment in start-up and early-stage companies more attractive. The scheme was aimed at the outside investor rather than the business owner, and was therefore significant as it represented further evidence that the Government was willing to retreat publically from its reliance on market forces. In June 1981 Sir Geoffrey outlined a set of amended rules (from those initially presented in the Budget) and commented: 'Investment [in early stage companies] is inevitably risky. I have therefore designed the new incentive to shift the existing odds dramatically in favour of the investor - to cushion the risk of loss and to multiply the opportunity of profit.'[114] The main principles of the scheme were quite straightforward. Investors recieved tax relief at their marginal rate, which for many involved in this scheme meant relief at 60%. Up to 50% of the ordinary share capital of the company qualified for relief and the investor was permitted to invest up to £10,000 under the scheme in any one year. In addition, only businesses which had been in existence for less than five years were eligible for investment under the scheme. Summarising the scheme, Howe said: 'I am sure that investors and their professional advisors will see that we are putting on to the statute book a tax incentive unparalleled in any major Western country.'[115] One company that was attracted was the Electra Investment Trust Ltd which set up a subsidiary, Electra Risk Capital (ERC), to operate under the provisions of the scheme. ERC was to invest in both the service and manufacturing sectors, although it would have specialist areas, including technology and marketing. ERC invested their £8 million fund in 32 companies between 1982 and 1983.[116] The fund was not a success, though, as table 2.4 illustrates; investors lost up to three quarters of their money.

Table 2.4 Electra Risk Capital ERC I Portfolio: Invested 1982 to 1983

Liquidations	15
Receiverships	1
Loss on Disposal	14*
Profit on Disposal	1
Other	1

* In 9 of these cases all of the capital was written off

Source: Adapted from *Electra Risk Capital Annual Report*, July 1992, pp27-31.

This fund had quite a profound impact on many involved in venture capital. ERC had been very bold in the investments that it had made, their portfolio being dominated by small, high risk companies. The sheer scale of the failure of this first fund taught many in the industry that there was a risk in believing their own rhetoric. Many in the industry liked to see themselves as being the entrepreneurial, adventuring section of the City, yet the ERC fund served as a warning that the industry did not have the 'golden touch' and that in some cases investment strategies needed to be re-evaluated.

Yet it was not this aspect of the scheme's performance that caused it to be abolished. The poor performance of the Electra portfolio, for example, was not immediately apparent, although by 1984 it seemed inevitable. The greatest problem for the Government at that time was that the scheme was not attracting sufficient investment. Over the scheme's two year life only £15 million was raised. This compared badly against the £100 million that the Government had anticipated at the scheme's inception. As a result, in 1983 it was abolished, and replaced by a scheme based on similar principles, the BES which it was hoped would create greater investment.

1983: Business Expansion Scheme

The creation of the BES indicated that the equity gap was still perceived to be a problem for the UK despite the revival in the economy. The Government stated that the aim of the BES was 'to encourage new and expanded activity in the small firms sector ... The aim of the scheme is, also, of course, to encourage investment in high-risk activities, where the risk to the investor will be at least to some extent commensurate with the generous level of tax relief.'[117] John Moore, the one-time heir apparent to Mrs Thatcher, added: 'We set up this scheme because we recognise the risky nature of this kind of investment [small or early stage unquoted independent companies]. So we designed it to be attractive. The investor gets his relief, up front, at his top rate or rates of income tax'[118] The intention of the scheme could not have been clearer. The Government wanted investors receiving tax relief of up to 60% to earn it by making investments in small firms, especially those where there was a high level of risk involved. It is against this ambition that the policy had to be judged.

Furthermore, the Government claimed to attach great importance to the scheme. Norman Tebbitt, in the early days of his reign at the DTI, said he regarded the BES 'as of major importance in stimulating the provision of risk capital to existing and potential small businesses. I take every opportunity to increase the awareness of the business expansion scheme among small private investors.'[119] The scheme had three main features, the first being the aforementioned tax relief. In addition to this the capital invested through the scheme had to be invested in the ordinary shares of a company, although under the BES it could be an established one. Thirdly, the scheme limited the amount that could be set against tax in any one year to £20,000, although this was increased to £40,000 shortly afterwards. In its early days the Government was upbeat about the scheme with £30 million being raised by fund promoters in the first four months. The then junior DTI minister, David Trippier, stated in November 1983 that 'more funds have been established since then and to this must be added the capital invested by individual investors. Although the figures may be small compared with the total investment placed by pension funds and the like, they are not insignificant in relation to the market at which they are targeted.'[120] Trippier followed up on those claims with a view that was supported by many in the venture capital industry at the time. This was that the BES had the additional value of raising the profile of venture capital, which even in 1983 was still a marginal financial activity. Trippier claimed this was 'to the benefit of small firms with good growth prospects.'[121]

The initial results of the scheme certainly seemed promising. It was announced by the DTI in 1984 that over 400 businesses involved with the scheme had attracted about £75 million in the first year. Half the total was said to have gone to young or start-up businesses.[122] In the following year,

1984-85, a further £150 million was raised. However, not everyone was impressed. One problem with the scheme was something known as 'bunching'. This was where the majority of investments were made at the end of the tax year, rather than being spread evenly over the twelve months. Oonagh MacDonald, the Labour MP, felt that the problem of 'bunching' reflected wider flaws in the nature of the scheme. In the House in 1987 she offered help to the then Chancellor, Nigel Lawson, on his speechwriting:

> If the Chancellor had been a little more frank he would have said, "We tried to get people to invest in new small companies by offering them tax relief. Of course, because people wanted the tax relief, but not to take any entrepreneurial risk, they were only willing to invest in asset-backed enterprises such as nursing homes. We did try to sort out the worst abuses last year, so give me some credit for that. However, because BES is just seen as a tax dodge [hence its popularity] people have been thinking about investments only in the last three months of the tax year ... This has meant that any half-baked scheme can raise cash in that period, but for the other nine months of the year virtually no project, however well thought out or beneficial to the nation, can raise a bean. Therefore, we shall patch up the BES a bit more by allowing people who invest in the period April to September to claim relief against their previous year's income."[123]

There were also concerns that the BES was slipping into the same financial habits for which the scheme had the potential to compensate. One such habit was the regional disparity in the provision of venture capital finance. The BES seemed to be reinforcing the trend of investors putting their money into businesses in the South-East of England. It was reported in 1987 that 62% of BES finance went to companies in the South-East, whereas only 5.5% went to companies in the North and North-West, with Northern Ireland companies receiving just 1.6%.[124] The disparity in the levels of finance being directed towards companies in the manufacturing and service sectors was also a concern to many observers. In the period to 1987 only 24% of BES investment was directed at manufacturing companies, compared with 61% directed at the service sector.[125]

The Government could well argue that these two concerns were beyond the remit of the BES; two other trends, however, certainly were not. Patrick Taylor, a BES analyst, argued in 1984 that the BES had immediately settled into a pattern where a very low proportion of the funds raised under the scheme were being invested in either start-up ventures or ventures that required only a small amount of finance. He concluded that 'it does seem that the start-up company, particularly one seeking a relatively small sum of money, say £50,000, will have difficulty in raising the required amount through an investment fund.'[126] Taylor had no doubt what the early evidence of the scheme meant for the BES's policy objectives: 'If the Government wants to encourage new businesses to be formed something more needs to be done to narrow the equity gap that still exists.'[127] A further concern was the lack of provision in the scheme for the investor to take an active role in the business. A common requirement of a business angel is that he be permitted to take an active part in the business, to have a hand in making his stake profitable. For many angels it is a pre-condition to investment; the BES did not allow this.

Furthermore, for the scheme to justify its tax relief it had to show evidence that the finance it raised was targeted at businesses which would otherwise not have been able to acquire that finance. In other words, there needed to be a high degree of additionality. It was this aspect that was to be the main focus of debate about the BES in its later years. This concern arose because in 1988 the Government made a decision that many believed effectively ended the scheme as a vehicle for raising small business equity. The decision was to open the scheme to companies which let residential property on the then newly created assured tenancy terms. The Government claimed that the move was important as the need to stimulate the private rented sector was widely recognised. Moreover, the increase in the availability of rented accommodation, it was said, would increase labour mobility, as accommodation would become more affordable. The BES initiative, therefore, had become part of a wider policy to revive the rented sector through deregulation. The decision to move the scheme into property was immediately seized upon by the Labour Party. Gordon Brown claimed to be bemused by the inconsistency of Government policy on the BES:

> Since the scheme was set up in 1983 - it was originally intended to provide tax concessions for high-risk investment in high technology industry to create jobs - Ministers have had to come to the House at least twice to say that, because of the increasing dependence on property and fixed assets, they intend to change the terms of the scheme ... Today, they appear to have turned a full circle. Instead of saying that they will limit the dependence of BES companies on property, they are saying that privately rented companies can be 100% dependent on property assets.[128]

There were a whole series of objections to this policy change. The most fundamental being that property investment was not what the scheme was set up to encourage. It was said that it was inevitable that the property aspect would dominate the original aims of the scheme, and that this was inexcusable when the economy was still suffering from a shortage in the availability of finance for genuine entrepreneurial ventures. One case emphasises this point. Patrick Eggle, a fast-growing guitar manufacturing company, had looked to the BES to avoid over-reliance on overdraft finance. The company wanted to raise £480,000. However, the managing director, Andrew Selby complained: 'I am finding it impossible to compete with the assured tenancy property schemes that have hijacked the BES. How can I compete when they are offering a 13% return virtually guaranteed. [And] even if I do find enthusiastic investors they are limited to placing just £40,000.'[129]

A second complaint against this policy U-turn was that the BES was not even an efficient way for a Government to revive the rented sector. The Labour Party contacted the Association of Metropolitan Authorities (AMA) and asked them to work out what they could do with the public money foregone under the new BES rules. AMA reported that if £40 million was foregone in tax relief the private rented sector would probably be able to build 1,000 rented properties in the first year. AMA also claimed that £40 million would have been enough for them to borrow sufficient money to build 10,000 local authority houses over the same period.[130] Gordon Brown reflected that it was 'a tragedy that the Government seem to feel that there is a psychological need to circulate cash around property developers and speculators before it can do any public good.'[131] A further rule change which contributed to complaints about the scheme's effectiveness in bridging the equity gap was the decision to restrict the amount a company could raise in a year to £500,000. The crucial point was that this rule excluded property companies, which were able to raise anything up to £5 million. It was a further distorting factor, ensuring that the scheme would drift further away from its original aims. To cap it all, in 1990 the general investment limit was raised to £750,000.

The arguments of Brown and others were not publically accepted by the Government and the said type of property companies continued to be covered until the scheme was abolished. It was no secret, however, that the demise of the scheme was linked to the post-1988 investment patterns. Despite all this, the Government still believed that the principles behind the scheme were sound and announced plans at the same time for the creation of two new schemes, the EIS and the VCT.

1991: Government Sponsored Business Introduction Services

This initiative launched by the DTI in 1991, is undoubtedly the least celebrated of the policies covered in this chapter. The decision to sponsor the operation of five BIS constituted a policy of non-financial intervention, a policy where the state intervenes but as a facilitator of investment rather than a financier or provider of incentives. The existence of BIS in the UK actually dates back to the late 1970s, although until the 1990s they were very few and far between. BIS facilitate informal venture capital investment by bringing together potential investors and (usually) small businesses. The need for such institutions was perceived after research showed that one of the chief obstacles to small business gaining informal equity capital was the ad hoc nature of its provision; investors and business simply did not know how to get together.

Table 2.5 Government Sponsored Business Introduction Services

TEC	Name of BIS	Area of Operation
East Lancashire	Capital Connections	North West
Devon and Cornwall	Devon and Cornwall Business Angels Programme	South West
Calderdale and Kirklees	Informal Register of Investment Services	Calderdale and Kirklees
South and East Cheshire	TEChINVEST	Cheshire and the Wirral
Bedfordshire	The Bedfordshire Investment Exchange	Bedfordshire

Source: BVCA, *A Directory of Business Introduction Services*, London, BVCA, 1993.

With the number of BIS existing in the UK in the early 1990s being very small and the number of deals facilitated insignificant in terms of bridging the equity gap, Eric Forth, the then Small Firms Minister, announced that the Government would be sponsoring five BIS to try both to increase the supply of capital and to establish the concept in the small business community. TEC up and down the country were invited to bid to receive the sponsorship, an invitation to which 19 responded. The successful bidders received £20,000 per year for two years, with the sponsorship being extended for a further year after an interim study. A number of these were joint-sponsored with private sector institutions. The impact of the scheme on the number of BIS in the UK was not limited to the creation of the above five services. Mason and Harrison note that a number of the unsuccessful bidders went ahead with their plans despite their failure in this scheme, something which the Government no doubt considered a virtuous by-product.[132]

A Third Attempt at Fiscal Intervention

The previously considered failure of the BES to direct finance towards small unquoted businesses and the belief that such businesses were still constrained by their inability to gain access to equity finance caused the Government to replace the BES with two new schemes, the EIS and the VCT. These two policies, announced in the second of the two 1993 Budgets, are successors to the BES in that they are further policies of *fiscal intervention*. Both policies use fiscal incentives to encourage *individual* investors to invest in the range of the equity gap. They also continue the Conservative policy of focusing this type of policy on individual investors, rather than targeting their initiatives at the institutional venture capital market.

1994: Enterprise Investment Scheme

The EIS was launched with the hope that it would operate more effectively than the BES in terms of raising equity capital for small business. As with the BES, the basic principles of the scheme are quite straightforward. The scheme allows unquoted trading companies to raise up to £1 million in new equity each tax year. This new equity is to be provided by individuals who can invest up to £100,000 per tax year in EIS qualifying companies. To qualify for investment under the scheme a company must be unquoted, its shares must be paid up, and it must be a trading company and not an investment company, although certain types of trading company are also disqualified. These qualifications need to be carried on for at least three years, although there is a concession made for start-up companies. The incentive to individuals to invest in such 'high risk' companies is the provision of tax relief at the lowest rate of income tax, 20%. In addition, if the investor holds the investment for five years then he will not be liable for capital gains tax on the realisation of the investment. Finally, if the company or companies that an individual invests in fails, then further tax relief is available. This is what is called loss relief, which is available at the top rate of income tax, 40%, and is based on the net loss after the original tax relief. Following the criticism of the BES, under the EIS it will be possible for an investor who previously had no connection with the company to become a paid director. This ruling is designed to encourage further the increase in investment by business angels. The Government hoped when it launched the EIS that this combination of tighter qualifying rules and accumulated tax concessions would tempt business angels into making investments in the small, high risk ventures deemed so important for the development of the economy.

1994: Venture Capital Trusts

VCT allow individuals to invest up to £100,000 a year in an investment trust which will contain unquoted companies. After the redrafting of the rules, announced in the 1994 Budget, a number of incentives are available for the VCT investor. Firstly, there is 20% income tax relief available on the amount invested in a trust, provided that the investor holds the shares for at least five years. Secondly, the proceeds from the investment, in both the form of dividends and capital gains, are tax free. Thirdly, tax on up to £100,000 of capital gains on other assets may be deferred when they are invested in new VCT shares. The procedure for becoming an investor in a VCT is again relatively straightforward in principle. The trusts are run by financial institutions which make public announcements about their flotation. A prospectus is issued and applications are invited. The investors are placing their trust in the ability of fund managers to invest the funds in small and, in the case of this scheme, medium sized businesses.

Conclusion

As can be deduced from this chapter the quest for state solutions to the problem of the equity gap has increased in pace over the past 20 years. Even within this recent period policies have been attempted from all four positions on the continuum of state intervention outlined in the previous chapter. A number of these policies have been given a high profile, like the NEB and the BES, whilst others have been largely concealed from the public gaze. The policies have, of course, been initiated in the knowledge that they will only be effective if the overall performance of the economy is at least sound. This is true of all microeconomic policies, but particularly so in the case of those which involve small business as they are especially vulnerable to adverse economic conditions. It is not the contention of this study that any of the considered policies can be a substitute for a positive economic climate.

What is of interest to this study is the relative performance of the various types of state intervention these policies represent. This will allow an assessment of both past and present policies, and more importantly provide evidence which can guide future policy in this area. There is still a great deal of evidence that there is a significant equity gap for small business and it can be said with confidence that future governments will initiate new policies in an attempt to find a solution. Indeed, the Labour Party has presented a proposal for a new business development bank. The evidence available on the policies outlined in this chapter is presented in the next four chapters. The most substantial evidence is available on the NEB, the Government's policy towards the institutional venture capital industry, and the BES. This is presented in separate chapters. Evidence on the other policies is less detailed but still worthy of consideration, and therefore presented in chapter six. The analysis of the evidence begins with the NEB.

Notes

[1] Macmillan Committee on Finance and Industry, *Report*, Cmnd 3897, 1931.
[2] *Ibid.*, pp173-4.
[3] *Ibid.*, p174.
[4] Whitebloom, S et al, 'City faces scrutiny of willingness to invest in British industry', *The Guardian*, 10 March 1994, p1.
[5] Longstreth, F, 'The City, Industry and the State' in Crouch, C (ed), *The State and the Economy in Contemporary Capitalism*, London, Croom Helm, 1979, p185.
[6] *Ibid.*
[7] *Ibid.*
[8] Hutton, W, 'An economic debacle on a grand scale', *The Guardian*, 25 August 1992, p2.
[9] Longstreth, *op.cit.*, p184.
[10] Lisle-Williams, M, 'The State, Finance and Industry in Britain', in Cox, A., *The State, Finance and Industry*, Brighton, Wheatsheaf, 1986, p252.
[11] Longstreth, *op.cit.*, pp161-2.
[12] Thomas, W.A, *The Finance of British Industry 1918-1976*, London, Methuen, 1978, p119.
[13] *Ibid.*

14. Coopey, R and Clarke, D, *3i: Fifty Years Investing in Industry*, Oxford, Oxford University Press, 1995, pp13-18.
15. *Ibid.*, p14.
16. *Ibid.*, p17.
17. *Ibid.*, p19.
18. *Ibid.*, p20.
19. *Ibid.*, p27.
20. *Ibid.*, p56.
21. Thomas, *op.cit.*, p123.
22. Coopey and Clarke, *op.cit.*, p40.
23. A full account of ICFC/3i's history is contained in Coopey and Clarke.
24. Cohen, N, 'Banks to sell 21 per cent of 3i', *Financial Times*, 9 June 1995, p22.
25. Gourlay, R, 'Banks reap profit of £176m with sale of 3i shares', *Financial Times*, 23 June 1995, p19.
26. Coopey and Clarke, *op.cit.*, p21.
27. National Research Development Corporation, *25 Years of Service to Innovation: Bulletin of the National Research Development Corporation*, Autumn 1974, pp6-7.
28. *Ibid.*, p27.
29. *Ibid.*, Foreward.
30. 'NRDC sets up small business fund with initial £2 million', *British Business*, 26 September 1980, p126.
31. Radcliffe Committee quoted in Thomas, *op.cit.*, p132.
32. Labour Party Study Group, *National Enterprise Board: Labour's State Holding Company*, Opposition Green Paper, London, The Labour Party, 1973, p12.
33. *Ibid.*, p9.
34. House of Commons Debate, 17 February 1975, col.937.
35. *Ibid.*
36. Wilson, H, *The Final Term: The Labour Government 1974-1976*, London, Weidenfield and Nicolson and Michael Joseph, 1979, pp141-2.
37. 'The NEB's guidelines favour the bosses', *The Economist*, 28 February 1976, p75.
38. 'Curate's NEB', *The Economist*, 6 March 1976, p71.
39. Interview with Lord Ryder, 1994.
40. *NEB Annual Report 1976*, p3.
41. Interview with Lord Ryder, 1994.
42. 'State enterprise - year one', *The Economist*, 7 May 1977, p77.
43. *NEB Annual Report 1979*, p25.
44. 'How wicked, public enterprise', *The Economist*, 10 December 1977, p92.
45. *NEB Annual Report 1980*, pp7&29.
46. *NEB Annual Report 1984-5*, p12.
47. 'BL's last battle ?', *The Economist*, 15 September 1979, p75.
48. House of Commons Debate, 10 April 1978, cols.1082-3.

[49] Grylls, M and Redwood, J, *The National Enterprise Board: A Case for Euthanasia*, London, Centre for Policy Studies, 1980, p47.
[50] House of Commons Debate, 18 January 1979, cols.2023-4.
[51] House of Commons Debate, 10 April 1978, col.1115.
[52] *Ibid*.
[53] House of Commons Debate, 18 January 1979, col.2046.
[54] 'Joseph tether NEB', *The Economist*, 21 July 1979, p83.
[55] House of Commons Debate, 19 July 1979, col.2005.
[56] House of Commons Debate, 6 November 1979, col.240.
[57] Halcrow, M, *Keith Joseph: A Single Mind*, London, Macmillan, 1989, p144.
[58] *NEB Annual Report 1980*, p3.
[59] *NEB Annual Report 1981*, p3.
[60] *Ibid*.
[61] 'Taxpayer's British Technology', *The Economist*, 25 July 1981, p18.
[62] Interview with Caroline Vaughan (former employee of NEB), 1994.
[63] Fairtlough, G, 'Exploitation of biotechnology in a smaller company', *Royal Society of London Philosophical Transactions: Series B*, Vol.324, 1989, p590.
[64] Dodgson, M, *The Management of Technological Learning: Lessons from a Biotechnology Company*, Berlin, Walter de Gruyter, 1991, pp27-8.
[65] *NEB Annual Report 1981*, p11.
[66] Curry, A, 'NEB - the risk taker', *New Statesman*, 26 February 1982, p4.
[67] *NEB Annual Report 1980*, p4.
[68] Dodgson, *op.cit.*, p25.
[69] *NEB Annual Report 1982*, p10.
[70] 'New role for BTG announced', *British Business*, 7 October 1983, p303.
[71] McLoughlin, J, 'Minister decides new role for NEB', *The Guardian*, 1 October 1983, p18.
[72] *NEB Annual Report 1990*, p10.
[73] *Trade and Industry*, 25 February 1977, p489.
[74] *Ibid*.
[75] *Ibid*.
[76] 'SDA offers low-interest loans', *Trade and Industry*, 10 February 1978, p262.
[77] *Ibid*.
[78] *SDA Annual Report 1981*, p33.
[79] 'A catalyst for industrial expansion', *Trade and Industry*, 3 March 1978, p36.
[80] 'Back to the private sector: Scottish Development Agency sells subsidiary', *British Business*, 25 January 1980, p10.
[81] *SDA Annual Report 1987*, p54.
[82] *Ibid*.
[83] British Business, 25 January 1980, *op.cit*.
[84] *SDA Annual Report 1982*, p11.
[85] *SDA Annual Report 1987*, p54.

[86] 'Office systems entrepreneurs backed by SDA and private funds', *British Business*, 29 August 1980, p747.
[87] *Ibid.*, p31.
[88] *Ibid.*, p33.
[89] Lonsdale, C, 'Re-assessing the role of government in bridging the equity gap', *Venture Capital Journal*, November-December 1995, p19.
[90] Scottish Development Finance, *Investing In Scotland's Future*, Company Publicity.
[91] *Trade and Industry*, 25 February 1977, p491.
[92] *Ibid.*
[93] 'Majority shareholding taken by WDA', *Trade and Industry*, 14 April 1978, p57.
[94] *WDA Annual Report 1978-9*, p3.
[95] *Ibid.*, p19.
[96] *WDA Annual Report 1980-1*, p8.
[97] *WDA Annual Report 1979-80*, p20.
[98] Small business finance from WDA', *British Business*, 14 May 1982, p56.
[99] *WDA Annual Report 1982-3*, p19.
[100] 'WDA 'seed loans' for new projects', *British Business*, 8 July 1983, p605.
[101] *WDA Corporate Plan 1984-1990*, p27.
[102] WDA Annual Report 1984-5, p8.
[103] *Ibid.*, p12.
[104] *Ibid.*
[105] *Ibid.*
[106] *Ibid.*, p13.
[107] *WDA Annual Report 1982-3*, p24.
[108] 'Scorched by dragon's breath', The Economist, 13 July 1985, p66.
[109] 'WDA earns 1000 per cent return on investments', *British Business*, 3 February 1984, p179.
[110] *Ibid.*
[111] Feasibility study written on the proposed Business Angel Network for Wales, September 1996.
[112] House of Commons Debate, 6 November 1979, col.242.
[113] *British Business*, Special Report, 30 October 1981, p6.
[114] *British Business*, 12 June 1981, p275.
[115] *Ibid.*
[116] *Electra Risk Capital Annual Report*, July 1992, p19.
[117] Mason, C and Harrison, R, 'The role of the Business Expansion Scheme in the United Kingdom', *Omega International Journal of Management Science*, No.2, 1989, p149.
[118] 'Business Expansion Scheme companies attract £75 million', *British Business*, 23 November 1984, p478.
[119] 'Parliament', *British Business*, 25 November 1983, p633.

[120] 'Government investment scheme strikes 'rich seam' says David Trippier', *British Business*, 2 December 1983, p678.
[121] *Ibid.*
[122] British Business, 23 November 1984, *op.cit.*
[123] House of Commons Debate, 30 April 1987, col.460.
[124] *Ibid.*
[125] *Ibid.*
[126] Taylor,P, 'The Business Expansion Scheme - is it filling the equity gap ?', *Venture Capital Report*, June 1984.
[127] *Ibid.*
[128] House of Commons Debate, 9 May 1988, col.43.
[129] Bethell, J, 'Clarke struggles to solve the BES riddle', *The Sunday Times*, 28 November 1993, p3.9.
[130] House of Commons Debate, 9 May 1988, col.47.
[131] *Ibid.*, cols.47-8.
[132] Mason, C and Harrison, R, *Promoting Informal Venture Capital: Some Operational Considerations for Business Introduction Services*, University of Southampton and Ulster, Working Paper No.4, July 1992

PART II

THE COMPARATIVE PERFORMANCE OF GOVERNMENT POLICIES TO BRIDGE THE EQUITY GAP

3 Labour's National Enterprise Board

The NEB as a Policy of Direct State Intervention

The NEB was a policy of direct state intervention as it involved the *direct provision of equity finance by the state*. The policy was born out of a lack of faith in the ability of market forces to solve the industrial problems of the mid-1970s. The eventual role of the NEB bore very little relation to the proposals that were agreed at the 1973 Labour Party Conference, which were an attempt to restructure the British economy. The plans were watered down between 1974 and 1975, with much of the radicalism of the original proposals removed. Yet the NEB throughout its active life (it was meaningfully active until about 1985) remained a policy of direct state intervention. The magnitude of its activity changed between 1975 and 1985 but its principal methods did not.

The NEB fulfilled a number of roles during its 10 years of active life. This study is most concerned with its role as a venture capitalist for small business. One of the problems perceived by the 1974 Labour Government was the existence of an equity gap and in an attempt to address the problem the Board made about 70 equity investments in such businesses and created a subsidiary Oakwood Loan Finance Ltd, which also made about 70 investments. This chapter will assess the record of the NEB as a small business venture capitalist. The record is assessed against the three criteria outlined in chapter one: its record of raising finance; its record in directing finance at the equity gap; and the financial performance of its investments. Further evidence, including a focus upon the Board's biotechnology investments, is also presented to assist in making a judgement. However, before this chapter proceeds it is necessary to bring attention to the fact that in the statistical data the figures for BL and Rolls Royce are omitted as they were firstly, transferred holdings rather than voluntary investments, and because, in any case, they would distort the study of the Board.

The Effectiveness of the NEB as a Small Business Venture Capitalist

It is important to see the small business role of the NEB in the context of its overall responsibilities. Its 'lame duck' role, especially in the case of Rolls Royce and BL, sapped the NEB of its time, money and, to a significant extent, its credibility. Nevertheless, the small business investment of the NEB has to be judged on its merits, and it is concluded in this chapter that the NEB enjoyed only limited success in this role. A number of minor successes were achieved, some in emerging technology, including biotechnology, but in general its performance was very modest.

The Financial Resources of the NEB

With a policy of direct state intervention the amount of finance that is raised is largely a political outcome and a product of a number of considerations. Firstly, it is determined by the government's view of how serious a problem is. This will usually have been worked out in Green Papers and other party policy statements prior to a general election. In the case of the NEB there were, amongst other statements, the 1973 *Labour's Programme for Britain* and the 1973 Green Paper *The National Enterprise Board*. Allied to this, the resources given to the policy will depend on the role given to the institution. The resources given to the NEB took into account the Board's responsibility for BL and Rolls Royce, which were in need of expensive restructuring. Secondly, resource levels may be determined by the fiscal position of the country. The NEB, however, seemed to remain unaffected by the fiscal crises that dogged the Labour Government with Eric Varley still granting the Board's wishes as late as 1979. Thirdly, the resources allocated to a body like the NEB will depend on the internal political balance of the party of government. The balance of a party affects its priorities, and this in turn can have an impact on resources. Under such circumstances the skill and standing of the minister responsible for the institution can be a crucial determinant and this can be seen in the case of the NEB. In the time before Labour was elected in 1974 the left clearly had the upper hand in the setting of priorities and the formulation of policy. As was seen in the previous chapter, the plans for the NEB, and by implication the resources it would have had, were extremely ambitious in the pre-government period. Once the party was in government, however, the right and the centre of the party gained greater control over what would actually be presented to Parliament and the plans for the NEB were limited, not least through the ruling out of any compulsory powers. The resources of the Board were as a result moderated accordingly.

The resources that the NEB eventually received were allocated in two main tranches. Firstly, in the 1975 Industry Act, the act that established the NEB, the Board was allocated £700 million. In addition a further £300 million was made available subject to parliamentary approval, by no means a foregone conclusion given the parliamentary arithmetic during the 1974-1979 term. Most of this was earmarked for the two main tasks the NEB had been charged with, BL and Rolls Royce (There would have also been Chrysler but for the fact that the Chairman Donald Ryder made its inclusion a resigning matter). The peak of the resources available to the NEB came with the 1979 Industry Act which increased its borrowing limit to £3,000 million, with a provision to come back to the House and increase it to £4,500 million, if necessary. The majority of the new resources dedicated by the 1979 Act were for BL and Rolls Royce. Indeed, the level of finance the Board invested on its own initiative was only a fraction of its overall investment, as is shown in table 3.1. The key point, however, is that for this type of policy the given resources are the outcome of a political process and depend on the ability of a government to push its legislation through the House of Commons. So it is not in this respect that such policies should be judged.

Table 3.1 Cost of the Purchase of NEB Investments 1976 to 1991 (Excluding Transferred Holdings)

Year	Investment (£m)
1976	19.30
1977	30.56
1978	51.71
1979	67.09
1980	50.01
1981	52.76
1982	12.04
1983	24.42
1984-85	2.44
1986 to 1991	Nil
Total	**310.33**

Source: Adapted from *NEB Annual Report,* 1976-1991.

The Effectiveness of the NEB in Targeting Finance at the Equity Gap

The distribution of the finance allocated to the NEB was also political. Although the NEB had a board that was theoretically independent of government, the aims of the Board were set by politicians (the autonomy of quangos such as the NEB is invariably relative in any case). The Board was given a number of aims, with that of providing capital to promising small companies being only one of them. Given that BL, Rolls Royce, and some of the other larger commitments of the Board involved many thousands of jobs, often in politically sensitive parts of the country, it is not surprising that the amount of finance dedicated to companies suffering from the existence of the equity gap was relatively modest. Table 3.2 shows the number of initial investments made over and under £200,000, an approximate equivalent to £400,000 in 1996.

Table 3.2 Number of NEB Initial Investments Made Under and Over £200,000

Year	Initial Investments Under £200,000	Initial Investments Over £200,000
1976	0	5
1977	9	11
1978	7	7
1979	6	14
1980	5	7
1981	2	6
1982	13	7
1983	26	7
1984-85	3	6
Total	71	70

Source: Adapted from *NEB Annual Report*, 1976-1991.

* Only includes companies for which full information is held
** The NEB also ran a number of subsidiaries charged with the responsibility of providing finance in amounts of less than £200,000. The most prominent of these was Oakland Loan Finance Ltd. Exact figures are not available for the number of investments the company made, but it is believed to be in the region of 80 to 100.

A table showing the proportion of the £310 million venture capital investment going into investments of less than £200,000 would be somewhat misleading as many of the companies received further injections of capital after the initial tranche. However, as the number of initial investments made under £200,000 was broadly similar to the number made above £200,000 it can be easily calculated that a greater amount of the capital invested by the NEB went into larger investments. Indeed, 49 of the investments made by the NEB were over £400,000, with 29 of these being in excess of £1 million.

Table 3.3 NEB Investment Thresholds

Total No of Investments	141
No of Investments > £200,000	70
No of Investments > £400,000	49
No of Investments > £1 million	29

Source: Adapted from *NEB Annual Report*, 1976-1991.

* Only includes companies for which full information is held

The statistics demonstrate that the NEB invested most of its finance in medium-sized and large businesses. This was especially so during the NEB's Labour years, and was for a number of reasons. Firstly, the NEB became involved in a number of rescues. These were often in large companies like the Fairey Group, which was acquired at the cost of £18 million in 1978. The motivation for ventures such as this were many. The NEB was not immune from political pressure, and that pressure was often directed at preserving jobs. This could be done very publicly through a rescue of a company that employed a large number of people. Indeed, the early actions of the NEB suggested it had a wish to be noticed. The Fairey investment was made despite a private sector bid from Trafalgar House. This gave the Board a tremendous amount of publicity, with the wrath that the investment incurred from the financial sector merely serving to emphasise the 'power' of the Board.

Secondly, the NEB made a decision to invest in microelectronics. Starting a microelectronics company from scratch is a very expensive business, and the Board's adventures in this field soon absorbed tens of millions of pounds. The general innovative role ascribed to the Board - there were also large investments in biotechnology - necessitated the making of large investments and furthered the shift away from small business venture capital. Thirdly, there was also a time factor. The staff at the NEB at no stage numbered more than about 80; consequently, there was a limit to the number of investments that it could consider. Given that small investments are proportionately more time consuming than large investments, and that the Board also clearly wanted to make an impact on the industrial scene, it is not surprising that only a relatively modest number of small investments were made. Overall, the experience of the NEB seems to show that if the state does want to invest venture capital in small business it is preferable for the institution doing so to be focused on that task rather than it being one of a number of commitments. On this evidence, political expediency and circumstance tends to crowd out the role in a wider organisation.

The Performance of Investments made by the NEB

The third criteria by which the NEB is judged is the performance of its investments. In this section the overall performance of the Board will be reviewed, followed by an analysis of their small business investment record.

The overall performance of the NEB as an investor

When the Board was set up it was given the target of achieving an annual rate of return of between 15 and 20% on capital employed by 1981. However, by 1980 the NEB had made little progress in reaching this target and, indeed, after 1978 returns had deteriorated sharply. After 1980 the Secretary of State decided that this was no longer the appropriate method of assessing the NEB, and from 1981 onwards the NEB was judged in terms its performance against the cost of government borrowing. This new measure of the NEB's performance did not produce a different result as the NEB continued to fall below the required targets. Indeed, the NEB did not achieve either of the two targets until 1985, when it had effectively ceased to exist as a venture capitalist. The absurdly good figures for the years 1988 to 1990 are meaningless because they are the result of a combination of inactivity and the sale of a few remaining, profitable investments. It is noticeable that the NEB's performance was particularly weak between 1979 and 1983. Some might be tempted to claim that this was due to the NEB being affected by the general recessionary conditions, rather than being the result of the Board's lack of judgement. This argument is investigated later in the chapter.

Table 3.4 Return on Capital Employed by NEB 1976 to 1980

Year	Return on Capital Employed
1976	7.3
1977	11.4
1978	11.3
1979	4.8
1980	-15.3

Source: Adapted from *NEB Annual Report,* 1976-1980.

Table 3.5 NEB Performance Against the Cost of Government Borrowing 1981 to 1990

Year	Annual Required %	Actual %	Annual Cumulative % #	Actual %
1981	13.07	-30.12	-	-
1982	13.40	2.16	13.25	-13.64
1983	13.20	0.18	13.23	-8.66
1985	13.12	19.70	13.21	0.06
1986	13.24	8.72	13.22	0.07
1987	12.91	18.96	13.22	9.05
1988	14.13	113,600.0	13.15	12.88
1989	14.13	11,800.0	13.13	23.75
1990	14.13	24,800.0	13.12	21.43

Cumulative for the previous five years

Source: Adapted from *NEB Annual Report,* 1981-1990.

Yet perhaps the most relevant statistics for a study that is concentrating on the NEB's role as a venture capitalist are those for the returns made on the disposal of its investments. The bulk of the disposals were made after

1979 when the Conservatives started to curb the Board's powers and required it to reduce its portfolio. The disposal figures (shown in table 3.6) varied a great deal from year to year. This was largely due to the fact that they were often strongly affected by the disposal of one of the NEB's larger investments. The overall figure for the investments disposed of between 1978 and 1991, bearing in mind that the NEB in 1991 still had a net book value of investments of £1.5 million, was a loss of £27.56 million. As this is a study of the NEB acting as an investor it is necessary to remove the returns on the investments that the NEB inherited from the Department of Industry. The NEB was given no choice but to accept these, and consequently they do not provide a fair test of the Board's judgement.

Table 3.6 NEB's Profit and Loss on Disposal of Investments 1978 to 1991

Year	Profit / (Loss) (£m)	Year	Profit / (Loss) (£m)
1978	0.30	1986	(12.52)
1979	(13.64)	1987	6.26
1980	4.42	1988	6.63
1981	(45.36)	1989	(8.66)
1982	(1.68)	1990	1.17
1983	1.13	1991	0
1985	34.39		

Source: Adapted from *NEB Annual Report*, 1978-1991.

The effect of doing this (shown in table 3.7) is to worsen, slightly, the performance of the NEB; the companies transferred were not all 'lame ducks' after all and some were even disposed of at a profit. The overall loss on disposal of the investments made by the NEB was, after this adjustment, £31.62 million.

The NEB's venture capital investment in small business

The focus of this study, however, is the provision of finance to small business. Two categories of investment by the Board have been chosen to analyse its performance in this role. These are initial investments of £500,000 and £200,000. The difficulties with such an analysis is the need to take into account the changes in prices since the time the NEB was investing. An investment of £200,000 in 1976 is not the same as one in 1997. This is important as the study into the NEB is in the context of a defined equity gap. The problems are made even more complicated by the fact that the NEB invested over a period of nine years of high inflation, meaning that the values of the Board's investments varied even within its own time. Consequently, it has been decided that it is not feasible to index every one of the NEB's 150 investments. Instead the policy of this chapter is to assume that prices have doubled since the Board's investments were made, whether it was made in 1976 or 1983. Although this assumption contains a significant degree of inaccuracy it is not felt that it will significantly affect the general picture that will emerge about the NEB's performance in this respect. The £200,000 and under category, therefore, represents those investments that were within the range of the equity gap.

Table 3.7 Adjustments to the NEB's Disposal Record (£m)

Profit / (Loss) on Overall Disposals			(27.56)
Minus the Transferred Companies:			
	Alfred Herbert Ltd	(57.36)	
	Brown Boveri Kent Ltd	(0.70)	
	Cambridge Instrument Co Ltd	(12.05)	
	Dunford and Elliott Ltd	0.16	
	Ferranti Ltd	49.80	
	ICL	24.21	4.06
Profit / (Loss) on Disposal of NEB Selected Companies			(31.62)

Source: Adapted from *NEB Annual Report*, 1978-1983.

Table 3.8 contains the outcomes of 92 investments the NEB made under £500,000 (a small number of other investments under that level were made but for various reasons they were omitted). The column entitled 'outcomes unknown' is necessary because of the decision in 1986 to transfer 27 investments to Oakwood Finance Ltd and the NRDC. Information about the eventual disposal of these investments is not available, as was the case in a few other instances. The investments that were transferred to Grosvenor Development Capital are also included in the table. The disposal outcome in those cases refers to the disposal by Grosvenor.

Table 3.8 NEB Investments Under £500,000 - Disposal Outcomes

Liquidations	20
Receiverships	8
Loss Making Disposals	20
Profit Making Disposals	16
Outcomes Unknown	28

Source: *NEB Annual Report,* 1978-1991.

The disposal record on these investments is at best mixed. Only 25% of the investments provided a return to the NEB, less than would have been expected in a category which included many established companies. Furthermore, even this modest performance includes a profitable investment in a company which only accepted finance from the Board as they were involved with one of the sector-based projects, and they were only involved in that because they felt they had no commercial choice. This company, which preferred to remain anonymous, would not have gone to the Board otherwise and could have easily have raised the finance elsewhere. In addition to this a director of the company was very scathing about the Board, claiming that the project had done little for their company. The Board should certainly not claim any credit for this investment. On the other hand there were a number of very successful investments, one of which was Celltech, featured later in the chapter. Although the £500,000 limit gives a broad picture of the NEB's investments in small and medium sized businesses, it is the investments of £200,000 or under that most concern the study. As these investments hold some significance for the assessment of a policy of direct state intervention they are set out in full.

Table 3.9 NEB Investments £200,000 or Less - Disposal Outcomes

Company	Initial Investment (£m)	Outcome	Profit / (Loss) on Disposal (£m)
Allen Thornton and Sons Ltd	0.03	Rec	(0.03)
Aqualisa Products Ltd	0.12 e/l	Profit	5.34
Automation and Technical Services Ltd	0.15	Profit	0.75
BTB (Engineering) Ltd	0.03	Liq	(0.03)
Barlin Consumer Products Ltd	0.05	Liq	(0.05)
British EKG Monitors Ltd	0.05 l	Liq	(0.05)
Caltec Insulations Ltd	0.05 e/l	Rec	(0.15)
RR Chapman (Sub Sea Surveys) Ltd	0.05	Profit	0.30
Epichem Ltd	0.02	Profit	0.07
Euromatic Machine and Oil Ltd	0.10	Loss	(0.02)
Excelarc Engineering Ltd	0.07	Loss	(0.08)
Focom Systems Ltd	0.12	Profit	0.68
Hemmings Plastics Ltd	0.10	Liq	(0.20)
Hivent Ltd	0.10 e/l	Liq	(0.11)
Imtec Group plc	0.18	Loss	(0.13)
J & P Engineering Ltd	0.15 e/l	Liq	(0.20)
Keland Electrics Ltd	0.16 e/l	Loss	(0.26)
Kongsberg Systems Technology Ltd	0.20	Loss	(0.48)
Mayflower Packaging Ltd	0.12	Rec	(0.17)
Microsell Systems Ltd	0.05	Loss	(0.04)
Mikro Industrial Instruments Ltd	0.05	Liq	(0.02)
Modular Office Systems Ltd	0.13	Rec	(0.27)
Momex (UK) Ltd	0.02 l	Rec	(0.05)
Multi-Arc Vacuum Systems Ltd	0.20	Profit	0.02
P Shapira Ltd	0.20	Liq	(0.20)
Pakmet International Ltd	0.15	Rec	(0.36)
Power Dynamics Ltd	0.18	Liq	(0.03)
Preformed Road Markings Ltd	0.09	Liq	(0.13)

Program Products Ltd	0.03 l		0.00
Protel Ltd	0.13	Liq	(0.46)
Rigby Electronics Ltd	0.07	Loss	(0.07)
Sandiacre Electronics Ltd	0.17	Liq	(0.51)
Shelton Instruments Ltd	0.12 e/l	Liq	(0.12)
Solglo Ltd	0.03		0.00
Technalogics Computing Ltd	0.04	Rec	(0.04)
Vicort of London Ltd	0.20 e/l	Liq	(0.12)
Whitecross Rubber Products Ltd	0.06 e/l	Profit	0.01

Source: Adapted from *NEB Annual Report*, 1976-1991.

Four investments of less than £200,000 were transferred to a part-owned subsidiary, Grosvenor Development Capital, in 1981. These are listed in table 3.10. The profit and loss on the investment refers to that incurred by Grosvenor Development Capital.

Table 3.10 Outcomes of Four of the Investments Transferred to Grosvenor Development Capital in 1981

Company	Initial Investment (£m)	Outcome
Doyce Electronics Ltd	0.08	Loss
FW Elliott (Holdings) Ltd	0.15 l	Profit
Hydraroll Ltd	0.06	Profit
Innotron Ltd	0.08 e&l	Loss

Source: *NEB Annual Report*, 1977-1979; and Grosvenor Venture Managers internal company statistics.

Key to Tables 3.9 and 3.10
l - loan; e/l - equity and loan package; liq - company went into liquidation; rec - company went into receivership

There were also a further 25 initial investments made by the NEB under £200,000, but the outcomes of these are unknown as they were among those transferred out of the NEB in 1986 to Oakwood Loan Finance and the NRDC; indeed they are many of the same companies that were listed in the unknown column in table 3.8. Sufficient is known, however, about NEB investment in small businesses for an assessment to be made.

The cross section of the NEB's small investments is a fascinating one as it offers ammunition to both the defenders and the critics of the Board. On the one hand the small investment portfolio is dominated by loss-producing investments, seemingly confirming the view that the state is a disastrous investor in industry and should keep out. Yet the available information on the NEB's small business investment suggests that its investment at this level did not really lose it any of its money at all, as a small number of spectacular successes more than offset the many loss-making investments. The portfolio contains fourteen companies that went into liquidation while involved with the NEB, with a further seven entering receivership. Seven more were sold by the NEB at a loss, two broke even, leaving only seven that were disposed of at a profit. However, one of these was Aqualisa Products Ltd. This company was founded in 1977, and the NEB made what proved to be a very wise decision to take 40% of the equity. The decision was wise because when the NEB finally disposed of its stake in the company in 1988 it was worth £5.34 million, a return on the investment of 4550%, about 400% per annum. This return transforms the whole nature of the NEB's investment under £200,000 as it alone covers the losses made on the other small businesses.

However, can it be said that because of this one overwhelming success the NEB's investment at this level was credible and that a recommendation should be made for a future government to carry out a similar policy ? There are two answers to this question. The first is that the NEB was lucky with Aqualisa Products Ltd, that any future attempt at state venture capital would be unlikely to have such a stroke of fortune, and that this very successful investment should not be allowed to deflect attention away from the two dozen or so others that were unsuccessful. The second answer is that the Aqualisa investment is what venture capital is all about. Although practices have now changed somewhat, at the time the NEB was operating it was accepted that a high-risk venture capital portfolio would contain a fair number of investments that were not successful, but that these would be more than compensated for by a smaller number of very successful ones. Indeed, it is the likelihood of failures in high-risk venture capital which makes equity rather than loan finance more appropriate. It is claimed that the NEB's portfolio reflected this expectation. There were in any case other very successful investments apart from Aqualisa. Focom Systems Ltd produced an annual return to the NEB of 567%, Automation and Technical Services Ltd an annual return of 167% and Epichem Ltd an annual return of 58%.

The NEB obviously hoped that more of the companies in its portfolio would be successful than was the case, but the expectation was never that nearly all would yield profits. The NEB believed that if they exhibited sound judgement then there would be enough successes to make the overall operation profitable. To some extent this was achieved in this area of investment, although the failure rate was clearly too high to be acceptable.

Aqualisa Products Ltd - An NEB success ?

Given that Aqualisa was such a success it is of some interest as to whether the Board's intervention was a significant factor. Aqualisa was set up in 1977 to produce shower valves. The arrangement that was worked out with the NEB was that each of the two founders would take 30% of the equity, with the Board taking the remaining 40%. The equity cost the NEB £70,000, and they also provided the company with a further £50,000 in the form of a loan. The founding directors were happy with this arrangement as it left them with a majority of the equity and therefore control over the business. An Aqualisa director said that the company would have gone ahead in 1977 even if the NEB had not provided capital as the prospects for the business were such that it would have been attractive to private sector financiers. Very few companies chose the NEB over private sector financiers, but, according to the director, involvement for them had a number of advantages. Firstly, high interest rates would have accompanied a private sector loan at that time. Secondly, the directors wanted the finance to include equity, and, thirdly, they felt that if nothing else the NEB had a reputation for fairness. The company was confident that they would be successful and did not want an investor that would interfere too much with the running of the business. This was an assurance that the NEB was to fulfil; according to the Aqualisa director the NEB took the attitude of 'leave well alone'.

The first three years of the company's life produced losses, but by the third year, 1979, the picture began to improve as sales increased from £40,000 to £640,000. It was in 1980, however, that the real value of the NEB's involvement was realised. During that year the company's sales rose strongly again to £810,000, despite the adverse economic conditions, and their losses were restricted to £50,000. The NEB stated in their annual report: 'The superior design of the shower valves produced by the company have enabled it to increase significantly its share of the market.'[1] The Board confidently expected future profits. It was at this time the company found that it needed more capital, albeit only £50,000. Despite their attempts, and their future prospects, the banks would not lend the company the money so it was the NEB that had to step in and provide further finance, in the form of ordinary and preference shares. An Aqualisa finance director commented how vital this second tranche of finance was, and insisted that the company would have gone into liquidation in 1981 if it had not been for the NEB stepping in. He also emphasised the loss there would have been to the British economy. The company, now part of Williams Holdings, turns over about £16 million annually, employs about 200 people and last year recorded a profit of £3 million. Its contribution to the taxpayer is about £2 million per year. The Aqualisa directors agreed that the NEB was useful as 'small companies often lack somewhere to go that gives them independent advice'. Overall the evidence here suggests that as far as this investment is concerned the NEB can take great credit from their involvement. It was a classic venture capital investment being high risk, yielding a high return, and producing economic gains to the economy that would not have been produced if conventional financial institutions had been the only option. Whether one can argue that it completely justifies the losses that were incurred on the other small business investments is another matter.

Assessing the Reliability of a Profit and Loss Analysis

The Aqualisa investment was an instance where the outcome was a profit for the NEB, profitable growth for the company, with the NEB deserving credit for the double success. Its involvement had not just been incidental, it had been crucial. However, this point has been an issue of debate with the NEB. On the one hand opponents of the NEB have argued that, in many cases, the profitability of the NEB's investments had nothing to do with the intervention of the Board, and therefore credit should not be claimed (an instance was described earlier in the chapter). On the other hand, defenders of the NEB claim that not all of the investments that lost the Board money should be blamed upon it. They claim other factors were at work, not least the 1980 to 1982 recession. An investigation into these claims reveals that the Board's record improves when the analysis goes beyond its basic profit and loss record. This section reveals that on most occasions it is wrong to deny the Board credit for its profitable investments, whereas not all of its loss making investments can be put down to its poor judgement.

In a number of the Board's profitable investments the company directors revealed that the NEB had made an important contribution to the success of their company, and in some cases a contribution that the private sector was not willing to undertake. For example, one director, who wishes to keep himself and his company anonymous, had discussions with 13 merchant banks; they all rejected the company's MBO proposal. One possible reason was the fact that the sales manager withdrew from the team, which may well have affected the confidence that the potential financiers had in the company. However, he felt that the company's track record was such that it should not have been too much of a consideration. Instead, the NEB invested in the company which eventually yielded a profit of over £600,000. The former director considers the involvement of the NEB to have been vital to the company. He admitted that 'had they not provided finance it is unlikely that the company would have remained in existence.'

A second director, who also requests anonymity, was also complimentary about the NEB's intervention. His company received about £300,000 in the form of equity from the NEB in 1979. The capital was used to deal with problems occurring in one of its divisions: a problem which was eventually solved by shutting it down. The company's performance after the intervention of the NEB was by no means perfect but justified the Board's intervention. Turnover was said to have been static between 1980 and 1982, but matters improved in the following three years and the company produced profits. The company fell back into a loss in 1986 due to an unsuccessful new instrument which was developed, and in 1987 they were taken over by a larger group. The director said that 'the involvement by the NEB had been beneficial to our company, although we had just as much help from our merchant bankers'. However, it seems that the NEB intervention was necessary as their bank and merchant bank rejected their application for finance back in 1979 saying that they should go elsewhere to spread the financing risks. A gain totalling over £900,000 was eventually made on the investment.

Epichem Ltd is also a case where the NEB stepped in where the private sector would not, with the problem in this case being the product. The silane gas that the company produced was highly unstable and hence the company presented a high risk to potential investors. Yet after the NEB's investment in 1983 the company went on to be very successful, and it was said that if the NEB had held on to its stake for another 18 months or so their profit on the investment would have been many times greater. Finally, Precision Systems Ltd benefited from a loan provided by the NEB finance company, Oakwood Loan Finance. Precision Systems was involved in the manufacture of high-tech welding systems and the £40,000 loan was for working capital. The former director interviewed said that the loan was important for the development of the company as it allowed them to expand to a position where they could raise second stage funding on the market. At this time the company was able to repay the loan, the profit for the NEB coming from the interest the company had paid. Since that time the company has been merged into a larger company, Precision Beam Technology. Precision System's former director added: 'There is a definite gap. I have been involved with a number of small businesses and there has been a real difficulty in getting finance between £100,000 to £200,000.'

It would appear, therefore, from this, admittedly small, sample that the NEB was by no means an unimportant factor in the achievements of the companies which provided it with a profitable return on its investment. The second claim often made was that the Board was not always at fault for the investments that it realised at a loss. From the evidence of a number of companies or former companies that were contacted, this would appear to be a fair claim, although a varied picture emerged. One of the most striking cases that acts in the Board's favour is Hemmings Plastics Ltd. Hemmings was a Merseyside manufacturer of plastic closures for the pharmaceutical industry and became involved with the NEB in 1977. The NEB subscribed for £100,000 of partly convertible redeemable preference shares. The finance was used to enable the company to expand its operations, both in terms of size and product range. This increased the workforce by about 30 to over 100. There were no problems about the finance at the time of investment, although in retrospect the businessman felt that more money was really needed for their plans. This, he said, was something that the NEB should have recognised. That they did not reflected the fact that the NEB did not use 'independent experts' to assess the proposal. He also recalled that the NEB had been a last resort for the company. The banks were not interested; in fact the NEB was suggested by their own bank manager. The banks did not lend to the company because it could not offer enough security. The banks wanted personal security which the directors were not willing to offer.

The company became quite profitable in the initial years after the NEB investment, with profits rising from £20,000 in 1977 to £80,000 in 1978.[2] Yet the company was forced into voluntary liquidation only three years later. The businessman had no doubt over what had caused this: it was nothing to do with the NEB but was the severity of the recession. He claimed that Hemmings could have survived in any sort of economic climate other than the one that was experienced between 1980 and 1982. The Board's investment was not totally wasted as he was able to salvage much from the liquidation and start again. In any case he believed that the NEB had been beneficial to the company, which, as he said, under normal circumstances was perfectly viable. When summing up his attitude to the Board he said that from his own experience he had been satisfied, but that he knew others who had been involved with it who had not felt so positive. He also blamed the politicians for causing uncertainty for businesses involved with the NEB; as has been recorded it became something of a political football. He said that there was still an equity gap for businesses like Hemmings in the 1990s, and that he would favour the setting up of a similar body to the NEB, but only if there were no political ties and that there was agreement that it should be there indefinitely.

A favourable verdict was also recorded in the case of Bull Motors Ltd. Bull Motors was purchased from the AO Smith Corporation in October 1977, and became a wholly-owned subsidiary of the NEB. The company manufactured industrial motors, mostly used for lifts. The initial transaction between the NEB and Bull was worth £500,000. Bull was also hit by the recession of the early 1980s, not least as it was especially vulnerable to the high exchange rates that were being experienced at the time, as they exported up to 80% of their output. The NEB persevered with Bull and increased its investment during 1979 and 1980 to nearly £2 million, mainly so that it could widen its range of motors. Its commitment eventually reached £3.02 million. Losses were incurred by the company between 1978 and 1981, but by 1982 the company had returned to profitability. In 1985 Bull showed a £900,000 profit on a £5.6 million turnover. The success was attributed to the motor that Bull developed at the time of the NEB's involvement, with one director arguing that Bull would have gone under, were it not for the Board's intervention. The company was bought back from the NEB in 1985, although the Board had to accept writing off over £2 million. It remains an important employer in its home town of Ipswich. The NEB lost money with Bull but the evidence suggests that it was not a fruitless investment and not at all an intervention to be ashamed of.

A director of Energy Equipment Co Ltd also acknowledged and defended the intervention of the Board. Energy Equipment manufactured fluidised bed boilers. Initially they did this successfully, and had British Sugar as one of its major customers, yet when the NEB disposed of the company to Petrofina (UK) Ltd in 1981 it had to accept a loss of £430,000. Despite this loss the company was a viable one when transferred and the NEB would have been justified in predicting that they had contributed to future success. According to a former director, however, problems arose almost as soon as Petrofina assumed ownership. This was largely due to their policy of scaling up the business too quickly. The company started to make boilers that cost £2 million, against their original ones that cost only £200,000, but this was done without making up the 'technology gap' that the leap involved. It became 'a civil engineering job and the company did not have the skills for that', the director commented. In the view of the ex-director the NEB could well have made a success of the company, as it was more likely that they would have allowed it grow naturally. He added that 'the basic product had potential, but the investors in the private sector would not allow it to take its natural course.' He also commented that the change from having the NEB as an investor to having a private sector one, caused 'something of a culture shock', although he did not reveal if that was to either of the parties' detriment. Therefore, not only was the Board not guilty of poor judgement, it was actually stated that the company's subsequent problems could well have been avoided if the Board had retained ownership.

There would also appear to be mitigating factors for the loss incurred from the investment in Agemaspark Ltd. In September 1976 the NEB invested £350,000 in the form of an equity and loan package in this spark erosion machine manufacturing company. The backing was intended to allow the company to expand, and in particular to increase its export sales. Agemaspark's performance in the first three years with the NEB seemed to confirm the Board's judgement as turnover increased from £1.71 million to £6.21 million.[3] During these years Agemaspark became increasingly profitable, expanded its production facilities, and in 1979 was awarded the Queen's Award for Export Performance. This encouraged the NEB to invest a further £250,000 in the business. However, the machine tool industry was badly hit by the 1980 to 1982 recession and over the years 1979 to 1981 turnover almost halved, taking the company back to where it was in 1977. By 1981 the company was making substantial losses, and in June of that year the NEB invested a further £1 million in an attempt to shore up the company's finances. However, it became clear by the end of that year that a substantial amount of money was going to be required to see Agemaspark through this period. Neither the NEB or the company's bankers were willing to do this so in April 1982 the company was put into receivership in the hope that a private company would come along with an offer. This is indeed what happened and Agemaspark was taken over by Hurco Europe Ltd. The NEB agreed to write off its £2 million stake. A Hurco director said that they felt the products offered by Agemaspark were sound, and they are still part of

Hurco's line at the time of writing. Hurco, in fact, still trade from the old Agemaspark premises.

There were instances, however, when the Board had clearly been at fault in both its judgement over and the management of the investment. British Robotic Systems Ltd (BRSL) is a case in point. This company was in its very early stages when the NEB invested in it in 1981. The company was a early starter in machine-vision, which is a technique whereby computers use visual images to monitor products during manufacture. The company very quickly gained a reputation as something of a leader in the field, and in 1984 formed a joint venture with the American company, 3M. A separate company, 3M Vision Systems, was formed. The problems with the investment were in the UK and included the fact that the NEB was a 100% shareholder in the company but was by that time looking to run down its portfolio because of political pressure. A private buyer was required, but the political uncertainty that surrounded the NEB was said to have put off many potential investors, and concerned 3M. The uncertainty also affected the orders that the company was receiving. Eventually the BRSL was sold to a company that acted as a distributor for the General Electric Company of the US. A director of BRSL argued that the company had good products but was hampered by the inconsistent policy of the NEB. The NEB was unable or unwilling to make a long-term commitment to the company so what they got from the Board was finance on 'drip feed', with even the initial capital of £260,000 not being sufficient for the company's needs. It is claimed by this former director that the company could have been a world leader if the Government had let the NEB invest in the company long-term.

The NEB would also appear to have been at fault over its investment in Doyce Electronics Ltd, a company founded in 1972 to make digital engine test equipment for the automobile industry. Between 1979 and 1980 the NEB invested £120,000 in Doyce, who had been unable to get finance from their bankers on the terms they required.[4] As a result the company was able to expand its range of equipment. In 1981, Doyce became another one of the eight companies that was transferred into the newly-formed Grosvenor Development Capital. However, partly because of an apparent over-valuation of the company's stock, Grosvenor put Doyce into receivership, and eventually lost £109,000 on the investment. The verdict from Grosvenor was that 'basically they never had a good enough product to win a sufficient market share in the field.'

Likewise, J and P Engineering is another example where the NEB simply made an assessment that proved to be wrong. J and P was the kind of investment that handed the NEB's opponents political capital as only a year after having put £200,000 into the business it went into liquidation. Unlike the Hemmings investment where 20% of the investment was recovered, the NEB lost all of the money it put into J and P. The business was well established and had spent many years supplying to nuclear research establishments, although the NEB finance was used to develop an operation in the medical field. In specific terms, J and P developed an isotope body scanner, of which the sales did not materialise, apparently due to a combination of a fall in demand in that market and the emergence of competition. Yet even before this situation became apparent, there were problems with the investment. One of the J and P managers recollects that 'the director appointed by the NEB and the MD just could not find any agreement as to how the finances should be handled.' All was not quite lost as the engineering division of the company was purchased by one of the management who started a new company.

A further mistake was made in the case of Mayflower Packaging, a company which manufactured automatic packaging machines. The Board invested £120,000 in the company in 1977 to alleviate the company's problems of under-capitalisation. A former director said that the company could have obtained the finance from other sources but this would have meant the management losing control over the business; the company seemed willing, however, to let the NEB take a 100% stake. The company went into liquidation because it lacked control over its costs. The director felt that the NEB was partly responsible for this, as it should have been recognised both before the money was invested and during the after-investment monitoring. This was especially so, he added, because the NEB representative on the Board was an accountant. A further £50,000 was committed by the NEB to Mayflower and the whole of this was lost when the company was put into receivership and then into liquidation in 1979.

From the evidence of this section a number of points can be made. Firstly, the information on profitable investments does not support the view that the NEB made little or no positive contribution to companies that provided them with a return. Indeed, if the Aqualisa investment is borne in mind, it seems that on many occasions the opposite was the case. Secondly, there is also some evidence that the NEB should not be held responsible for all of the investments that provided them with a loss. There were clearly some cases where the NEB acted in a way which was unhelpful to the company, although even in one of these cases, BRSL, this was partly due to the political pressures that were placed upon the Board after 1979. It was not, though, a commonly held view that the Board had contributed to individual misfortunes or shown poor judgement in investing at all. This was partly due to a third point that can be made: the claim that other factors intervened to contribute to the poor performance of many of the companies, and consequently the Board's investment. One of these factors was the 1980 to 1982 recession, the significance of which is now assessed.

The NEB and the 1980 to 1982 Recession

Many defenders of the Board argue that the performance of its investments must be seen in the context of the recession that ravaged the economy between 1980 and 1982. Three points are made. Firstly, it is argued that many of the NEB's investments were in early-stage companies, or in companies that were going through what were thought to be short-term financial difficulties. It is claimed they were especially vulnerable to such a harsh economic climate. Secondly, it is claimed that it is credible to use the recession in mitigation against the shortcomings of the Board as it was unusually severe, especially in the manufacturing sector which was the focus of much of the Board's investment. The key point is that while it is accepted that all economies go through recessions and that it is a company's responsibility to ensure they are strong enough to survive it, this recession was so severe that viable businesses went to the wall. Some of these viable businesses, it is suggested, were in the NEB's portfolio. Thirdly, many suggest that it is ironic that some of the harshest critics of the Board were in the party that caused the recession, and the consequent losses.

Again, it is possible to provide some evidence on this contention. It has already been noted that some of the Board's investee companies believed that the recession was the dominant reason why their business went to the wall, or was taken over by another company; both the directors of Hemmings Plastics and Agemaspark made this claim. The financial performance of these two companies does indeed go some way towards supporting their view as their performance during the years of recession were out of character with previous years. Agemaspark had a steady if unspectacular profits record between 1976, the date of the Board's investment, and 1979, and its turnover also built up over that period. The recession of the early 1980s dramatically reversed that growth, however, and caused the company to incur a huge loss in 1981 - £1.8 million on a turnover of only £3.2 million. Receivership quickly followed in 1982, and as previously documented, the company was taken over by Hurco Europe. The situation was similar in the case of Hemmings Plastics Ltd. Their profits turned to losses in 1980 and three years later the company went into liquidation. A similar picture is seen in the cases of The Mollart Engineering Co Ltd, North East Audio Ltd, and Sandiacre Electrics Ltd, which all saw profits turn to losses in 1980 and 1981. Mollart and Sandiacre suffered the most, with Mollart's losses reaching almost £1 million in 1982. All three firms went out of business.

Whilst there are dangers in taking into account factors such as this, the above examples show there is some evidence to suggest that there were companies in the NEB portfolio that were potentially viable but for the unusually severe recession between 1980 and 1982. This factor must not be allowed to obscure, though, the fact that investments like J and P Engineering were simply poor investments, and that the NEB made a fair number of them.

The NEB and its Sectoral Approach: The Case of Biotechnology

One way in which the NEB sought to maximise the impact of its limited funds was to invest in emerging sectors; this often involved high technology. The NEB sought to act as a catalyst for future private sector development which fitted in with its role of bridging important gaps with which the private financial sector would not get involved. This approach was said to have been applied to micro-electronics and computers, with the setting up of Nexos Office Systems, Insac, Inmos and Q1 (Europe). A number of established computer companies were also financed. The most successful part of this approach was the creation of Inmos, an investment which was realised at a very large gain, whilst the least successful part was Nexos Office Systems which struggled to sell its wares and lost the NEB about £30 million.

Another example of the NEB's sectoral approach was biotechnology, with its centrepiece being the formation of Celltech Ltd. A prime mover behind Celltech, Gerard Fairtlough, head of the NEB division dealing with science, believed that 'the NEB made a significant impact on biotechnology'.[5] In this section this claim is examined for two reasons. Firstly, it forms part of the assessment of the NEB, but secondly, it is also interesting to explore whether this attempt at a sectoral strategy provides any lessons for the investment policy of any future state investment institution. The starting point for an analysis into biotechnology is to ascertain what existed in the way of an industry prior to the intervention of the NEB. The answer is that there was not a great deal. A number of companies were operating in the field, but there were no companies in the UK that had been set up solely to concentrate on developing biotechnology advances, as was the case in the United States.

Celltech Ltd

The NEB felt that the UK's inadequate presence in the field was unnecessary given the country's research record. As a result the NEB put a plan together for a company called Celltech. Because of rules imposed by Sir Keith Joseph the NEB had to find private sector backers to form a joint public-private venture, something they managed with Prudential Assurance, the Midland Bank, British and Commonwealth Shipping, and Technical Development Capital (an arm of 3i). All of these investors committed themselves to taking 14% of the equity. To be able to claim that the NEB was successful in this sector, however, it has to be shown that it made a crucial contribution to the formation of Celltech. According to Dr Norman Carey, Research and Development Director of Celltech at the time of its formation, and now an independent biotechnology consultant, it did make such a contribution. He said: 'The NEB was very important. Certain people at the NEB picked up the suggestions of people in the academic world and worked out the idea of forming the company. They were able to show that the potential existed to form a company.'[6] Dr Spencer Emtage, a long time employee at Celltech, agrees. He insisted: 'If it wasn't for Gerard Fairtlough, Celltech wouldn't have started. He was the driving force behind the company.'[7] Dr Hamish Hale, a director of Apax Partners and an authority in the field, goes some way to explain why the NEB's intervention was so important: 'None of the major drug companies was interested in developing companies like Celltech; indeed they still remain uninterested, unlike large companies in the US, Sweden and Switzerland.'[8]

Mark Dodgson, who has written the definitive work on Celltech, came to the same conclusion: 'The NEB/BTG's financial support was critical to the company.'[9] He notes, however, that this was nearly put at risk, by both the NEB/BTG and the Government:

> Celltech emerged from a public policy for science and technology disrupted by the Conservative election victory in 1979 ... Celltech was the brainchild of two public-sector organisations - the NEB and MRC - [yet] political dictum did not allow it to be public sector owned. Private sector backing was required, and the

combination of severe time pressures placed on the NEB organising team by numerous bureaucratic delays, and the limited enthusiasm in the City for investing in biotechnology and in NEB initiatives, ensured that Celltech began its life with its uneasy group of shareholders. To add to its insecurity, Celltech's major shareholder, the NEB, had made assurances [to the Government] that it would attempt to divest its holding within three years. After it had made its initial investment the NEB came under political and economic pressures to reduce its shareholdings as rapidly as possible. And senior NEB/BTG officials were trenchant in their view that Celltech should become a short-term, commercially-orientated company. 'National interest' considerations came more to the fore when BTG, relieved of the pressure of being the dominant shareholder, and more secure in the knowledge that it would enjoy financial returns, began to make its decisions about its shareholdings in line with the needs of the company.[10]

Despite these far from ideal developments out of which Celltech still managed to emerge, Dodgson was in no doubt that 'the NEB/BTG's occasionally reluctant, but continuing support was instrumental for Celltech's survival and growth.'[11] There appears to be a consensus about the importance of the NEB's contribution to Celltech and it is also suggested that the private market would not have initiated a company like Celltech, and certainly not at the time Celltech was formed.

How important has Celltech been for the UK biotechnology industry?

This still leaves the question of how important Celltech was to the development of a biotechnology industry in the UK. Hamish Hale said that again the issue was clear cut: 'There is no doubt that Celltech was seminal in getting the industry going in the UK. The NEB were right to get things going through Celltech ... Celltech was important in the sense that it was the first company to be formed in the UK specifically to develop biotechnology. Celltech was similar to how biotechnology was done in the US.'[12] Dr Norman Carey concurs:

> Celltech showed that it was possible to do such a thing. It was not a common thing in the biological sciences to go into something like Celltech - it was the kind of thing that they did in the States rather than here ... It is no longer true to say that a biotechnology company can't be formed without an institution like the NEB, there are now many others around. But the question to be asked is would the industry have developed if Celltech had not shown the way?[13]

Dr Carey suggests possibly not. Dodgson also directly associates the development of Celltech with the development of the UK biotechnology industry. The position of Celltech, sixteen years after its formation, however, is questionable. Some think that the company cannot go on for much longer telling its investors that the returns will come in the future. Hamish Hale says that 'despite having been going for over ten years they have not yet had any major product sales. They do contract manufacture monoclonal antibodies but they are only 'small beer', contracts for about £1 million. They should be producing products that will make them £100 million given the amount of money they have spent. Some are sceptical about the company. Other companies have caught them up, and in fact have probably passed them.'[14] Indeed, as table 3.11 reveals, their financial record is not an impressive one, even for a company that is always going to promise high returns in the future.

Table 3.11 Celltech's Performance 1981 to 1992

(£m)	1981	1982	1985	1986	1987	1990	1991	1992
Turnover	0.07	0.37	3.84	7.60	11.41	19.87	17.04	12.30
Profit / (Loss)	(0.93)	(1.88)	(1.42)	(1.16)	1.34	(16.5)	(9.35)	(9.16)

Source: Adapted from *NEB Annual Report,* 1982; *Directory of Directors*, East Grinstead, Reed Information Services, 1990 and 1994.

In the summer of 1994 Celltech announced that they had made 'the biggest corporate deal yet to be signed by a UK biotechnology company'.[15] This was a collaboration with the US drugs manufacturer, Merck, on a drug for asthma, a sector apparently worth 'at least $4 billion a year and growing at 15% annually.'[16] The deal, it was said, represented 'a vote of confidence in its product pipeline, as well as bringing in cash.'[17] Merck is to pay for the later rounds of trials that the drug will need to go through. Don Seymour, a former non-executive director at Celltech, reflecting on the Merck deal and other recent developments, thought that the company's prospects were promising. He said: 'Recently they have done some good joint ventures with US companies, which seeing as they are very successful augers well for the state of Celltech.'[18] Further to the claims that have been made thus far, the NEB's investment in Celltech was a financial success for the Board itself.

Pressure to relinquish its investments forced the Board to make a gradual withdrawal from Celltech and by 1987 it had divested the whole of its stake realising a profit of £8.4 million.

The NEB's gradual withdrawal from Celltech

In 1980 the NEB took a 44% stake in Celltech; table 3.12 shows the Board's gradual withdrawal. After the Celltech investment had been made Arthur Knight, the then NEB chairman, told the investment team that they should consider their task of promoting biotechnology completed, and that they should focus their attention elsewhere.[19] However, the publicity that accompanied the Celltech investment led to a number of other biotechnology proposals landing on their desks. A number of these were deemed worthy of investment.

Table 3.12 The Withdrawal of the NEB from Celltech

Date	Remaining Stake (%)	Profit on Sale (£m)
1983	28.0	0.66
1985	15.1	3.02
1987	0.0	4.72
Total Profit		8.40

Source: Adapted from *NEB Annual Report*, 1983; 1985; and 1987.

In 1981 the Board made a joint investment with Rank Hovis McDougall to commercialise the latter's development of a new protein food. The Board invested a total of £960,000 in the consequent company, Dytes, and the NEB's stake was sold in 1984/85 at a profit of £120,000.[20] The Board also invested in Speywood Laboratories Ltd, a joint investment between the NEB and Prutec, the venture capital subsidiary of the Prudential Assurance Company. The company acquired a method to gain a product called Factor Eight, a substance that exists in blood which when absent from the human body leads to haemophilia. As a result of the investment, the company was able to expand its premises and a director named Heath predicted that if the research went to plan 'we may never have to collect blood plasma from donors again.'[21] However, the company got into financial difficulties. Don Seymour, who was brought in to be chairman at this time, explains that the financiers invested without understanding fully what was required for success in a biotechnology company. His view was that the investment in the company had been inadequate for its requirements: 'It was clear to me that a few million had been invested when really thirty million plus was needed.'[22] Seymour recommended that the company should be sold to a larger concern, and indeed this is what happened with a deal agreed with Porton International. The NEB lost £180,000 from this investment.[23]

Finally, the NEB financed IQ (Bio) Ltd., a company formed in Cambridge in 1981 by a team of former Cambridge University researchers and the owners of Acorn Computers Ltd. The company developed a biological amplification process that enabled the convenience of enzymatic immunoassay tests to be combined with a high degree of sensitivity. A small research site was set up in Cambridge. This company also ran into financial difficulties, however, due largely to the lack of financial control within the company.[24] Don Seymour was again sent in to chair the company, and again he decided that the only future for the company was with a larger concern. As a result the company was sold to Novo, a Danish pharmaceuticals company.

The NEB and a biotechnology strategy

There is some disagreement over whether the clutch of investments the NEB made in the area of biotechnology constituted a strategy for the sector. Roger Hay, who was part of the team that set up Celltech, believes that the Celltech investment was initiated with the strategic intention of developing the industry. The later biotechnology companies (there were a number that were rejected as well) were encountered unintentionally, however, and Hay said that if anything it was 'an untidy strategy.'[25] Don Seymour, who was brought into deal with the problems of Speywood and IQ (Bio), was less impressed with the NEB. He said that the Board never had the competence to develop a biotechnology strategy, and that this was demonstrated in the investments it made. They betrayed, he believed, a fundamental lack of understanding of the realities of biotechnology, including an idea of the scale of investment required. From the evidence it would appear that the investment in Celltech was made with strategic intent. It was a deliberate attempt to increase the UK presence in biotechnology, a sector considered to contain great economic potential, and its attempt met with some success. Beyond this it is difficult to view the other investments as constituting a continuation of the strategy. The publicity caused by Celltech led to the Board receiving further opportunities to invest in biotechnology companies, but the decision to invest was based on viability rather than strategic factors.

The development of the UK biotechnology industry

Before coming to a conclusion about the contribution of the NEB to the development of the UK biotechnology industry, the extent of that development, post-NEB, needs to be ascertained. In February 1994 Arthur Andersen produced a report entitled *UK Biotech '94 - The Way Ahead*, which included a calculation of the size of the industry. Arthur Andersen predicted that there would be a sector turnover of £878 million in 1995-96.[26] It commented that 'the strength of the sector's product development pipeline indicates that even faster growth could follow, particularly when recombinant drugs and plants currently progressing through clinical and field trials reach the market in 1996 or thereafter'.[27] The growth of the industry was also reflected in the level of research and development carried out in the sector. This was set to rise to a level of £202 million by the year 1996.

Table 3.13 1994 Projection of Growth in the UK Biotechnology Industry

	Estimated Revenue (£m)	Estimated R&D Expenditure (£m)	Estimated Employment Growth
1992/93	470	130	8,300
1995/96	878	202	10,700

Source: Adapted from Arthur Andersen, *UK Biotech '94*, London, Arthur Andersen, 1994, p13.

The contribution of the NEB to the development of the UK biotechnology industry

The UK's presence in this sector was virtually non-existent at the end of the 1970s, and it took the NEB's intervention to change matters. Celltech does seem to have had an important influence on the development of the industry, seminal according to Hamish Hale, and now the UK has a significant presence in the industry, even if it is not comparable to that in the US. Even Don Seymour who was critical about the way in which the NEB intervened in this area admitted that 'there is some substance to the claim that the Board had a catalytic role in the development of the industry.'[28] His criticism was that the Board did not understand the scale of investment biotechnology companies needed, and, in common with other private sector financiers, they did not appreciate the time scale for a company becoming profitable. Celltech is also widely given credit for having broken the mould in the way publicly financed research is exploited in the UK. It is important, though, that the NEB's contribution to the development of biotechnology in the UK should not be exaggerated. Its role as a catalyst for future private sector development, its success in raising the profile of biotechnology, not least in the City, and its provision of finance for Celltech, and the other companies, seems to be the limit of its achievements.

The implications for a future state investment institution

The implications of the NEB's investment in biotechnology, and to a lesser extent microelectronics, for a future state investment institution depend on whether one believes that the financial markets are still unwilling to invest in embryonic, high-tech sectors. If there is still an unwillingness on the part of the private sector to invest in emerging industries, then it would seem to be a role that a state institution could usefully fulfil. A recent episode suggests that an unwillingness does indeed still exist. In 1989, Ronald Hamilton and Bill Seden patented a new technological development, a one-day disposable contact lens. By 1995 the product was on the market, sold by Boots the Chemist. Sales of £900,000 by August 1995 meant that Hamilton and Seden's company, Award, broke even only part way through their first year; sales are expected to have topped £6 million in 1996.[29] The potential of the product appears almost limitless, with the UK alone having 35 million spectacle-wearers. However, this is not a success story for private finance and the institutional venture capital industry; on the contrary, it is an example of British finance at its least effective. In 1988 Hamilton approached 3i. Initially they appeared enthusiastic, but this enthusiasm evaporated when they could not acquire joint funding commitments from other venture capitalists. Instead, Hamilton turned to BTG, then still in the public sector, who had patented the lens, and the DTI, who gave Hamilton's company a SMART award for promising technological developments.[30] When further finance was required in 1993 - and by that time they were already involved with Boots - it was again the public sector which delivered. SE, Lothian and Edinburgh Enterprise, and British Coal Enterprise provided the bulk of the £1.5 million finance package.[31] The only help from the private sector came through an overdraft from the Bank of Scotland. Hamilton was again rejected by 3i.[32]

Hamilton says: 'We're looking at a business whose potential is measured in hundreds of millions of pounds', yet private finance, including the institutional venture capital industry, could not recognise the potential.[33] SE, incidentally, made a profit of £4.8 million on their investment of £450,000 (£300,000 in a first round deal; £150,000 second round), which was made at an IRR of over 200% per annum.[34] The establishment of a formalised public sector fund, or funds, for high-tech innovations may go some way towards ensuring that others like Hamilton do not have to go through such an unsatisfactory and uncertain process again.

Comments on the Practices of the NEB as a Venture Capitalist

There are a number of other issues concerning the NEB as a state venture capitalist on which the recipients of its finance were able to provide evidence. They concern the NEB's competence during the actual venture capital process, upon which some of the Board's critics cast doubt. Evidence was sought for three stages of the venture capital process: the due diligence stage; the decision about the terms on which the finance was to be offered; and the after-investment monitoring. Twenty of the NEB's investee companies gave evidence on these issues. The impression is given by some of the Board's critics that the NEB, in its desperation to make investments, paid insufficient attention to the quality of the companies in which they invested. A number of the NEB's investee companies were asked to recollect their experience of applying for finance to the NEB to see whether this criticism is justified. In a majority of cases the companies felt that they had been adequately scrutinised. In only a quarter of the companies was there the belief that insufficient research had been carried out. Indeed, in the case of the investment in Mather Machinery, where the NEB was the lead investor in a syndicated deal, it was the company's view that the NEB were 'the ones who knew most about engineering, manufacture and exporting.'[35] A number of the other interviews revealed a picture of the NEB acting in a similar way to the private sector, requiring the companies to provide business plans, make personal presentations, with the NEB staff themselves looking into the products and markets. There was one instance where the company said that the NEB had made a decision 'on our own figures', but the overall impression is that the NEB was not by any means an easy touch for money.

The willingness to provide finance on terms that reflected the needs of the recipient company was part of the Board's claim to be a distinctive investor; the opposite accusation has often been made against the private sector. From this sample of the NEB's investee companies, the claim about the Board seems to be justified. Only two of the companies felt that the finance was not suitable for their needs, and in both of these cases it was because the companies had not asked for sufficient finance. In the other cases the companies reported that the finance was specifically tailored to their needs. This was despite the fact that the companies had required from the NEB radically different finance, from start-up capital to finance for a MBO. It does not appear, from these companies at least, that the NEB acted inadvisedly in this respect.

Thirdly, the investee companies were asked if the NEB had interfered in the affairs of their company in a manner that was to its detriment. Again the NEB came out very well with only two of them expressing dissatisfaction on this matter, one of these complaints being that it was a lack of interference by the NEB that had been the problem. This was in the case of the NEB's investment in Mayflower Packaging, which went to the wall within two years of its making. In this instance the director felt that, in retrospect, the NEB representative should have recognised, and then interfered to improve, the company's manufacturing cost control.[36] In addition, a director of Aycliffe Engineering recalled that the NEB had 'occasionally' interfered unhelpfully and unnecessarily.[37] The other directors, however, were positive about the way the NEB had handled its responsibilities. The overwhelming view of the companies was that they did not want excessive interference from the NEB, and that happily they did not suffer it. The NEB appeared to have limited their involvement to attending board meetings, as was their right, and to offering advice when required. A former director of Keland Electrics said that the NEB had 'monitored performance on a very regular basis, participated in board meetings, but encouraged managers to get on with it.'[38] A former director of JJ Electric Components described the relationship they had with the NEB as 'hands off', a familiar term to students of the private venture capital industry.[39] That view would appear to sum up the NEB's approach, beyond the appropriate level of monitoring. On these criteria, therefore, the NEB scored highly over the way in which it operated as a venture capitalist. This should not be too much of a surprise as many of the former NEB investment executives have gone on to prominent positions in private venture capital institutions.

Conclusion: The Effectiveness of the NEB as a State Venture Capital Policy

The overall performance of the NEB was clearly mixed. Indeed, it is fair to say there was more failure than success. However, as the balance sheet loss of just over £30 million shows, the Board was by no means the financial disaster it was often presented as. This loss figure also does not include the savings that were allegedly made as a result of the appointment to BL of Michael Edwardes. It is said that although Edwardes did not solve the problems of BL overnight, his management prevented the company from descending into chaos. Many in the Board claim that if it had been up to the Department of Industry, who would have been in charge of BL but for the NEB (and who, indeed, was again in charge after 1981) Edwardes would never have been appointed. It is claimed that he would have been too bold an appointment to have been made by a government department. In addition there is some evidence that the NEB saved the taxpayer money in the case of Rolls Royce as a sharper focus was put upon the company's claim to more public money. These incalculable gains may well dwarf the £30 million official balance sheet deficit, and are at least worth considering.

It is, though, the performance of the NEB's smaller investments that most concerns this study. The first comment to make is that the NEB did not bridge the equity gap; indeed it did not even make a discernible impact upon it. The Board only made about 140 investments, and only about 90 (plus the loans made under the Oakwood scheme) below a level that would now would be equal to about £1 million. There was insufficient focus on the equity gap within the NEB for it to make a significant contribution. The chapter's main focus was the Board's investments of less than £200,000. Despite the Aqualisa investment which was a huge success, and the handful of other successes, the NEB's investment record here was poor, although not disastrous.

The success of a state venture capital institution is measured, largely, by its ability to pick winners. Here the NEB was found wanting. Only seven out the 37 investments for which information is available (nine out of 41 if those transferred to Grosvenor Development Capital are included) were disposed of at a profit to the Board: a 'hit rate' of 18.9%. If this is the rate at which a state institution picks winners then it radically changes the way such a policy has to be planned. It cannot be set up with the thought that a certain number of investments will achieve its aims. Instead all calculations will have to be multiplied by five. For example, if it is thought that providing 100 growth companies with equity finance will have the desired impact on the equity gap, then 500 investments will have to be made, and so on. Evidence on SE (see chapter 6), however, suggests that the success rate need not be so low. Overall, the NEB really needed 2 or 3 more Aqualisas to be comfortable about its performance.

Beyond the straight statistical analysis the record of the NEB does in fact improve. The claim that the Board made little contribution to its successful investments was largely rebutted by the companies concerned and there were also a number of businessmen, whose companies caused the Board to lose money, who neither held the Board responsible for their failure, nor believed that the NEB was wrong to invest in their company. This was argued as they believed there were external and often exceptional circumstances that led to their demise or poor performance. The chief culprit was said to have been the unusually severe recession of 1980 to 1982. Furthermore, Daniel Kramer argues in his book on the NEB that the Board's record needs to be judged with an understanding of how it had been a 'national blessing'. What he means by this is that even where the investment failed some advances were still made, whether it be through products being integrated into other companies' lines, techniques being developed, or equipment being salvaged for new ventures. The evidence from the investee companies supports this perspective, although it would be unwise to consider it as a significant factor.

It must also be borne in mind that the NEB dealt mainly in high-risk investments; consequently, its performance should be expected to be more uneven than those of venture capital companies that invest in later stage and 'safer' companies. Furthermore, the NEB often made higher risk investments than even they themselves wished to. This was because the NEB was under political pressure to invest, particularly in the regions, where there were great expectations from the left that the Board would attack unemployment head on. Another mitigating factor offered to explain some of the failure of the NEB was the requirement, after 1979, to sell investments as soon as practically possible. This, many believe, led to the NEB not getting full value for the investments they made. However, one senior ex-employee, sympathetic to the Board, said that not too much store was to be set in this argument. The effect of having to dispose of investments early was not always a disadvantage; sometimes it meant the Board got a price for their stake that included a premium for the promise the company was apparently showing, promise that in many cases was never fulfilled. He certainly did not consider it to be the multi-million pound factor that Kramer argued it to be in his study of the NEB.[40]

Finally, research shows that the NEB did enjoy some success, in the area of biotechnology. It seems to be quite widely recognised in the biotechnology field that the NEB made a positive contribution to the industry at a time when it was struggling to have its potential recognised by the traditional private financiers. The NEB involvement was clearly something of a painful process, partly due to its own faults and partly due to the obstruction of others, and in 1994 it was said that even its flagship company, Celltech, had by no means a secure future. Nevertheless, this was an instance where the NEB recognised potential, acted upon its beliefs, and was proved right about that potential by subsequent events. Indeed, it should be remembered that Celltech was a start-up investment, that despite being over £200,000, was related to the issue of the equity gap. The NEB's contribution to biotechnology was catalytic rather than substantial but nevertheless important.

As with many political policies, the reality of the NEB's performance lay in between the extremes. The NEB was not the complete disaster that the Right portrayed it as, nor was it particularly successful. The NEB showed that a policy of direct state intervention is faced by many problems, the most important being firstly, that it is difficult for the state to make a very large number of investments, and secondly, that it is not always easy to pick winners in the small business sector. Given the fact that the NEB was also treated sceptically by the business community, any government implementing such a policy should not expect to get too much gratitude for its efforts.

Notes

[1] *NEB Annual Report 1980*, p9.
[2] *NEB Annual Report 1978*, p25; *1979*, p13.
[3] *NEB Annual Report 1977*, p18; *1979*, p7.
[4] *NEB Annual Report 1981*, pp42-43.
[5] Interview with Gerard Fairtlough, ex-employee of Celltech Ltd, 18 May 1994.
[6] Interview with Dr Norman Carey, biotechnology consultant, 21 July 1994.
[7] Interview with Dr Spencer Emtage, ex-employee of Celltech Ltd, 21 July 1994.
[8] Interview with Dr Hamish Hale, Director of Apax Partners, 21 July 1994.

[9] Dodgson, M, *The Management of Technological Learning: Lessons From a Biotechnology Company*, Berlin, Walter de Gruyter, 1991, p130.
[10] *Ibid.*, pp129-130.
[11] *Ibid.*, p130.
[12] Interview with Dr Hamish Hale, *op.cit.*
[13] Interview with Dr Norman Carey, *op.cit.*
[14] Interview with Dr Hamish Hale, *op.cit.*
[15] Green, D, 'Merck - Celltech deal on asthma drug', *Financial Times*, 21 July 1994, p23.
[16] *Ibid.*
[17] *Ibid.*
[18] Interview with Don Seymour, ex-chairman of Speywood Laboratories and IQ (Bio), and ex non-executive director of Celltech, 23 August 1994.
[19] Interview with Roger Hay, ECI Ventures and ex-NEB employee, 23 August 1994.
[20] *NEB Annual Report 1984-1985*, pp16-17; p12.
[21] *British Business*, 25 December 1981, p12.
[22] Interview with Don Seymour, *op.cit.*
[23] *NEB Annual Report 1984-1985*, p12.
[24] Interview with Don Seymour, *op.cit.*
[25] Interview with Roger Hay, *op.cit.*
[26] Arthur Andersen, *UK Biotech '94*, London, Arthur Andersen, 1994, p14.
[27] *Ibid.*
[28] Interview with Don Seymour, *op.cit.*
[29] Buxton, J, 'Sights focused on expansion', *Financial Times*, 29 August 1995, p8.
[30] *Ibid.*
[31] *Ibid.*
[32] *Ibid.*
[33] *Ibid.*
[34] Hamilton Fazey, I, 'Award takes first prize', *Financial Times: Survey - Venture and Development Capital*, 20 September 1996, p5.
[35] Interview with DL Uttley, Mather Machinery, 23 April 1994.
[36] Interview with LC Sawdy, Mayflower Packaging, 21 April 1994.
[37] Interview with K Altringham, Aycliffe Engineering, 30 March 1994.
[38] Interview with J Perfect, Keland Electrics, 15 April 1994.
[39] Interview with JM Jessop, JJ Electric Components, 15 April 1994.
[40] Kramer, D, *State Capital and Private Enterprise: The Case of the UK National Enterprise Board*, London, Routledge, 1988, pp44-47.

4 The Conservatives and the UK Institutional Venture Capital Industry

Government Policy Towards the Institutional Venture Capital Industry: A Laissez-faire Approach

Government policy towards the institutional venture capital industry - in terms of it bridging the equity gap - has been laissez-faire since the election of the Conservatives in 1979. There has been no discriminatory government policy initiative aimed at channelling the investment finance of the industry towards the equity gap. Discriminatory policy could, for example, have included tax incentives or subsidies directed at the disproportionately high costs of making small or early-stage deals, but neither of these has been offered. There have been some measures of government policy that have affected the industry generally. Capital gains tax reductions, for example, have in the view of many benefited the industry. But these reductions were not directed specifically at the industry; they were reductions aimed at business in general. The laissez-faire policy has been pursued despite many voices within the small business community lamenting the lack of investment being targeted at the equity gap. Indeed, concessions have been made by the Government to these concerns in the private investor market, through the BSS, the BES, the EIS and the VCT. The institutional market, however, has been left to go it alone.

The Development of the UK Institutional Venture Capital Industry

Up until the 1980s private venture capital had mainly been associated with the US economy where the industry had first come to prominence in the 1960s. The US venture capital industry, which had originally financed start-up and early-stage high technology companies, had made its name by making some spectacularly successful investments. The best known was Apple;

another was Genentech, a biotechnology company. The venture capital company Kleiner and Perkins invested $200,000 in Genentech in 1975; nine years later that investment was worth over $47 million. In 1982 the US Senate requested a report on the industry because of the impact it was having on the economy and venture capital's potential for high investment returns seemed to be vast. In the UK, a shortage of risk capital available to small business had long been identified, and although the situation had greatly improved since the time of the Macmillan report, the development of a recognisable institutional venture capital market after 1979 promised a solution at last to this long standing problem.[1]

The rise of the UK institutional venture capital industry was, by any standards, remarkable. That it should have risen so quickly, and at that particular time, seems to be attributable to a number of factors that occurred simultaneously. There is a political element in the development of the industry as many commentators believe that one of the key factors was the election of a Conservative Government in 1979. The boost this gave to the industry was said to be two-fold. On the one hand the Conservative victory was said to have released a burst of energy among private financial institutions and entrepreneurs. Further to this many argue that there was a belief at that time that the Conservatives understood the crucial importance of the small firm to the economy. This was said to have led to over 100 measures being introduced for small businesses during the first term, making such businesses more attractive both to run and to invest in.

A second factor promoting the industry's development was said to have been the establishment of the Unlisted Securities Market (USM). The USM was more flexible in its rules than the main exchange, allowing companies with only three years business experience to seek a quotation. This made it easier for investors to realise the gain on their investment, which had previously been a disincentive to investing in unquoted companies. Thirdly, the experience of the US industry was also a factor in that it raised the profile of venture capital. Many British financial institutions, having invested in American venture capital funds, began to consider whether there might be similar opportunities in the UK.

These factors were stimulus enough for the industry, but perhaps the most important factor that contributed to its rapid growth was the economic climate during the second half of the 1980s. Although the long-term benefits of that period have since been questioned, there can be no doubt that at that time long-term investment was considered a more attractive proposition than at any time in the previous twenty years. The growth in the market took the size of the industry from an estimated £20 million in 1979 to a 1980s peak of £1647 million in 1989. In 1994 over £2 billion was invested by the industry, the first time this figure had been passed. These overall figures do not tell the full story and there has been a great deal of criticism over the way the industry has developed. The criticism centres around the accusation that, to a significant extent, the UK institutional venture capital industry has ceased to be a venture capital industry. It is alleged that many of the institutions in the industry have moved away from investing in start-up or early-stage companies, and from investing in amounts below £400,000, the high-risk investments that many expect a venture capital industry to undertake. The industry, it is claimed, has moved towards later-stage investments, in particular MBO, which have often yielded very high profits in exchange for limited amounts of risk. It is this situation that has allowed many commentators to claim, that even though an institutional venture capital industry investing over £2 billion a year has grown up in the UK, an equity gap for small businesses still exists, with some even suggesting that the situation has got worse.

In this chapter it is argued that the policy of laissez-faire adopted towards the institutional venture capital industry has been ineffective in the impact it has had on the equity gap for small business. Keith Joseph claimed when the Conservatives came into office in 1979 that the removal of obstacles to enterprise would see problems like the equity gap disappear. As much as can be expected in a mature capitalist economy, these conditions have been enjoyed by the institutional venture capital industry, and during the 1980s there were periods of high economic growth as well. Yet the evidence suggests that the equity gap is still as significant a problem as ever, with the investment trends of the unhindered venture capital industry a major factor behind it. Before this view is substantiated it is necessary to briefly set out the structure of the industry.

An Anatomy of the UK Institutional Venture Capital Industry

Venture capital fund status

In 1996 the BVCA reported that there were just over 100 full members acting as venture capitalists in the UK. In the 1994 guide to venture capital prepared by Stoy Hayward, 164 funds are recorded.[2] These funds are different in a number of respects. One difference is that there is a variation in the status of venture capital funds. Firstly, there are *captives*. These are funds that are divisions or subsidiaries of larger financial institutions, for example banks and insurance companies, and are provided with finance by their parent institution. An example is Nat West Ventures, the venture capital arm of the Nat West Bank. There are also *semi-captives*, which combine captive finance with independently raised funds. Secondly, there are *independents* which are funds which raise their finance on the market. These funds seek to persuade investment institutions to provide them with capital. The defining point is that private independents are not legally connected to the institutions that have provided their finance. These type of funds are in some cases actually listed on the stock exchange. Finally, there are a number of *public sector venture capital funds* operating in the UK. The most significant of these is SE, which as was mentioned in a previous chapter, has recently raised a joint fund with the private sector. It is also worth noting that at the local level the public sector is, in some areas, active in the provision of seed capital. Many borough councils in the Birmingham area, for example, run funds that provide such capital.

Venture capital stages

There are also a number of venture capital investment stages which require different types of finance. *Seed capital* finances the earliest stage of a business, which, in practice, often means product development. An entrepreneur may have a new method or concept which he believes, if developed, could prove profitable. The amounts of capital that are committed to seed projects are usually quite small; it is not usual for a seed project to require more than £200,000. Seed capital is arguably the most risky form of investment, as there is a very strong possibility that the project will not progress beyond this stage. However, against this the potential returns of seed capital are huge, with returns of 1000% plus being within the bounds of possibility.

Start-up capital is for the establishment of a business. It is defined as finance provided to a company that has not yet started selling its product commercially. It may be used to take the development of a product further, to buy machinery, or to finance early marketing costs. Again start-up finance usually, but by no means always, involves a relatively small amount of finance. Normally a start-up investment will be under £500,000. As with seed capital, the investment contains an above average level of risk, with the company by definition having no track record. However, as with seed capital, the investment can produce spectacular returns, with the investor unlikely to commit money to the business unless he feels there are strong growth prospects.

Early-stage capital is provided to launch a company into commercial production. It is to provide a bridge between the time of launching a product on the commercial market and the time when the product begins to provide the company with income. This again is capital provided to a company with little or no track record, and so once more it carries an above average level of risk. As with seed and start-up capital, this greater than normal risk is offset by the possibility of greater than average returns.

Expansion capital can be used to further a business in a number of ways. A company may come to the stage where it can no longer satisfy demand for its products from its existing capacity; the new capital may be used therefore to expand production facilities. A company may also find that its machinery has become obsolete; the capital in this case will be used to replace it. Working capital is also considered to be in this category. Expansion capital is finance to companies that already have a sales record, and is, thus, considered a less risky stage of investment than the previous three. Expansion investments can vary from the provision of working capital to a small business, which may only be £50,000, to investments of many millions of pounds.

Finance for *MBO* and *management buy-ins (MBI)* are two further types of capital. MBO and MBI have, since the mid 1980s, dominated the institutional venture capital industry, and, in the view of some, brought the name of venture capital into disrepute. In an MBO, finance is provided to the existing management to enable them to become the owners of the business. In an MBI finance is provided to an outside management team to enable them to buy into the company. Capital can also be provided by the institutional venture capital industry for the purchase of existing shares in a company. This is known as a *secondary purchase.*

Sector preferences

Most venture capitalists will consider companies from any sector of the economy, but there are some which concentrate on more specific areas. Perhaps the most common are those venture capitalists who concentrate on high technology investments. An example is Venture Founders Ltd who claim only to invest in projects which are computer, electronics, biotechnology, or medical/health related. Usually though most venture capital companies will invest in any project they believe will be profitable.

Regional preferences

A number of institutional venture capitalists restrict their investment to certain geographical areas. Many of these regional funds have either been born out of, or are still part of, the industrial development policy of a local authority. An example is Yorkshire Enterprise Ltd, which was set up by the old West Yorkshire Metropolitan County Council, in 1982, to combat the effects of the collapse of the area's traditional industries. There are other regional funds, however, without such historical ties, Ulster Development Capital Ltd being one example.

Summary

The UK institutional venture capital industry, as has been stated, was left during the 1980s and 1990s to its own devices. The Government stated its confidence in the ability of the private sector to provide capital and bridge any funding gaps that may temporarily exist. The rest of this chapter investigates whether or not the industry has repaid this faith and provided a satisfactory flow of capital to small business.

The Effectiveness of the Institutional Venture Capital Industry in Raising Finance

The institutional venture capital industry has, since its development into a recognisable industry in the late 1970s, enjoyed considerable success in raising capital. Figures for the amount of finance raised are not available, but those for the investment of the industry offer an acceptable guide. Table 4.1 shows that, apart from the recessionary years of 1990 and 1991, the investment of the industry has been rising since the late 1970s. 1994 was a record year for the industry, with £2 billion having been exceeded for the first time. The aggregate figures, however, do not tell the whole story. To assess the effect the industry has had on the equity gap, the way in which the finance has been targeted must be investigated.

Table 4.1 Total Aggregate Investment of BVCA Members 1979 to 1994 (£m)

Year	Aggregate Investment	Year	Aggregate Investment
1979	c 20	1989	1647
1984	190	1990	1394
1985	325	1991	1153
1986	584	1992	1434
1987	1029	1993	1422
1988	1394	1994	2070

Source: Adapted from BVCA, *Guide to Venture Capital*, London, BVCA, 1992, p2; and BVCA, *Report on Investment Activity*, London, BVCA, 1984-1994.

The Effectiveness of the Institutional Venture Capital Industry in Targeting Finance at the Equity Gap

The performance of the institutional venture capital industry in targeting finance at the equity gap can be approached in a number ways: in terms of investment size; investment stage; and by region.

Investment size

The raw figures for the average size of investments made by the institutional venture capital industry seem to explain why there are so many people who criticise the industry for having failed to make an impact on the equity gap. In the early days of the industry, the average investment size was low enough to suggest that it might make an impact on the gap, particularly given the fact that the industry was, at that time, investing close on 30% of its funds in start-up and early-stage investments. However, there was always an upward trend and by 1989 the average venture capital investment was over £1 million. This declined during the 1990 to 1992 recession, but by 1993 the one million mark had been exceeded again, and the trend seems to be firmly upwards once more.

Yet if the figures are broken down it is seen that, despite the average figure for the industry as a whole having increased dramatically, the figure for the average size of start-up and early-stage investments has increased less significantly over the period. The increase in the overall average size of investments was largely caused by the increase in the average cost of MBO. There has been some increase in the average size of start-ups and early-stage investments, but taking into account inflation, they are far smaller. The 1994 figures, however, cast some doubt as to whether this will continue indefinitely.

Table 4.2 Average Size of UK Investments 1984 to 1994

Year	Average Size (£000)	Year	Average Size (£000)
1984	271	1990	840
1985	540	1991	783
1986	605	1992	948
1987	773	1993	1013
1988	957	1994	1331
1989	1051		

Source: Adapted from BVCA, *Report on Investment Activity*, London, BVCA, 1984-1994.

Table 4.3 Average Size of UK Investments - By Stage 1984 to 1994 (£000)

Year	Start-up	Early	Expansion	MBO/MBI	Secondary
1984	250	202	259	332	412
1985	343	282	402	1108	418
1986	512	371	362	1325	725
1987	393	341	436	2364	865
1988	347	330	629	2600	647
1989	486	375	674	2604	792
1990	382	365	633	1712	565
1991	223	195	584	1889	414
1992	331	425	461	2338	367
1993	280	308	472	3300	849
1994	450	403	588	4920	450

Source: Adapted from BVCA, *Report on Investment Activity*, London, BVCA, 1984-1994.

It would appear, therefore, that if the industry is leaving a gap for investments under £400,000, it is not because the investments it is making in start-up and early-stage companies are being made at much higher levels of finance. Information contained in the BVCA directory does not indicate a problem either. In 1994 77 of their 117 members announced themselves willing to invest in amounts less than £400,000; indeed, 49 accepted proposals for investments of less than £200,000.[3] Yet this is a classic case of where statistics can be misleading. Firstly, many of the venture capitalists who claim to be willing to make such investments are found not to have done so for a number of years. Secondly, there are other venture capitalists that do indeed make such investments, but they only make up a very small part of their overall investment activity. Finally, many of the venture capitalists who exclusively invest at that level are investors which are only managing a small fund.

Investment stage

As was described earlier, venture capital investment is divided by stage into six categories; seed, start-up, early, expansion, MBO and MBI, and secondary purchases. Over the period 1984 to 1994 the industry made a decisive shift away from investment in start-up and early-stage ventures, as tables 4.4 and 4.5 reveal. This is important because it is usually these deals that are below £400,000, the range of the equity gap.

Table 4.4 UK Investment by Financing Stage - % of Amounts Invested 1984 to 1994

Year	Start-up	Early	Expansion	MBO/MBI	Secondary
1984	17.8	9.3	44.1	20.8	8.0
1985	11.7	6.5	38.5	37.3	6.0
1986	15.1	7.3	27.1	45.2	5.3
1987	8.0	4.9	29.4	55.0	2.4
1988	5.0	5.0	31.0	56.0	3.0
1989	6.0	9.0	23.0	61.0	1.0
1990	7.0	5.0	31.0	52.0	5.0
1991	4.0	2.0	27.0	55.0	5.0
1992	3.0	3.0	26.0	65.0	3.0
1993	3.0	3.0	25.0	62.0	7.0
1994	3.0	2.0	25.0	67.0	3.0

Source: Adapted from BVCA, *Report on Investment Activity*, London, BVCA, 1984-1994.

132 The UK Equity Gap

Alarm has also been noted over the amount of seed capital that is available in the UK. There are only a small number of institutional venture capital funds that advertise themselves as offering seed capital, and even fewer that are specialist providers. A study of seed capital carried out in 1988 by Venture Economics showed how limited its supply was in the UK. They reported that in 1987 only 24 seed capital investments were recorded. These amounted to £1.9 million by value, or 0.2% of the total investment activity that year.[4]

Table 4.5 UK Investment by Financing Stage - Amounts Invested 1984 to 1994 (£m)

Year	Start-up	Early	Expansion	MBO/MBI	Secondary
1984	24.7	12.9	61.4	28.9	11.1
1985	31.6	17.5	104.0	100.8	16.3
1986	57.9	28.2	104.0	173.6	20.3
1987	75.1	45.3	274.9	513.0	22.5
1988	70.0	60.0	402.0	733.0	33.0
1989	86.0	129.0	319.0	867.0	19.0
1990	76.0	52.0	343.0	582.0	53.0
1991	35.0	23.0	333.0	544.0	54.0
1992	43.0	39.0	322.0	807.0	40.0
1993	34.0	35.0	307.0	769.0	86.0
1994	45.0	31.0	421.0	1112.0	59.0

Source: Adapted from BVCA, *Report on Investment Activity*, London, BVCA, 1984-1994.

It cannot be disputed that the institutional venture capital industry has, to a significant extent, turned its back on start-up and early-stage ventures over the last ten years. The fall in the percentage of total investment going into start-ups has been so dramatic over the period that the actual amount of finance in real terms invested in start-ups in 1994 was barely higher than that invested in 1984, taking into account inflation. There seems to have been two separate stages of the decline in start-up investment. Firstly, in the mid-1980s the amount of finance devoted to start-up ventures increased significantly, three-fold between 1984 and 1987. However, the increase was not as rapid as that for the overall investment of the industry, so there was a *relative decline* in start-up investment. The second decline that occurred was an *absolute decline* in start-up investment. This occurred after the peak amount had been reached in 1989, and has been a fairly consistent trend up to the present day. The pattern has been very similar for early-stage investment by the industry. Again, a stage of relative decline occurred, followed by a stage of absolute decline. Again the peak was reached for early-stage investment in 1989, since when there has been the absolute decline. It would appear that start-up and early-stage investments have suffered from both the boom of the mid to late 1980s, and the bust of the early 1990s. During the period of very strong economic growth that occurred in the mid to late 1980s, the industry found that there were safer, and quite significant, returns to be had from making later rather than early-stage investments.

This was particularly true in the case of MBO/MBI. These investments increased by exactly thirty fold between 1984 and 1989, on the back of wider trends in the economy. When the economic bubble burst after 1989 it seems that the industry felt the economic conditions recommended a slow down in this type of investment and almost a total halt to early-stage investment. The subdued economic conditions served only to make the industry even more cautious about early-stage investment, considered a high and clearly unacceptable risk.

Regions

The equity gap in the UK is often said to be more acute in the less prosperous regions. Many have argued that this has been exacerbated by a South-East dominated institutional venture capital industry. On the face of it the regional statistics for the industry (see table 4.6) seem to back up this belief. The breakdown of the amounts invested, and the corresponding percentage figures, show that the majority of venture capital investment in nearly all of the ten years featured went to London and the South-East. In contrast, the whole of the north of England, that is the combination of the North West, the North, and Yorkshire and Humberside, has never seen more than 18% of the total level of investment in any one year, and often a good deal less.

Despite its London dominance, the institutional venture capital industry denies that it has unduly concentrated its investment in the South-East to the detriment of other regions. They argue that the reason why such a large number of the industry's investments are made in the South East is that the South East is where a higher proportion of companies are situated. Statistics taking into account the level of regional economic activity back up the industry's contention and show that the South East was not, in 1993, a

134 *The UK Equity Gap*

disproportionately favoured region in this respect. This is well illustrated by table 4.7.

Table 4.6 UK Investment by Region - % of Amounts Invested 1985 to 1994

	SE	SW	EA	WM	EM	N	Sco	Wal	NI
1985	64	7	6	7	2	6	7	3	0.1
1986	64	5	5	3	3	10	7	3	0.1
1987	57	7	3	4	8	12	5	4	0.2
1988	50	4	3	9	7	18	6	2	1
1989	48	7	3	6	7	12	15	1	1
1990	61	3	5	6	6	11	7	1	0.2
1991	52	7	3	9	5	14	7	2	1
1992	44	10	3	7	7	16	8	3	2
1993	53	3	4	6	4	18	10	1	1
1994	37	9	2	13	4	24	5	4	2

Key: SE - South East; SW - South West; EA - East Anglia; WM - West Midlands; EM - East Midlands; N - North; Sco - Scotland; Wal - Wales; NI - Northern Ireland.

Note: The category 'North' includes the BVCA regions 'North', 'North West' and 'Yorkshire and Humberside'.

Source: Adapted from BVCA, *Report on Investment Activity,* London, BVCA, 1985-1994.

Indeed, it is interesting to note that the most favoured area of the country was Scotland, with almost twice as many investments taking place than the number of businesses justified, so to speak (The high figure for Scotland might have been due to the investment activity of the public sector organisation SE, which is a member of the BVCA). Furthermore, the other areas with higher than average levels of investment were also in the north of the UK, namely the North and Yorkshire and Humberside. What the BVCA does not provide, however, is a table giving the amount of finance invested in each region indexed against the number of companies. If they had, it would have shown that a great deal more was invested in the South East per company registered for VAT than in other parts of the country. 35% of VAT registered companies are located in the South East whereas the area received 53% of the finance.[5]

Table 4.7 Investment Activity by Region 1993: Comparison with Total Number of Registered Businesses

	VAT Registered Businesses 12/92	No. of Venture Backed Companies 1993	Average Per 1000 of VAT Registered
South East	560,597	383	0.68
South West	150,431	54	0.36
East Anglia	64,719	35	0.54
West Midlands	136,415	70	0.51
East Midlands	109,707	63	0.57
Yorks. and Humb.	119,896	92	0.77
North West	145,636	95	0.65
North	60,542	54	0.89
Scotland	118,083	151	1.28
Wales	81,759	48	0.59
N.Ireland	53,515	21	0.39
Total	1,601,300	1,066	0.67

Source: BVCA, Report on Investment Activity, London, BVCA, 1993, p12.

The Performance of Investments made by the Institutional Venture Capital Industry

The success of the institutional venture capital industry in providing equity capital relies, of course, on its ability to make profitable investments. Venture capitalists that do not make a competitive return on the finance they have raised on the market or acquired from their parent institution, are unlikely to attract further funds to invest. This will undermine any effect the industry might have on the equity gap. For a long time the BVCA decided against publishing details of the investment performance of their members, but there was a change of heart in 1992 and a study was commissioned into funds raised between 1980 and 1990. This study was published in 1995 and updated in 1996. The results were merely a confirmation of what everyone in the venture capital field already knew: later-stage investments had proved more profitable than earlier-stage investments. It is now possible that the announcement of these results will further entrench the practices of the industry to the detriment of small business.

BVCA Performance Measurement Survey 1994 and 1995

The main driver behind the decision to produce annual performance surveys was the constant demands by the industry's institutional investors for information. They stated clearly to the industry that they could not guarantee indefinite funding if they were not given the information to allow them to compare this sector with others they could invest in. It was also suggested that other institutions were waiting for such information before they even began to put money into the sector. This proved to be the decisive factor, although many in the industry were still against the idea. The opponents believed that a survey would show the industry in a poor light, as it would be grading investments made in its early years when many lessons were being learned. They also argued that measuring non-realised investments, which would have to be prominent in the survey, was meaningless as anything could happen to them after they were measured. The BVCA dismissed this view, countering that the industry had standardised valuation techniques as adequate as any other part of the financial sector and the survey went ahead.[6]

The 1994 survey was confined to independent funds, and only included those which invested over 60% of their capital in the UK and had been running for more than four years. This may seem very restrictive but the survey still covered 94 funds and £2,851 million of raised capital.[7] This represented 90% of the funds raised during the period. The 1995 survey was based upon a similarly selected sample with the total funds considered amounting to £3,271 million.[8] The data is presented in two ways, by year and by investment stage, with the most value for this study coming from the latter. The overall returns reported in 1994 was 12.1%, which Maurice Anslow argues was a higher figure than many in the industry feared.[9] It was the breakdown of the figures, however, which showed the real picture of how the industry had performed since 1980.

The figures dividing the funds by year show a large diversity in performance, as can be seen in table 4.8. Anslow commenting on the 1994 survey said: 'The best "vintage" years for fund formation were 1985 and

1990, according to the BVCA figures, with both periods presumably coinciding with the optimum pricing conditions which followed for venture capital deals ... By contrast, the worst years for fund formation were 1986 and 1987 where the pooled internal rate of return (IRR) came out at 5.8% and 1.1% respectively, presumably a reflection of the high pricing conditions which prevailed at the end of the 1980s boom.'[10]

Table 4.8 UK Venture Capital Industry Performance by Year: 1994 Survey

Year of Formation	No. of Funds Surveyed	Total Raised £m	Pooled IRR %
1980-1984	9	131	10.2
1985	12	407	19.5
1986	9	144	5.8
1987	8	276	1.1
1988	18	601	10.8
1989	15	656	14.6
1990	13	636	19.5

Source: BVCA, *Performance Measurement Survey*, London, BVCA, 1994.

As far as this study is concerned, the second presentation of the data holds the greater interest. It revealed that the industry's record in investing in start-up and development capital (defined as expansion capital and small MBO of less than £2 million) has been modest, to say the very least, and explains why so little finance has been directed at such investments, with the proportion decreasing all the time. The 1994 figures (see table 4.9) of 4% and 5.6% for these types of investments are not the kind of returns that institutional investors will be looking for from this part of the financial sector. It is suggested that institutions look for their return from venture capital holdings to be 2.5% higher than the FT All Share Index. This index in the ten years to September 1995 returned 15.7%.[11] The shortfall is huge, therefore, with even start-up funds lying in the top quartile of the pool not meeting this requirement. It is also worth noting that the mixed investment, generalist funds were also modest performers which is disappointing as one hope for start-up and early-stage funding is that it can be 'carried' within mixed funds.

The release of the data for 1995, despite revealing a similar picture of venture capital investment in the UK, does offer some grounds for optimism. The IRR for start-up and development capital (see table 4.10) were slightly higher in 1995, something which the BVCA claims is likely to continue in the future: 'Early-stage fund returns lag behind later-stage funds partly because a higher proportion of their portfolio remains undistributed and is conservatively valued, and also because the returns are heavily influenced by the readiness of public markets to accept high-technology and biotechnology companies in their development phase. In the last two years it has become much easier to float such companies in the UK. If US experience is anything to go by, it is likely that the returns of early-stage funds will show a significant improvement as a result.'[12]

Table 4.9 UK Venture Capital Industry Performance by Investment Specialisation: 1994 Survey

Category	Number of Funds Surveyed	Total Raised £m	Pooled IRR %
Start-up	17	183	4.0
Development	23	415	5.6
Mid-MBO	16	558	14.7
Large MBO	10	1177	23.1
Generalists	18	518	7.1
Total	84	2851	12.1

Source: BVCA, *Performance Measurement Survey*, London, BVCA, 1994.

Table 4.10 UK Venture Capital Industry Performance by Investment Specialisation: 1995 Survey

Category	Number of Funds Surveyed	Total Raised £m	Pooled IRR %
Start-up	17	258	4.3
Development	31	483	6.9
Mid-MBO	18	578	16.2
Large MBO	12	1,344	23.8
Generalists	22	607	9.7
Total	100	3,271	13.0

Source: BVCA, *Performance Measurement Survey*, London, BVCA, 1995, p9.

Category definitions for the BVCA Performance Measurement surveys: Start-ups - includes funds that invest in seed, start-up and early-stage companies; Development - includes expansion and small MBO with less than £2 million of equity invested; Mid-MBO - include equity investments of £2-5 million; Large MBO - includes equity investments over £5 million; Generalists - invest in a variety of stages

Table 4.11 UK Venture Capital Industry Upper Half and Upper Quarter Performance by Investment Stage: 1995 Survey

Stage	Pooled IRR of Upper Half	Pooled IRR of Upper Quarter
Start-up	9.7	16.1
Development	14.1	18.3
Mid-MBO	25.6	26.9
Large MBO	32.5	40.4
Generalist	13.6	16.4
Total	18.8	25.2

Source: BVCA, *Performance Measurement Survey*, London, BVCA, 1995, p10.

It will be necessary to wait for the improved figures to materialise, however, as there have been many claims made by the industry over the years about start-up and early-stage investments and very few of them have been realised. Table 4.11 shows that healthy returns are possible, though, with the top quarter of the start-up and development capital focused funds performing quite well. In summarising the overall findings the BVCA draws an up-beat conclusion from the survey:

> This survey shows that long-term returns, superior to those available from other asset classes, can be achieved by venture capital fund investment, together with acceptable levels of liquidity ... Surveys have shown that venture capital funds' unique provision of both finance and experience to the companies in which they invest, helps them to grow and develop more quickly and successfully than other types of company, thus creating good returns to their investors ... The BVCA believes that there is a strong case for venture capital having a role in any balanced portfolio.[13]

The problem is that the venture capital in the balanced portfolio is likely to be in the form of larger and later-stage investments and this trend can only be consolidated by these statistics. Institutional investors now know for a fact that start-up and early-stage funds deliver *significantly* lower returns on investment, and that they will need to be able to identify one of the very top performers to ensure they receive even a decent return on investment. As table 4.12 shows, there is every chance of these investors actually receiving negative returns. An across the board improvement in returns for start-up and smaller development capital will have to continue for some time yet before this segment of the market is able attract significant levels of finance and have a significant impact on the equity gap.

Table 4.12 UK Venture Capital Industry Lower Quartile, Median, and Upper Quartile Performance by Investment Stage: 1995 Survey

Stage	No. of Funds	Lower Quartile IRR (%)	Median IRR (%)	Upper Quartile IRR (%)
Start-up	17	-2.3	5.8	10.6
Development	31	-4.8	2.3	10.6
Mid MBO	18	10.3	17.6	22.9
Large MBO	12	14.5	21.3	26.1
Generalist	22	1.2	4.5	10.1
Total	100	-0.2	6.2	17.4

Source: BVCA, *Performance Measurement Survey*, London, BVCA, 1995, p11.

As was mentioned, the discrepancy in the performance of early and later-stage investments was no secret. It was already known that a number of funds which invested in small and early-stage companies had done badly and in many cases had gone to the wall. The Avon Enterprise Fund is a classic example. This fund invested between £100,000 and £250,000, and although Avon claimed in 1990 to be holding a portfolio that had appreciated from £1.53 million to £2.20 million since purchase, there were difficulties with many of their investments. In their submission to the 1991 *Venture Capital Report Guide to Venture Capital in the UK* they had to admit that 12 of their investee companies had gone into liquidation, and that they had incurred a loss on realisation of £839,000 on investments originally made at £1,984,000.[14] This relatively poor performance meant they were unable to raise further funds, and went out of business.[15] Many other similar funds suffered the same fate. For example, East Anglian Securities and Foundation Development Capital went into liquidation in the late 1980s, whilst JMI Advisory Services, which invested in amounts as small as £50,000, and Metrogroup Capital, who went down to £20,000, both found that they were unable to raise any further funds.[16] Others can be added to the list, including Oxford Seedcorn Capital, Oakland Investment Management, PA Developments, and Syntech Information Technology Funds.[17]

The aforementioned Prutec Ltd, a fund run by the Prudential insurance company was a further fund which invested in small, early-stage, and high-risk investments and was one of the earliest to fail. Prutec invested a total of £45 million, which was divided between two main activities. 40% of their finance was invested in research projects at universities and other research establishments, with the remaining finance going into 20 early-stage high technology companies. One of these was Speywood, the biotechnology joint venture with the NEB mentioned in the previous chapter. The fund, however, was a disaster with *The Economist* commenting: 'Some of [their investments] may yet prove profitable, but so far Prutech has made money on only one - Biosearch, which makes machines that produce synthetic genes. It has made one big write off: a Welsh microcomputer firm called Dragon in which Prutec invested more than £8 million. Dragon went bust last year [1984].'[18] Prudential announced that it was to wind down Prutec in 1985. Another celebrated small and early-stage venture capital failure was Electra, although its disastrous ERC 1 fund was actually finance raised under the BSS (see chapter 2). It is worth mentioning this fund, however, as it had a considerable impact on the industry as a whole. Many in the industry, including Electra themselves, learnt that venture capitalists did not have a 'golden touch', and that small, early-stage investments were high-risk, no matter how skilful the executives. Many venture capitalists who began their operations in the mid to late 1980s refer to the Electra Risk Capital fund when discussing how they decided on their position in the market. The fund reinforced the doubts many had over high-risk venture capital.

Yet it was by no means the case that all small and early-stage venture capital funds failed. One was even successful in the 1970s, not remembered as the best decade for industrial investment. This was Abingworth's fund launched in 1973. The company specialised in high technology ventures, with most of its funds invested in the United States. However, they did make some investment in the UK, about 13% of their portfolio in the 1970s. At the time of the flotation of Abingworth in 1983 only two of their 13 realised UK investments had been disposed of at a loss, with the profitable investments easily making up for them and a good deal more.[19] The company's performance indicates that it was possible to invest successfully in relatively small amounts in the 1970s - something to reflect upon in respect of the NEB.

A further example of success at this level is Yorkshire Enterprise Ltd, which was set up in 1983 at the initiative of the old West Yorkshire Metropolitan County Council to answer a concern that an equity gap was opening in the area. It was believed that there was a shortage of working capital available for small companies. The first fund, launched in 1983, backed 130 companies, and the company reports that a gross internal rate of return of 23% has been achieved to date.[20] It was said that they had realised proceeds of £5.92 million, whilst the book value of an original £9.89 million fund still stood at £7.84 million.[21] The results achieved by Yorkshire Enterprise have been made largely from investments in the range of the equity gap. The company has an investment ceiling of £500,000, and is addressing, as was its intention, the equity gap in a part of the country that was once reliant on a number of heavy industries. Their venture capital has been required to develop new companies and innovation, and they have provided it successfully.

For every success like Yorkshire Enterprise there were a great number of small and early-stage venture capital funds which performed badly in the 1980s, and the relatively poor IRR for start-up and development capital in the BVCA survey is easy to understand. The much higher IRR for later-stage investment can also be understood by analysing a sample of venture capital funds. Candover Investments, for example, was set up in 1980 to invest in large MBO and provide development capital. Candover became a public company in 1984 and its current policy is to look for investments of above £1 million. Over the last ten years Candover has been consistently profitable, a record reflected in table 4.13.

Table 4.13 Candover: Profits After Tax 1984 to 1992

Year	1984	1986	1988	1990	1991	1992
£ Million	0.19	0.59	1.50	2.27	2.84	3.15

Source: Adapted from *Candover Investments Annual Report,* 1989 and 1992.

Equity Capital For Industry, now ECI, is another example. ECI is one of the older venture capital funds having been founded in 1976 with initial capital of £41 million. The high demand for the ECI funds was indicative of the situation in the 1970s. Lord Plowden reported in 1977 that in the first 12 months ECI had received over ninety applications for finance.[22] Currently ECI considers proposals between £1 million and £8 million and in 1992 was able to announce that 'realisations from the ECI portfolio over the last eleven years have achieved an overall compound return of 28% a year from 99 companies.'[23] Murray Ventures, investing between £500,000 and £10 million, have also been successful. In the 1992 Annual Report the Chairman, Ian Denholm, stated: 'In spite of continued difficult trading conditions [1992 was] a record year for realisations of unlisted investments with £15.7 million realised for a net gain on cost of £7.5 million.'[24]

Success has also been achieved by those at the very top of the market. The Electra Investment Trust, investing between £5 million and £30 million, is one case, with the fund producing a profit every year between 1982 and 1992. In the years 1989 to 1992 the yearly profits were in excess of £10 million.[25] Their profits are likely to continue as in 1992 their twenty largest holdings (representing 44% of their assets) were valued at nearly three times their original cost.[26] The case of Legal and General Ventures, investing between £1 million to £50 million, is also worthy of note. The venture capital arm of the firm released the following information in 1994: 'Over the period January 1990 to September 1994 the annual equity portfolios returned an annual IRR of 46.3% ... Over the same period the portfolio IRR on realised investments was an annualised 96%.'[27]

All the figures available on the UK institutional venture capital industry are consistent with the fact that the industry has moved away from smaller and early-stage investments to the more profitable world of MBO and other large and later-stage investments. This is why many observers argue that the development of a £2 billion venture capital industry has had little impact on the equity gap for small firms. In the light of these facts, the next section provides a platform for venture capitalists themselves to have their say about the equity gap.

The Institutional Venture Capital Industry and the Equity Gap: The Industry's View

The accusation that the industry does not assist small and early-stage businesses is one with which all venture capitalists are familiar. Quite naturally many have come to their own opinion about its validity. Jan

Berglund, who was prepared to identify a gap, said that the gap was more about companies losing time, with the inadequate supply making the search harder, rather than viable projects not ultimately being able to acquire finance. He says that one should not assume that just because institutional venture capital companies reject a overwhelming majority of those who come to them for finance, that this means that viable projects are being turned down. He laments that 'a lot of the companies that approach us are, it has to be said, very poor. They seem to have no management experience or acumen. We cannot take on these sorts of companies.'[28] Edmund Johnston, of Ulster Development Capital, made the same point: 'Often it is shortcomings in the projects offered that are to blame.' He notes one weakness, however, that he does believe the market has yet to correct: 'High-tech projects with good entrepreneurs putting them forward may be an area where there is a shortage, but it is difficult to pick these as winners.'[29]

Keith Williams, of British Steel (Industry) Ltd, broadly agrees with Berglund; he says that 'a very good proposal will nearly always be snapped up.'[30] The weakness he sees in the market is in the provision of equity finance under £100,000; here he believes companies with ordinary, solid proposals may find it hard to get backing. He makes the comment, though, that it is difficult for the institutional venture capital industry to move into investments that may be on the margins of viability as 'some that we do back fail, and if they are perceived to be the best, then what were the rest of the ones which we looked at like ?'[31] Derek Harris, whose venture capital fund, Birmingham Technology, makes mainly high-tech investments, believes that any gaps that do exist are due to rigidities in the market. For example, he states that 'complicated deals can cost as much as £60,000 in legal fees' and that this is a substantial disincentive to making smaller investments.[32]

Informal Venture Capital: A More Likely Bridge ?

One of the arguments of those who believe in the ability of free markets to solve economic problems is that the market constantly adapts to new circumstances and demands - problems that exist are only ever temporary. The development of a recognisable *informal venture capital market* in the 1990s seems to vindicate this view. The difference between this market and the institutional venture capital market is that informal venture capital is not provided by an institution but by a *private individual* or a group of individuals known as *syndicates*. If responsibility for bridging the gap is to be shifted towards the informal market then this, again, would indicate a lack of belief in the ability of the institutional market to provide a solution. Yet it would still be consistent with the view that natural market processes can to solve economic problems. Evidence on informal investment is at present rather patchy, largely because it has only recently been an area of academic interest; consequently, its ability to provide a solution to the problem of the equity gap is unproven. Yet as the finance is directed mainly at small business, and as many experts in the field, including Colin Mason, believe that an untapped pool of up to £2 billion exists in the UK, the emergence of this sector is clearly worth attention.[33] A reason as to why the pool remains largely untapped is the absence of an infrastructure to facilitate the coming together of business and investors. Since the beginning of the 1990s, this situation has been improved by the establishment of a significant number of BIS.

Business Introduction Services

Up until the 1990s there were very few BIS in the UK. Indeed, one of the early pioneers, Lucius Cary, set up his Venture Capital Report service in 1978 because he himself had suffered from a lack of established sources of this type of investment. In recent years a critical mass of BIS has begun to emerge, including those sponsored by the Government in the aforementioned 1991 initiative. According to a 1995 BVCA source, there are 25 BIS currently in the private sector, compared with 9 in 1993, and it would appear that this number is going to increase in the future (A full list of public and private sector BIS and their activities appears in the appendix). BIS can operate in one or more of three different ways. These are the publication of an investment bulletin, which vary in the depth of information provided; investment meetings, where business people seeking finance give a presentation to an investor audience; and database matching, where the compatibility of investor and potential investee are decided by a computer.

The development of an infrastructure for informal venture capital, and the previously mentioned government incentive schemes have brought a lot of attention on the market. For a time no small business page, it seemed, was complete without an article on informal venture capital. This has reflected the hope that the informal venture capital market will be able to make a significant impact on the equity gap for small business. The view is often expressed that the institutional venture capital market will continue to raise its lower investment limits leaving the informal market to provide the equity for requirements of under about £200,000. The question to be asked, however, is whether this is likely to happen.

Business Introduction Services and the existence of an equity gap for small business

There is certainly no doubt amongst BIS executives that there is a gap to fill; the existence of a gap for small equity investments is proclaimed as the reason for their existence. The only disagreement is over the level at which the gap exists. The following two comments were typical of the overall view. Chris Hodgson of Investors in Hertfordshire said: 'The basis of our operations is that there is a gap for small business.'[34] Claude Brownlow of Winsec Management Services agreed, saying: '100%. The gap is the main reason why we set up the service.'[35] Like Lucius Cary nearly fifteen years earlier, the setting up of Winsec's service came about after a particular incident, in this case a sports car project needing about £200,000. The need for such a service in the Essex area was recognised from that project and Winsec now produce about four investment bulletins a year.

Many of the service executives admitted that most of their client companies had come to them as a last resort. Steve Gallagher, of the Gloucestershire Enterprise Agency service, said: '80% are coming to us as the last resort.'[36] Chris Hodgson added: 'It is unusual if they haven't already been to the banks.'[37] However, the executives argued that this should by no means indicate that the companies are merely the risks that no-one else is willing to take. Hodgson continued by arguing that rejections by conventional financiers are often due to the size or the nature of the request, rather than the quality of the company. Indeed, David Ward, of Principality Financial Management, said that it was quite right that BIS should attract such businesses: 'Our niche is where the banks won't lend and in the area below the traditional venture capitalists' lower threshold. This typically means investments of between £50,000 and £300,000.'[38]

Although the BIS executives interviewed were almost unanimous in their identification of a gap, they stressed that a lack of finance was not the only problem small businesses faced. Indeed, many argued that a belief that it was their only problem was in actual fact a problem in itself. Michael Thompson of Capital Connections said: 'It is not always money that is required. Often a bit of expertise and guidance from those that know about small business can reveal other factors.'[39] Consequently, Capital Connections and most of the other BIS offer consultancy help and stress that an informal investor often has more than just finance to offer their business. Investors often have a great deal of experience in business, and one of the reasons why many of them take equity in a small business is that they wish to contribute to the company in a wider sense than just being an injector of capital.

Initial evidence on informal venture capital

Relatively little is known about the performance of informal venture capital investments, and in many cases it is far too early in the investment cycle to make a judgement anyway. Mason and Richard Harrison, in particular, have begun to address the issue, and in February 1995 (with Peter Allen) brought out some initial findings. They were interested in three areas of informal investing: the investment process; the post-investment experience; and investment performance. Their findings were as follows:

The investment process

The study found that involvement with a business angel forced the small business to formulate a clear and, by definition, commercially acceptable business plan. They said that it needed to be 'comprehensive, realistic [and] investor-orientated'.[40] Informal investment is also 'a relatively quick process, particularly when compared with institutional venture capital'.[41] This is important for small businesses as they need to proceed quickly during the years of early growth. Thirdly, the investor angel often provides a second round of finance.[42] Mason and Harrison also comment on other advantages of informal investment: '[It] is relatively inexpensive for both entrepreneur and investor. Informal venture capital is also a very flexible source of finance. The form that the investment takes is varied, including equity, loans, debt-equity arrangements and even factoring.'[43]

The post-investment experience

Mason, Harrison and Allen commented: 'The study has provided further evidence that business angels make a valuable hands-on contribution to their investee businesses, typically in the form of strategic advice, business skills and networking. However, it is important not to overlook their contributions as "coach"/"mentor" which are equally valuable ... There were only a minority of situations where the entrepreneur felt that the investment agreement favoured the investor.'[44]

Investment performance

There were three main findings about investment performance. Firstly, Mason and Harrison admitted: 'No investor in the study has made significant financial returns from any of the investments that were examined, although this is influenced in part by the recession which seems likely to have contributed to the high failure rate of investments made prior to 1991.'[45] Secondly, they commented: 'Investors have lost money in a significant proportion of investments, although in some cases this can be attributed to naivety and inexperience.'[46] These two findings are reflected in table 4.14.

The table needs to be read with an understanding that the first column is heavily populated because most of the investments in the survey were made very recently and, therefore, have not had much time to demonstrate their potential, or lack of it. Thirdly, they commented: 'Although investors are seeking significant capital gain, a significant proportion nevertheless obtain some form of earnings stream, either through dividends or interest or, more commonly, directors fees and consultancy fees. This effectively "recycles" some of their investment and also provides partial financial recompense in the event that the investment fails'[47]

Table 4.14 Informal Investment Performance: Aggregate Evidence 1988 to 1994

Year of Investment	Still trading: Investor still with company	Company failed	Unable to trace: Presumed failed	Company still trading: Investor sold investment
1988/1989	2	3	6	0
1990	0	2	2	0
1991	1	1	1	0
1992	11	6	2	2
1993/1994	18	0	1	0
Total	32	12	12	2

Source: C. Mason, R. Harrison and P. Allen, *Informal Venture Capital: A Study of the Investment Process, the Post-investment Experience and Investment Performance*, Working Paper No12, University of Southampton and Ulster Business School, February 1995, p30.

Summary

Any attempt to extrapolate the findings of this survey must be carried out with great caution. The survey involves a limited number of companies, and many of the investments have only just been made. Nevertheless, it is possible to deduce from the findings that informal investment is high risk. On the one hand, this is bad news for the investor, yet on the other it is good news as it suggests that the informal venture capital sector is going to provide genuine high-risk venture capital. The extent to which this risk will limit the amount of the investment made by the sector remains to be seen. From the evidence of this survey, it remains to be seen whether angels can have serious expectations of a substantial capital gain. Studies like this one are valuable, but it is going to be some years before more authoritative research can be carried out.

The effect of the informal venture capital market on the equity gap

Despite the tentative start, the BIS have made many involved in the area believe that they can, in the coming decade, increase their operations and make a significant contribution to bridging the equity gap. David Ward of Principality Financial Management, based in Swansea, said this, as did a number of others, but he qualified his statement by saying that it would take time. The aforementioned Michael Thompson went some way towards explaining why: 'We should have some impact, and the investments we promote can act as a catalyst; an equity participation can often draw in bank loans. It is a slow hard grind though. Three or four successful matches a year would be a reasonable return at the moment ... So we must widen our organisation if it is going to succeed. The problem is that you can't force it; informal venture capital is a personalised business.'[48] Claude Brownlow agrees, saying that it takes time to build up the two client bases - the pool of investors and a large number of investment proposals. The service can do very little until it has a substantial pool of potential investors, as only then can it talk with any credibility to companies seeking finance. Brownlow said that Winsec had worked very hard on its investment pool with the reward being that it now totals about £30 million. He argued that the predominantly local services needed to have a few high-profile successes to make a breakthrough. An investment that led to high growth would raise the profile of the service and increase the recognition of what private equity could do for a company.

One word that many of the executives used was 'networking', the linking of various BIS. To many this was the key to the future ability of informal venture capital to bridge the equity gap and indeed for some time it was said that unofficially the DTI was pushing that line. One development that brought the issue to the surface was the founding of a national database, VentureList, by Enterprise Adventure (which grew out of the old Enterprise Initiative run by the DTI) in June 1994. VentureList works on the same principle as the local databases, with the companies seeking funds providing standardised information which is put onto a database. Enterprise Adventure's chairman, Peter Benton, announced at the birth of the network that it was not intended as a competitor to the already existing introduction services, but rather that it would seek to involve them in a larger critical mass of investors, which, as mentioned by Claude Brownlow, is essential if the industry is going to promote deals efficiently and with credibility. However, since 1994 very little has happened to suggest that a network is going to be formally created. This is not least because many of the established BIS understandably see it as a threat to their hard fought for investor and client bases. It is also the case that the various BIS are operating at different levels of service and with different standards of investigation.

The ability of BIS to bridge the gap is further undermined as there are suggestions that they are not commercially viable as private sector services. Colin Mason said that 'the government must recognise that it is very difficult to cover the costs, let alone make money, when doing this kind of thing. Therefore, the government should go some way towards underwriting the costs of the operation.'[49] Claude Brownlow agrees; the service that his company provides is only one part of a wider financial management company and he admits that 'a company like us has to be involved in other activities; a business introduction service has to be run on a part-time basis.'[50]

Conclusion: The Effectiveness of the UK Institutional Venture Capital Industry in Bridging the Equity Gap

The government has pursued a laissez-faire policy towards the institutional venture capital industry. This has meant there have been no specific policy initiatives aimed at encouraging the industry to invest a greater proportion of its capital in small and early-stage investments. This chapter has sought to find out whether this policy has been effective in bridging the equity gap. The evidence produced suggests that it has not.

Assessing the policy of laissez-faire

There is no denying that the UK industry, as defined by the BVCA, is thriving. In 1994, venture capital institutions in the BVCA invested a record £2.07 billion, a 46% increase. These figures, however, assume a very broad definition of the term venture capital; much of the finance is capital for MBO. All but a tiny fraction of the finance raised by BVCA members is of no relevance to the equity gap. The average investment size of the industry is over £1 million, only 5% of the industry's resources are being directed towards start-up and early-stage investments, whilst the industry's seed capital investment is almost immeasurable. Indeed, the limited amount of finance the industry has directed towards the gap is one of the reasons why so many believe that the gap still exists today. Further evidence on the industry goes some way to explaining why it invests as it does. The recent performance surveys produced by the BVCA have shown that the greatest profits lie in MBO and larger, later-stage investments. The returns for start-up and smaller development investments have, *on average*, been very low and well below that necessary to attract further finance from the City institutions.

A sensitive question arises, therefore, over whether these lower returns are inevitable or whether they are the result of venture capitalists underperforming in this respect. Those in the industry argue that there is a lack of quality amongst the small businesses that approach them for finance. They state that some of the smaller businesses they have invested in turned out to be of a poor quality and lost them money, rationalising from this that the ones they turn away must be even worse. In particular the industry complains about a generally poor standard of management in the small business sector. One venture capitalist said that a 'good' small business had a better than 50% chance of gaining finance, and this despite the fact that the general consensus was that winners were more difficult to pick in this part of the market. Others involved in the industry, who understandably did not wish to be identified (and who do not appear at any other stage of this book), argue differently and suggest that there is a lack of high quality small investors in the institutional venture capital industry. Obviously, it is very difficult to substantiate this view, except to say that there is a very wide spread of performances between the funds of this nature.

It is perhaps fairest to comment that three main conclusions can be made about the institutional venture capital industry and the efficacy of a laissez-faire approach to bridging the equity gap. Firstly, it can be said with confidence that the industry is having only a very limited impact on the equity gap. Secondly, there would appear to be both demand and supply factors causing this limited impact. On the supply side the levels of finance being targeted at the gap are very low and falling. A number of reasons have been given for why this is so, most of them concerning the incentives in the market which are pushing the finance ever further away from the gap. However, a demand element must also be considered as many business surveys report that small businessmen and women are unwilling to surrender a stake in their business to outside investors for fear of losing control of their company, and as has just been mentioned, the industry claims that much of the demand is of poor quality. Thirdly, given what has been said, it can be concluded that the laissez-faire approach to the institutional venture capital industry has been largely unsuccessful. Furthermore, the lack of success has been predictable, with only common business sense needed to forsee it. The incentives in the market were always clear, and pointed firmly in the direction that the industry has gone. Indeed, the experience was not in any way peculiar to the institutional venture capital industry; it could have easily been predicted from other episodes in the history of the financial system. A virtually apolitical view of the limits of markets would have indicated that the policy would not have a significant impact on the equity gap.

The alternative of informal venture capital

Although the BVCA still waxes hopeful about the future prospects of the institutional industry having an impact on the gap, many writing on the subject almost discount it from their calculations. Instead, they are increasingly focusing on the role of the business angel and the informal venture capital market. The growth of this market and its infrastructure has largely been a market development, although the Government was involved during the early days and provided a lot of publicity. It will be some time before it is possible to judge whether the informal market (in this latest guise) will have a significant impact on the equity gap as it is not known yet how successful BIS and other services will be in promoting investments, nor how successful those investments will be. Colin Mason and Richard Harrison have provided some excellent initial evidence, with their findings showing that there is some doubt as to whether many investors will make substantial returns from informal venture capital investment. It will be some time though before it will be possible to ascertain to what extent the market's potential can be tapped.

The problem of definition

In the *Daily Telegraph* in April 1995 a headline reported: 'Venture funding at record £2 billion'.[51] The article explained: 'Venture capital investment by British companies rose 46% last year to a record £2.07 billion, according to the British Venture Capital Association ... UK venture capitalists have invested as much as the rest of Europe together'. To the average small business entrepreneur this article would, understandably, suggest that this sector has much to offer his type of business and its requirements. In reality, as this chapter has demonstrated, the prospects for small and early-stage business acquiring low levels of finance are not anywhere as promising as the £2 billion figure suggests and perhaps there would be something to be said for the BVCA being more specific in their press releases. To aid clarity the term *venture capital* could be limited to the first three categories outlined earlier in the chapter. These are seed capital, start-up capital and early-stage capital. These investments usually involve higher than average risks and mark out the investments as distinct from most of the industrial and service sector investments made by the financial sector as a whole. It was this type of finance that was in short supply before a recognisable 'venture capital' industry emerged, and this type of finance that the industry was expected to provide. If this definition was used, it would mean that in 1994 £76 million of venture capital was invested, and this would surely give a better indication of what small business people ought to expect, should they explore this particular financing option.

Notes

[1] The term 'institutional venture capital industry' is used to describe the providers of venture capital which are *financial organisations* as against *investing individuals*. Individual investors are covered by the term 'informal venture capital industry' adopted later in the chapter.

[2] Stoy Hayward, *Venture and Buy Out Capital 1994*, London, Stoy Hayward, 1994.

[3] BVCA, *Directory 1993-4*, London, BVCA, 1993.

[4] *UK Venture Capital Journal*, 'Special report: two gaps in the UK venture capital market', November 1988, p9.
[5] BVCA, *Report on Investment Activity 1993*, London, BVCA, p11.
[6] Anslow, M, 'Performance data shows wide spread of IRRs for UK independent funds', *UK Venture Capital Journal*, November/December, p12.
[7] *Ibid.*, p13.
[8] BVCA, *Performance Measurement Survey 1995*, London, BVCA, 1996, p7.
[9] Anslow, *op.cit.*, p14.
[10] *Ibid.*
[11] *Ibid.*, p15.
[12] BVCA, Performance Measurement Survey 1995, *op.cit.*, p1.
[13] *Ibid.*, p8.
[14] Cary, L, *Venture Capital Report Guide to Venture Capital 1991*, pp125-126.
[15] Anonymous industry source.
[16] Anonymous industry source.
[17] Anonymous industry source.
[18] *The Economist*, 'Scorched by Dragon's breath', 13 July 1985, pp66-67.
[19] Abingworth plc, *Issue to the Public*, June 1983, pp4-5.
[20] Yorkshire Post, *The First Ten Years*, 23 March 1993, pB6.
[21] Yorkshire Enterprise internal company data.
[22] Equity Capital for Industry, *Annual Report and Accounts*, 1977, p4.
[23] ECI Ventures, *Annual Report*, 1992, p3.
[24] Murray Ventures, *Annual Report and Accounts*, 1992, p7.
[25] Electra Investment Trust, *Annual Report and Accounts*, 1992, p38.
[26] *Ibid.*, p13.
[27] Legal and General Ventures, *Company Statement*, 9 March 1995.
[28] Interview with Jan Berglund, Industrial Technology Securities, 12 December 1993.
[29] Interview with Edmund Johnston, Ulster Development Capital, 14 December 1993.
[30] Interview with Keith Williams, British Steel (Industry) Limited, 15 December 1993.
[31] *Ibid.*
[32] Interview with Derek Harris, Birmingham Technology (Venture Capital), 19 January 1994.
[33] Interview with Colin Mason, 30 June 1994.
[34] Interview with Chris Hodgson, Hertfordshire TEC, 2 March 1994.
[35] Interview with Claude Brownlow, Winsec Management Services, 16 May 1994.
[36] Interview with Steve Gallagher, Gloucestershire Enterprise Agency, 13 March 1994.
[37] Interview with Chris Hodgson, *op.cit.*

[38] Interview with David Ward, Principality Financial Management, 28 March 1994.
[39] Interview with Michael Thompson, ELTEC, 8 March 1994.
[40] Mason, C, Harrison, R, and Allen, P, *Informal Venture Capital: A Study of the Investment Process, the Post-investment Experience and Investment Performance*, Working Paper no 12, University Of Southampton and Ulster Business School, February 1995, p34.
[41] *Ibid.*, p35.
[42] *Ibid.*
[43] *Ibid.*
[44] *Ibid.*, p35; p36.
[45] *Ibid.*, p37.
[46] *Ibid.*
[47] *Ibid.*, p38.
[48] Interview with Michael Thompson, *op.cit.*
[49] Interview with Colin Mason, *op.cit.*
[50] Interview with Claude Brownlow, *op.cit.*
[51] Becket, M, 'Venture funding at record £2bn', *Daily Telegraph*, 12 April 1995.

5 The Conservatives' Business Expansion Scheme

The Business Expansion Scheme as a Policy of Fiscal Intervention

The BES was a policy of *fiscal intervention*. Such a policy is initiated when a government identifies a specific area in which it wants to increase investment, but feels that fiscal inducements are required to precipitate such an increase. By definition, it comes as a clear admission that an equity gap exists. The record of the BES is one that cannot be taken at face value, and indeed should not be, as large amounts of taxation were foregone in its name. In this chapter the scheme will be tested against the three criteria used in this study so it can be evaluated as a state venture capital policy. The evaluation, in comparison with that of the NEB and the institutional venture capital industry, is limited in terms of the data employed. The information provided by the Inland Revenue is useful, but restricted to certain aspects of the scheme, and information on the performance of investments is rather difficult to come by. Nevertheless, the evidence that is presented in this chapter reveals that the BES, despite the huge amounts of finance raised by the scheme, was largely ineffective in its task of bridging the equity gap; this ineffectiveness led to its abolition in 1993.

The Effectiveness of the Business Expansion Scheme in Raising Finance

When the raw figures for the BES are considered it appears that the scheme has been reasonably successful. Using Inland Revenue statistics it can be seen that between 1983 and 1993 just over £4 billion was raised. Nearly £2 billion of this was raised in the final 20 months. A further estimation is that for this £4 billion plus to be raised, the Treasury had to forgo well over £1 billion in tax revenue. It needs to be mentioned at this stage that there were three ways in which BES investments could be made. Firstly, finance could be invested directly in a business; it was possible to avoid the need for a middle man. Secondly, it was possible for an investor to put his stake into a

BES fund. A BES fund accumulated BES stakes and then acted as a fund manager, in the same manner as the institutional venture capitalist. An example of a BES fund manager was Capital for Companies situated in West Yorkshire. In 1994 they were still managing a fund of £9 million. The investor, when he put his money in a BES fund, placed his trust in the fund managers that they would be able to make and manage investments that would be profitable. The investors had no say over the investments that were made on their behalf.

Table 5.1 Investment Raised Under the BES 1983/84 to 1993/94

Year	Amount of Investment (£m)	Cumulative Total (£m)
1983/84	105.0	105.0
1984/85	148.0	253.0
1985/86	157.0	410.0
1986/87	169.0	579.0
1987/88	201.0	780.0
1989/89	421.0	1201.0
1989/90	216.0	1417.0
1990/91	324.0	1741.0
1991/92	410.0	2151.0
1992/93	897.0	3048.0
1993/94	960.0	4008.0

Source: Inland Revenue Statistics 1995, London, HMSO, 1995, p81.

This aspect was the difference between BES funds and BES prospectus issues - the third way of investing under the scheme. When an investor put his money into a prospectus issue he was investing in a specific project, the details of which were laid out, quite naturally, in a prospectus; the fund manager had a specific financial target for a specific project which he tried to achieve. Many prospectus issues were in hotels, regrettably in the view of many. The significance of there being three different types of BES investment is revealed later in the chapter.

The Effectiveness of the Business Expansion Scheme in Targeting Finance at the Equity Gap

The BES, therefore, clearly had some success in facilitating the raising of equity capital, but this could never be the end of the matter as the Government had clear targets for where the capital was to be channelled. In this section it will be shown that the Government for a long time fought a battle with investors over the destination of capital, before finally giving up in 1988. The BES never satisfactorily financed the small, unquoted, and risky independent companies it was set up to finance, and, indeed, this was one of the main reasons for its abolition in 1993.

Sectors

After the first year had led to a preference for asset-backed ventures, the Chancellor of the Exchequer, Nigel Lawson, made no fewer than four attempts between 1984 and 1988 to try to target the tax relief on early-stage, high-risk businesses. In 1984 he outlawed farming ventures, which had been popular in the first year of the scheme. A year later he outlawed property development. In 1986 he made a further regulation that BES companies could not have more than 50% of their net assets in property. Finally, in 1988 he imposed a limit of £500,000 on the amount that could be raised by a company each year (although not shipping or rented property companies). However, in 1988 a further change was made to the scheme's rules. It allowed companies providing rented property under the new assured tenancy terms to qualify for BES relief. The ruling was criticised for being at variance with his previous efforts to return the scheme to its original objectives, and this criticism increased when it became clear that the change had produced a devastating effect on the way finance was raised under the scheme. This effect is reflected in tables 5.2 and 5.3.

Prior to the 1988 rule change there was a reasonable balance to the investments made under the scheme, by this criterion at least. Service and manufacturing companies both received about a third of the finance raised, and there was also room for other types of business as well. As table 5.3 illustrates, however, after the 1988 property rule change the overwhelming majority of funds raised under the BES was for rented property under the assured tenancy scheme. Between 1988 and 1993 property investment never accounted for less than 75% of the overall finance raised. One key group of players which contributed to this domination were British universities and colleges. In the period after 1988 these bodies raised £891.68 million. In addition 22 housing associations raised £299.29 million over the same period.[1] Furthermore, it could be argued that many of the risky ventures that the scheme was meant to be promoting would have come into the manufacturing category. Yet between 1988 and 1993 less than £75 million was raised under the scheme for any kind of manufacturing company. The evidence suggests that very little of the BES relief went to high-risk small firms, with the prime cause being the introduction of assured property ventures into the scheme after 1988. All contact with the original ambitions for the scheme were lost after this date.

Table 5.2 BES Investments by Economic Sector 1983/84 to 1985/86 (% of Total Investment)

Sector	Amount of Investment: Start-ups	Amount of Investment: Established companies
Construction	7.4	15.2
Distribution	16.2	11.3
Manufacturing	23.3	34.5
Services	48.0	35.4
Other sectors	5.1	17.3

Source: Adapted from C. Mason and R. Harrison, 'The role of the Business Expansion Scheme in the United Kingdom', in *Omega International Journal of Management Science,* Vol 17, No 2, 1989, p153.

Table 5.3 Amounts Invested Through the BES 1988/89 to 1993/94 (£m)

	1988-89	1989-90	1990-91	1991-92	1992-93	1993-94
Private Rented Housing	368	162	284	368	868	937
Agriculture	2	2	1	-	1	-
Construction	2	-	1	-	1	6
Manufacturing	15	13	11	20	13	-
Wholesale / Retail	8	7	6	5	5	11
Service Industries	26	31	20	16	9	3
Others	-	1	1	1	-	3
Total	**421**	**216**	**324**	**410**	**897**	**960**

Source: *Inland Revenue Statistics 1995,* London, HMSO, 1995, p81.

Investment size

The record of the BES was also mixed when it came to encouraging investments that were of a size that would relate to the equity gap. Earlier in the chapter it was mentioned that there was much concern over the size of BES investments, with the Chancellor, in 1988, imposing a limit of £500,000 on the amount that could be raised by a company (excluding shipping and private rented property companies) in any one year. Concern over this issue pre-dated that decision, however, and Patrick Taylor produced figures in 1984 to illustrate the emerging problem.

Table 5.4 Average Investment Sizes of BES Funds 1983/84

Fund Managers	**Amount Raised (£m)**	**Average Investment (£000)**
Electra Risk Capital	10.0	360
Lazard Development Capital	5.0	452
Charterhouse Development Capital	3.0	375
County Bank	2.4	274
Mercury (Warburg)	2.4	138
Stewart Fund Managers	2.0	200
Granville	1.9	269
Baronsmead	1.6	183
Singer and Friedlander	1.5	221
Guinness Mahon	1.5	188
Ravendale Bexfund	1.5	122
Minster Trust	1.2	200
Buckmaster and Moore	1.0	143

Source: Adapted from P. Taylor, The Business Expansion Scheme - is it filling the equity gap ?', *Venture Capital Report*, June 1984.

In the first year of the scheme, 1983-84, the average levels of many of the funds were not outside the terms that have been used in this study to locate the equity gap. However, it was hoped at that time, that the BES might allow businesses to raise equity under £100,000, leaving the £100,000 to £400,000 range to the growing institutional venture capital market. From the very start of the scheme this did not appear to have happened, and the 1988 ruling to limit investments to under £500,000 seems to reflect this. Indeed, the 1986 Peat Marwick report into the BES identified the BES's very own equity gap. It said: 'Our study indicates that it is difficult to raise BES finance over £50,000 directly and the BES funds typically do not invest below £150,000.'[2] Furthermore, even at that early-stage Peat Marwick felt they needed to add that 'the trend since 1983-84 appears to have been towards larger and perhaps less risky investments.'[3] It was a view Colin Mason, Richard Harrison and John Harrison were able to back up two years later. They reported: 'The average size of investments under the scheme has increased from £147,000 in 1983/84 to £234,000 in 1985/86 ... While the majority of companies have raised small amounts of finance through the scheme, much of the finance invested has not contributed to a reduction in the size of the equity gap. In 1985/86 ... 70% of the finance invested through the scheme was in companies which each raised over £500,000.'[4]

Mason et al were in no doubt as to the reasons for the increase in the average level of investment. They commented: 'These features of the scheme are largely a reflection of the increasing significance of prospectus issues, which are typically used by companies to raise amounts in excess of £500,000, and of a relative decline in fund investments, which predominantly make investments in the £50,000 to £500,000 range.'[5] A pattern emerged from the very early years of the BES: the proportion of finance invested directly and through BES funds declined, whereas the proportion of finance invested in prospectus issues increased markedly. The average investment under a prospectus issue was over £1 million; indeed by 1986 it was around £2 million.

With direct and fund investments catering for much smaller investment sizes the implications for the equity gap of the movement towards prospectus issues was clear. Colin Mason and Richard Harrison commented that within the first few years the scheme's aim of promoting direct venture capital investments by individuals had been eclipsed by other methods of investment. The effect of the existence of three different methods is shown in tables 5.5.

After the 1988 property rule change matters deteriorated even further, in terms of investment size. As has been reported, most BES investment was channelled into property companies after 1988, and as they could raise up to £5 million a year, it followed that most investment was in large ventures. Finance was still raised in amounts under £400,000 after 1988, but this was only a fraction of total investment, and, as table 5.3 suggested, much of it went into property ventures anyway. Furthermore, during the 1990s an ever increasing amount of investment went into ventures with a lower limit of £1 million.

Table 5.5   Average Investment per Company Under the Three Methods of BES Investment 1983/84 to 1987/88 (£000)

	Funds and Schemes	Prospectus Issues	Direct Investment
1983-84	203	1132	52
1984-85	226	1078	36
1985-86	204	1055	26
1986-87	281	2215	-
1987-88	321	1821	-

Source: Adapted from C. Mason and R. Harrison, 'The role of the Business Expansion Scheme in the United Kingdom', *Omega International Journal of Management Science*, Vol 17, No 2, 1989, p151.

Table 5.6 Finance Raised by Investment Size 1988/89 to 1993/94 (£m)

Range of Investment per Company (lower limit)	1988-89	1989-90	1990-91	1991-92	1992-93	1993-94
0	9	9	9	9	7	8
£50,000	137	14	12	11	10	9
£100,000	43	32	27	24	21	22
£250,000	33	32	23	16	16	19
£500,000	35	28	18	11	16	29
£1,000,000	164	101	235	339	827	873
Total	421	216	324	410	897	960

Source: Inland Revenue Statistics 1995, London, HMSO, 1995, p81.

Stage of investment

The record of the BES was also chequered when it came to the stage at which investments were made. Even as early as the first year Peat Marwick reported: 'BES has not been a significant source of seedcorn capital. Within our sample only 3 out of 43 companies raising £50,000 or less did so as seedcorn capital to finance a new trade start up; in contrast, BES has been used predominantly to provide working capital to companies suffering from liquidity crises and seeking to expand and, companies seeking to finance the purchase of existing businesses.'[6]

Over the ten year period of its existence the scheme did raise a great deal of finance for start-up ventures, but this merely illustrates that this indicator is not particularly reliable for the BES as most property ventures were start-up ventures - they just happened to be very large ones. By the end of the scheme the average start-up investment under the scheme was over £1 million and nearly all BES investments were rented property start-ups.

Table 5.7 BES Investment by Investment Stage 1983/84 to 1993/94 (£m)

	Start-ups: Amount	Start-ups: Average Size	Established Companies: Amount	Established Companies: Average Size
1983/84	63	0.12	42	0.21
1985/86	142	0.24	15	0.15
1987/88	186	0.26	15	0.13
1989/90	209	0.23	7	0.12
1991/92	407	0.49	3	0.05
1992/93	893	1.09	4	0.07
1993/94	957	1.09	4	0.08

Source: Inland Revenue Statistics 1995, London, HMSO, 1995, p81.

Levels of risk

Much about the risk, or lack of it, involved in investments made under the BES has been implied in the three previous sub-sections. For the tax relief foregone under the scheme to be justified - and remember, prior to the 1988 Budget most BES investors received 60% relief - there had to be a substantial element of risk involved in the investments. There is no equity gap for sure-fire profitable opportunities. The fact that most of the investments made, especially in the later-stages of the scheme, were either in property, or in later-stage or asset-backed businesses, suggested that the BES did not always promote apparently risky investments. This was the view of Mason et al who said: 'The scheme has not assisted significant numbers of high-risk businesses. Instead the bulk of the finance raised through the scheme has been invested in service sector businesses, often asset-related and predominantly in the wholesale, retail, real estate and leisure sectors ... the proportion of total finance invested in the manufacturing sector has declined from around one third in 1983/84 to under one quarter in 1985/86.'[7]

Regions

Although it was never one of the explicitly stated aims of the BES, it was in a sense implied that if the scheme was to make an impact on the perceived shortage of risk capital available to small, high-risk businesses, it would have to direct capital towards the regions. This, it has been reported on many occasions, is where a part of the shortage of equity capital lies. This did not happen though; indeed, if anything the BES made matters worse. Mason et al were able to report in their 1988 assessment: 'BES investors are concentrated in Southern England. Nevertheless, the proportion of BES investments in the South East is much greater than its share of BES investors; conversely in the rest of the country the proportion of investors is greater than its proportion of investments. Hence, a further adverse impact of the scheme on UK regional economic development has been to produce a north-south flow of risk capital.'[8] The regional pattern that Mason et al describe was established in the very early years of the scheme. The South-East always enjoyed a markedly disproportionate share of the finance raised, with this being at the expense of much of the rest of the country.

Additionality

A further crucial test of the scheme was whether the funds raised were genuinely additional. In the Peat Marwick report, written prior to the 1988 rented property rule change, the issue was dealt with. It concluded that the additionality of BES funds was high. The report said: 'Of the gross amount of £105 million invested through the BES in 1983-4, approximately £99 million was additional to the particular companies, approximately £98 million was additional to the UK unquoted company sector, and approximately £76 million was additional to direct UK equity holding.'[9] The report added that 'the vast majority of private investors [of 1983-84] had not previously invested in unquoted companies prior to making their BES investment. Many of the investors interviewed made BES investments again in 1984-85, and most are considering further investment under BES.'[10] However, once the 1988 rule change had been made, so little finance was raised for high-risk ventures, largely because of the rush into property ventures, that the concept of additionality became almost irrelevant, especially in terms of bridging the equity gap.

The Performance of Investments Promoted Under the Business Expansion Scheme

Another crucial aspect of the BES was the performance of investments made under the scheme. The BES has already been criticised for not being successful in targeting funds at high-risk ventures so one might have thought that the performance of the funds raised under the scheme would have been quite impressive. In fact they have been mixed, as table 5.8 illustrates.

Table 5.8 1992 Value of BES Investments Made Between 1983/84 and 1987/88

Year	Value in 1992 (%)	Failure Rate in 1992 (%)
1983-84	97	25
1984-85	92	22
1985-86	97	24
1986-87	74	38
1987-88	55	28

Source: Adapted from M. Bose, 'A cautionary tale for investors', *Investors Chronicle*, 24 July 1992, p14.

Whilst bearing in mind the statistics in table 5.8 are from 1992, the results of the first three years were acceptable, at least as far as investors were concerned. The small depreciation in the value of the investment would be more than compensated for by the tax relief (of course, the figures in the table are averages and some investors will have done better than others). The fourth and fifth year funds, however, have been unquestionably disappointing. The values of 74% and 55% for investments made in 1986-87 and 1987-88 respectively are very poor, and mean that many investors will almost certainly have lost money, notwithstanding the tax relief. The depreciation of the value of BES finance is not surprising given the failure rate of investments made under the scheme. There was a significant failure rate throughout the period, and according to figures from Harrison and Mason, investment was most unsuccessful in Wales and Northern Ireland.

The consequences of these statistics have been seen on the ground. In the summer of 1994, Johnson Fry gave their 12,000 investors a warning that their investments were only worth between 30% and 69% of the amount they invested in 1989.[11] The investments made with Johnson Fry were largely in property, under the assured tenancy scheme, permitted under the BES after 1988. These investments have, of course, been hit by the slump in the property market. It is very unlikely indeed that these investors will see all their money again. The irony is, of course, that investments in property were criticised for falling outside the 'high-risk' spirit of the scheme when they were made in the 1980s. The degree of underperformance of BES investments can be seen in figures published recently by BESt Investments. They report that out of the 1300 publicly-funded trading companies set up under the BES, fewer than 20% have returned any cash to their investors.[12] Alan Ruddock of the Sunday Times expresses this modest performance slightly differently, saying that research has shown that only 20% of BES-funded companies have survived.[13]

Table 5.9 BES Results from Guaranteed Schemes: Annual Tax-free Return per £1 Share

Companies	Maturity Date	Contracted Return per £1 Share
Homes for Tenants 1-10	March 1998	n/a
Homes for Tenants 11-12	December 1998	n/a
Tweed Premier 1-6	December 1998	122p
Lyonsdown Properties 1-2	June 1997	115p
Lyonsdown Properties 3-12	October 1997	120p
Executive Estates 1-6	March 1998	106p
Principal Portfolios 1-4	March 1998	105p
Shannon Residential 1-3	February 1998	107p

Note: Tax relief has not been taken into account. A typical higher rate taxpayer would have paid only 60p per pound invested because of tax relief. Most investors will have left the schemes this year but the schemes will continue to maturity.

Source: Adapted from *The Times*, 21 September 1996.

Quite naturally, some of the better returns were achieved by those investors which had joined guaranteed schemes - those schemes in which the return on investment was fixed at the outset. This was only possible, however, for certain types of assured tenancy scheme investments where the property had been pre-sold at a fixed price. It was possible, for example, for the student accommodation schemes. Figures were released recently by Johnson Fry which showed how these investments had fared. These are seen in table 5.9.

The Cost Effectiveness of the Business Expansion Scheme

The cost effectiveness of the benefits which, despite its drawbacks, the BES has still delivered also need to be assessed. The impact that schemes which allow tax relief have on the public finances is often overlooked. This tendency was especially negligent when the relief on offer under the BES was related to income tax, which meant that until 1988 some investors were receiving tax relief of up to 60%. The tax forgone on the scheme totalled well over £1 billion, not an inconsiderable amount. Again, this was an issue that the Peat Marwick report considered. They made the following calculation:

> Extrapolating the results from the companies surveyed, we estimate that one year following the investment of BES, approximately £100 million in turnover and over 4000 jobs were attributable to BES investment made in 1983-84. This represents, in those companies which received BES finance, additional output and employment that would not have existed in the absence of the BES ... the crude cost per job of additional employment attributable to BES investment in 1983-84, calculated by reference to the amount of estimated tax relief given to BES investors, is in the range of £8,000 to £13,000.[14]

This cost per additional job, which increased after the scheme became dominated by property ventures, was said by Mason et al to be 'higher than for other small firm schemes'.[15]

Conclusion: The Effectiveness of the BES as a State Venture Capital Policy

The fact that the BES was altered a number of times and then eventually abolished underlines the problems that were experienced with it. There was no shortage of funds raised under the scheme, but as has been demonstrated the scheme had a number of shortcomings. Firstly, too little of the money was raised for high-risk projects. No-one would have expected all of the finance raised under the scheme to have gone into high-risk ventures, but the amount that did in no way justified the taxation that was foregone. The post-1988 explosion in assured tenancy scheme investments brought the BES into disrepute. Secondly, despite the conservative nature of much of the investment made under the scheme (very few envisaged the collapse in the property market after 1989), BES funds were by no means all successful; many people have lost a lot of money through the BES. Yet perhaps the most important lesson of the BES, certainly as far as the aims of this study is concerned, was that it showed that a government not only cannot force investors to put their money into risky projects, but also can not necessarily depend on them responding to tax incentives either. The temptation in schemes like this is always going to be to find a proposal which has an excellent chance of at least retaining its value, thereby allowing the investor to make his/her profit from the tax relief.

In its defence, it is true to say that not all was lost. The vast amount of taxpayers' money was not completely lost, and some even went to its intended target - small high-risk businesses. The problem was that, as Mason et al comment, it was not a cost effective way to help the economy and a fairly disastrous way to bridge the equity gap. A further benefit of the BES is said to have been its contribution in 'waking up' the venture capital industry, at a time when it had a low profile. The exact contribution of the scheme in this respect is, of course, impossible to measure but there does seem some justification for the view. Even in the early 1980s venture capital was a backwater in the financial sector and very few institutions took it too seriously. The BES precipitated the involvement of a number of notable financial institutions, including the County Bank, Electra and Warburg, and increased its profile in general. Finally, the scheme, following on from the BSS, also introduced the individual investor to venture capital. There are now commentators arguing there is pool of informal venture capital in the UK amounting to £1 or £2 billion; venture capital investment is an option which is no longer considered to be an afterthought. There were, therefore, redeeming features to the BES, but these cannot, and indeed did not, obscure the simple fact that the BES was ineffective at the task it was set and its abolition was as necessary as it was inevitable.

Notes

1. BES Association, *BES Factsheet*, October 1993.
2. Peat Marwick, *Report on the Business Expansion Scheme*, London, Inland Revenue, 1986, p27.
3. *Ibid.*, p9.
4. Mason, C, Harrison, J and Harrison, R, *An Assessment of the Business Expansion Scheme*, London, Small Business Research Trust, 1988, Executive Summary.
5. *Ibid.*
6. Peat Marwick, *op.cit.*, p14.
7. Mason, Harrison and Harrison, *op.cit.*
8. *Ibid.*
9. Peat Marwick, *op.cit.*, p181.
10. *Ibid.*, p7.
11. MacErlean, N, 'BES firms seek market rescue', *The Observer*, 5 June 1994, pB2.
12. Gourlay, R, 'The shape of things to come', *Financial Times*, 18 January 1994, p12.
13. Ruddock, A, 'Shares' bull run pushes start-ups to sidelines', *The Sunday Times*, 6 February 1994, p3.9.
14. Peat Marwick, *op.cit.*, pp7-8.
15. Mason, Harrison and Harrison, *op.cit.*

6 Further Evidence on Government Policy to Bridge the Equity Gap

In this chapter the limited evidence that is available on the performance of the SDA/SE, the WDA, the BSS, the government sponsored BIS, the EIS and the VCT is presented as part of the overall assessment of the government policy approaches in this area. This information is a supplement to the more substantial evidence provided on the NEB, the BES, and the Government's policy towards the institutional venture capital industry. As this study is concerned with assessing the relative efficacy of alternative approaches to bridging the equity gap, the reader is reminded of the type of intervention each policy or institution represents prior to the presentation of the findings.

Scottish Development Agency / Scottish Enterprise

The venture capital role of the SDA, which has now been replaced by SE, is an example of direct state intervention. The agency has invested public sector venture capital directly in an attempt to solve the funding problems of Scottish business. In the 1980s and 1990s this finance was often provided as part of a syndicated investment along with private money. It was mentioned in the assessment of the NEB that, under a policy of direct state intervention, the amount of finance raised by the policy and the extent to which that finance is targeted at the equity gap, is in the hands of the policy makers, rather than the outcome of market operations. The amount of finance available to any public body is set out in the parliamentary legislation, whilst the investment ranges are usually established in the guidelines governing its overall operations. It is, therefore, not in terms of the amount of finance raised/invested, or in terms of the targeting of that finance, that a policy of direct state intervention should be judged. Instead, the success or failure of this type of policy has to be judged on the performance of the investments made: how effective the public bodies are in 'picking winners'.

Such information on the performance of the organisation responsible for economic development in Scotland, once the SDA, now SE, is presented in two parts. Firstly, the returns on capital employed are shown for the overall investment activity of the organisation when it functioned under the name of the SDA. This covers the period between 1977 and 1991 and includes non-equity investment and investment away from the range of the equity gap (more specific information is not available). The figures in table 6.1 are for the SDA's investment between 1977 to 1991 and have been compiled from information revealed in the organisation's annual reports.

Table 6.1 Scottish Development Agency Return on Capital Employed 1977 to 1991

Year	Return on Capital (%)*	Cumulative Returns (%) #	Year	Return on Capital (%)*	Cumulative Returns (%) #
1977	7.6	-	1985	3.9	4 year 3.4
1978	-3.3	-	1986	4.1	5 year 3.6
1979	-14.3	-	1987	1.7	5 year 3.3
1980	-0.8	-	1988	5.9	5 year 3.9
1981	-1.9	-	1989	-8.8	5 year 1.3
1982	2.8	-	1990	38.7	5 year 8.3
1983	2.8	-	1991	27.1	5 year 11.3
1984	3.8	3 year 3.2			

* SDA's headline figure.
# Cumulative percentage return for the said number of years to the relevant date
Note: These figures were no longer presented in the annual accounts after 1991 when the Scottish Development Agency became Scottish Enterprise.

Source: Adapted from *SDA Annual Report*, 1977-1991.

The second part of the evidence relates to the activities of Scottish Development Finance (SDF), which was established in the early 1980s when the development body was known as the SDA. SDF provides venture capital for new and growing companies, focusing on 'equity gap' investments below £500,000. It either invests as the sole venture capital provider, or acts as a catalyst to introduce other venture capital investors by playing a lead role in the due diligence process and by sharing the financial risk. Often it is the first round investor, funding companies to the stage where more significant amounts of venture capital can be raised, once commercial success has been achieved and where the risks are lower. SDF has operated profitably, and has successfully combined its economic development role with a commercial approach to investment.

Until 1996, SDF was funded entirely through SE, but last year it raised a £25 million limited partnership venture capital fund, the *Scottish Equity Partnership*. This involved £12.5 million from SE and £12.5 million from 15 corporate, financial, and high net worth individual investors. That initiative, which will represent SDF's main source of funding for the rest of the century, has been followed up by the establishment of a high risk seed capital fund, *The Scottish Technology Fund*, formed in collaboration with the 3i group. This fund is managed by SDF and focuses upon the commercialisation of Scotland's science and technology base. Finance is available to firms seeking less than £100,000. Evidence on the investment performance of SDF is available for the period 1991 to 1997. During that period 91 equity investments were made by SDF, with 28% of the finance being directed towards start-ups, 45% towards development capital investments, and 27% towards management buy-ins and buy-outs.

The IRR achieved by SDF for those investments has been estimated as 25%. This is a compound IRR, which gives a measure of discounted cash flow yield over the period, and has been stated gross of costs. The IRR has been built up using cash inflows and outflows, and the valuation of those companies in the portfolio at 31 March 1997, using the valuation guidelines provided by the BVCA. Furthermore, the IRR does not include any investments which were already in the SDF portfolio in 1991. This means, for example, that a £6.6 million profit realised on Spider Systems during the 1991-1997 period is not included.

During the period 1991-1997 there were a number of major successes which made a significant contribution to the IRR achieved by SDF. SDF was the lead backer of the 1996 BVCA/Financial Times Venturer of the Year winner, the previously mentioned Award plc, which produced for SDF an IRR of about 200% and a profit of £4.3 million within 3 years. Calluna plc, an electronics company, provided SDF with a profit of £3.3 million, with other higher achievers being the Core Group and Deep Sea Leisure. Since 1991, SE's investment activity has achieved leverage of £5 of external finance for every £1 it has invested itself. This is claimed by SE to be indicative of the confidence the private sector has in its operations.[1]

Welsh Development Agency

The venture capital role of the WDA, for the same reasons as given for the SDA, represents a policy of direct state intervention. Like the SDA, the WDA also made a lot of its investments in the 1980s and 1990s as part of investment syndicates. When judging the performance of the WDA's investment a number of factors need to be taken into account. The WDA was affected by the restrictions it was placed under: its requirement to dispose of profitable investments as soon as possible, the fact that it spent until 1987 acting as a lender of last resort, and the fact that it targeted its funds at high risk investments. Nevertheless, the annual rates for total investment were recorded in the annual reports and accounts, and are consequently reproduced in table 6.2. These rather poor figures are somewhat counter-balanced by considering the agency's casualty rate. In 1984 the agency reported that its casualties represented 5% of its total investment clients, a rate which compared favourably with private sector rates at that time.[2] A good deal of economic activity would appear to have been promoted.

Table 6.2 WDA Annual Rate of Return on Investment 1980 to 1990 (%)

1980-81	-4.7	1985-86	-12.7
1981-82	2.2	1986-87	-3.0
1982-83	9.1	1987-88	-12.1
1983-84	-13.4	1988-89	-21.9
1984-85	-4.1	1989-90	6.4

Source: Adapted from *WDA Annual Report*, 1980-1990.

The current activity of the WDA (discussed in chapter two) includes three new developments: the new joint public and private high technology fund; the proposed business angel network; and the working capital initiative. Despite investing at a relatively low level and seeing the activity as only one of their numerous development tools, the continued activity of the WDA in investing risk capital follows from their view, stated in 1995, that the Agency's 'small business venture capital, seed capital, and development loan activities compare very favourably, in terms of value for money, with alternative job creation techniques'.[3]

Business Start-up Scheme

Whilst considering the performance of the range of government equity finance initiatives it is worth re-stating the limited achievements of the BSS. The BSS was the first of the four policies of fiscal intervention which have been implemented since the election of the Conservatives in 1979. The BSS fits into this category as under the scheme investors were offered tax relief as an incentive to put money into particular types of companies. The scheme was very restrictive in its rules and only promoted the investment of £15 million in the two years of its operation. This compared against Government predictions of £100 million.[4] Furthermore, as the Electra Risk Capital fund showed (see chapter two), some of the impact of the limited funds raised was lost as they were invested in companies that went into liquidation. That the scheme would be abolished was rarely in doubt, and this task was undertaken in 1983.

Government Sponsored Business Introduction Services

The policy adopted by the Government in 1991 of sponsoring five BIS represents an example of non-financial intervention. The Government provided the operating bodies with a small amount of finance, £20,000 each per year for three years, but this was used exclusively to set up the services and was not distributed to either the participating small businesses or investors. The role of the services was merely to facilitate the coming together of businesses and investors and having done that, not least because of the 1986 Financial Services Act, retreat from the scene. The DTI recently commissioned Richard Harrison and Colin Mason to assess the impact and the cost effectiveness of this policy and in this section the main findings are presented. Harrison and Mason record that the overall objective of the policy was 'to test the proposition that Business Angel Networks [another name for Business Introduction Services] are a worthwhile way of enabling business angels to channel financial resources and hands-on expertise to small firms by removing the financial constraint which had handicapped matchmaking initiatives'.[5] This they argued could be measured according to three criteria: the policy's direct impact in terms of registrations and matches; the induced investment effects in terms of additional financial and non-financial investment; and the indirect effects. Clearly, despite the importance of the latter two criteria, it is by the policy's direct impact that it must be judged.

The first issue to be addressed was the number of registrations secured by the five BIS. At the time of the final review in March 1995, the services had collectively 264 investors on their books. As investors only stay on the register for about six months, mainly due to either disappointment or success at investing their funds, it is acceptable to consider the total number of investors registered over the period. The figure for this measure was just under 350. The capital available from the 264 investors on the books in March 1995 was £26 million.[6] From the other perspective it has been calculated that the five services have promoted almost 500 investment opportunities over the three years under study. At any one time there were between 20 and 30 under active consideration. The average investment opportunity was in a manufacturing company, in its early stages, seeking about £50,000 (£45,763 to be exact).[7]

Table 6.3 Current Client Base of the Government Sponsored BIS

	Current Investors	Estimated Amount Available	Current Businesses
Bedfordshire	35	£7m	23
Capital Connections	36	£4m	37
Devon and Cornwall	78	£5m	114
IRIS	45	£4.6m	15-20
TechInvest	70	£6m	20-25
Total	**264**	**£26.6**	**209-219**

Source: Adapted from R.Harrison and C.Mason, 'Developing the informal venture capital market', *Regional Studies*, Vol 30, No 8, 1996, p779.

Whilst the creation of a critical mass of investors and opportunities is a crucial element of a BIS's operation, it was important for the policy that a significant number of matches were achieved. The task of measuring these is complicated by a number of practical problems, not least the problem of retaining contact with the two parties after the introduction. In order to avoid problems under the 1986 Financial Services Act, the BIS withdraw after contact has been made, yet as negotiations can take several months contact can often be lost. This is made more likely by the fact that businesses are not always forthcoming if they are obliged to pay a success fee. Nevertheless, it has been recorded that in all 64 investments were facilitated by the five services; this involved the investment of £3.7 million (see table 6.4).[8] Harrison and Mason qualify this by admitting that four of the investments were made by institutional venture capital funds rather than business angels. As a result the figures have been amended to 60 investments and £2.7 million. In addition to this investment, there were also reports of offers of finance being rejected by businesses. Furthermore, it was found that the rate of investment increased in both the second and third years suggesting that it takes time for a BIS to become known and accepted in the local business community, but once it has been, the deal flow increases rapidly. This is a particularly important finding. Finally, it was noted that the overall rate of investment of the BIS compared well with comparable bodies, including the Midland Enterprise Fund.[9]

Table 6.4 Number of Investment Matches Facilitated by the Government Sponsored BIS

	Total Number of Investments	Amount Invested (£000)
Bedfordshire	4	205
Capital Connections	5	65
Devon and Cornwall	25	1,300
IRIS	11	333
TechInvest	19	1,793
Total	**64**	**3,696**

Source: Adapted from R.Harrison and C.Mason, 'Developing the informal venture capital market', *Regional Studies*, Vol 30, No 8, 1996, p780.

A number of the 'induced investment effects' are also recorded. These include a leverage effect, which in the case of TEChINVEST meant that for every £1 invested through the service £2 was raised for the business elsewhere. There was also evidence of follow-on investment, with many angels providing second-round finance. Businesses also benefited from contact with investors at investor clubs and venture capital seminars, and finally, there was the valuable hands-on involvement which was often available from the business angel. Angels offered assistance including financial and marketing expertise, as well as general management advice.[10] Harrison and Mason also argue that the five BIS have contributed to a growing, and much needed 'equity culture' in the local business communities. Furthermore, they contend that some credit can be claimed by the Government for the doubling of the number of BIS in the UK since 1993.[11]

A further important criterion for a government policy is its cost-effectiveness. The five BIS performed well in this respect with the cost per job to the taxpayer being only about £1,000 to £1,500. The degree of additionality was also impressive; nearly all of the investment would not have been made in the absence of the services. Finally, there was a low displacement effect as it was predicted that little of the finance would have been used for equivalent purposes.[12] Despite the growth in the number of BIS in the UK over the past few years, Harrison and Mason argued that the evidence still supported the view that public sector involvement was crucial. Firstly, there were still doubts over the ability of services to be self-financing in the long-term. Secondly, a number of the private sector services were favouring certain types of investment, leaving a number of gaps. Finally, there were many areas in the UK that were inadequately served in this respect; Yorkshire and Humberside was an example of this.[13]

Whilst recognising that this evidence only comes from two academics and that it was a survey commissioned by and written for the DTI, the evidence suggests that this policy has been quite successful in terms of its ability to raise finance and in its applicability to the equity gap (it is as yet too early to assess the performance of investments made through the services). Furthermore, the evidence suggests that the services take time to become established in the local business community, but once accepted significantly increase their activity. For this reason, this type of policy would appear to have a good chance of being effective and cost-effective in the medium to long-term. It must be remembered that what was achieved was done with only a very small amount of central government funding; further evidence is needed, however, to assess the extent of this effectiveness. It is also worth noting that there was a great difference in the performance of the five services, particularly in terms of the number of matches promoted. Any extension of this type of policy in the future should take this fact into consideration.

A note must also be made of the evidence concerning the ability of business angels to achieve a return on their investment. This evidence, revealed in a study of informal investment in general, suggests that many angels will not see a large return on their investment, and indeed a large number lost money. For this type of investment to be influential in the long-term, this record will have to be improved upon. Nevertheless, Harrison and Mason would appear to have some justification for their upbeat conclusion: 'Overall, based on the direct and indirect impacts of the initiatives, the informal investment demonstration projects can be considered to have been very successful in terms of the mobilisation of a significant pool of investment capital, stimulating demand for equity finance from SME that might otherwise have remained latent, and facilitating a significant level of informal venture capital activity relative to other SME equity finance initiatives.'[14]

Enterprise Investment Scheme

The EIS is a direct replacement for the BES and is, thus, a policy of fiscal intervention. This is because the state is seeking to influence private sector investment through the use of fiscal incentives. The EIS (along with the VCT) is the third attempt to encourage investors to invest in small business in this way, and as such may well represent the last chance for schemes of this nature to be taken seriously as a policy to bridge the equity gap. When judging this policy, it has to be kept in mind that it has only been running since 1994; the performance of the scheme may well change over the coming years. The experience of the BSS and BES, however, suggest that early problems are not easily rectified.

The Inland Revenue announced in March 1996 that £42 million had been raised by about 400 companies under the EIS since its inception. This figure is considered to be substantially less than the Government expected when it announced its formation in the November 1993 Budget and even this low figure does not accurately represent the impact the scheme is having on the equity gap. According to leading authorities on the EIS, about half of this finance has been raised through public offers. Much of this finance has been used for property development projects like Johnson Fry's 'Pathfinder' scheme, which raised about £3 million. As far as small business is concerned only about £20 million has been raised.

There are a number of reasons for the low amount of investment raised under the scheme. Firstly, the scheme is extremely complicated. Many involved with the scheme have complained to the Inland Revenue that the sheer weight of the rulebook is putting off many of its intended targets. Small business people are put off by this complexity, and this situation is made worse by the fact that accountants are largely ignoring the scheme as well; it was hoped that they would point their business clients in the direction of the scheme. Accountants have claimed that it is not economic for them to stay up-to-date with the scheme when it may only be applicable to one or two of their clients. It has also been suggested that the complexity of the scheme will lead to some firms finding their project being rejected by the Inland Revenue when they believed they were well within the rules.[15] Secondly, the EIS is suffering from living under the shadow of the BES. Many people who invested under the BES had bad experiences and either lost money or found that they could not realise their investment at the desired time. Thirdly, and most important, is the fact that the tax relief on offer under the EIS is considerably less than that which was offered under the BES. The up-front tax relief of 20%, many believe, is not enough to compensate for the risks that are involved in the kind of investments that it seems will have to be made under the scheme; no loopholes have been found (yet) of the kind that were discovered during the tenure of the BES. Supporters of the EIS point to the loss relief that is available at 40%, but Barry Anysz of Capital for Companies, which was set up to run BES funds, said: 'The main problem is the lack of tax relief up front. It's not the best marketing message to say that if you lose your money you can get tax relief on the losses.'[16]

Despite the modest beginning of the EIS, there is a chance that, although the overall totals of finance raised under the scheme will be appreciably lower than those raised under the BES, a greater proportion of the funds raised under the scheme will be in genuine high-risk trading companies. This has been born out to some extent by the Inland Revenue's announcement in March 1996 that the average investment under the EIS, excluding the aforementioned public offers, has been £75,000, well within the range of the equity gap. As Richard Gourlay commented in 1994: 'At the very least, genuine trading companies are less likely to see their proposals swept aside by artificial financial products, such as the assured property schemes that so discredited the BES.'[17] As far as the study's third criteria is concerned, it is, as yet, too early to tell to what extent the investments made under the scheme will be profitable.

At the moment, many involved in the area of SME finance believe that the most positive aspect of the EIS is the fact that it shows that the Government is at least aware of the sector's problems in acquiring equity. In particular, the Government apparently listened to the views of the experts and enabled investors to become directors in the companies they financed, a situation which makes many feel more comfortable about risking their money in a small or early-stage company; it was not permitted under the BES.

In conclusion, the Inland Revenue has let it be known that it is satisfied with the early performance of the EIS. Others, however, take different view. One leading expert on the EIS commented that the scheme had, in fact, been something of a "damp squib". Indeed, because of the reduced attraction of the EIS as a tax shelter, the scheme is unlikely to raise funds at anywhere near the level of BES. The question is, can it raise funds at a level which makes it have a significant impact on the equity gap - at present the answer to this question is still unknown, although the early signs are not greatly promising. The rules should ensure, however, that some of the finance is raised for the intended type of high-risk company, even if the property development schemes announced in the first two years are an ominous reminder of the BES.

Venture Capital Trusts

The scheme facilitating the creation of VCT is also a policy of fiscal intervention as it again involves the offer of tax relief to encourage specific types of investment. The difference between the two schemes is merely that with the VCT the investor puts his money into a trust which is invested by a trust manager in qualifying companies.

Table 6.5 Venture Capital Trusts Launched in 1996

Trust Name	Minimum-Maximum Fund	Maximum Investment in Company
Advent	£7.5m - £25m	£1.0m
British Smaller Companies	£5m - £15m	£1.0m
Capital for Companies	£4m - £10m	£1.0m
Close Brothers	£10m - £30m	£1.0m
Gartmore	Max £20m	£1.0m
Hodgson Martin	£5m - £13m	£1.0m
Johnson Fry	£5m - £20m	£1.0m
Pennine AIM	£3m - £8m	£0.3m
Quester	£6m - £15m	£1.0m

Source: Adapted from C. Watts, 'Putting the bite on venture capital trusts', *Small Company Investor*, March 1996, p25.

When the Government launched the scheme the Chancellor of the Exchequer, Kenneth Clarke, set a target for the VCT of raising £2.5 billion in the first five years.[18] This target was a stiff one and the scheme in the first two years showed no signs of raising anywhere near that amount. In 1995 only three trusts were launched, raising a total amount of only £41 million. In 1996 nine more trusts have been launched and if these are fully subscribed a further £156 million will have been raised.[19] While the policy struggles to match up to expectations in terms of capital raised, the VCT may also perform poorly in its targeting of capital at the equity gap. It is still believed that most of the finance invested under the VCT will be targeted at investments close to the £1 million limit and that this is some way above what is believed to be the range of the equity gap. It is expected that start-up and early-stage companies will do particularly badly under the scheme. One expert in this field argued that the tax free status for dividends under the scheme would mean that the trusts would invest in later-stage companies, on the basis that that type of company would more likely to deliver immediate dividends; earlier stage companies would be squeezed out. Furthermore, it is expected that funds raised under the VCT will become part of syndicated investments which may be in total £3 million or £4 million - a development which would cast doubt on the scheme's additionality. As with its sister policy, the EIS, many doubts remain over the scheme's effectiveness as a policy to help bridge the equity gap.

Notes

[1] Internal Scottish Enterprise information.
[2] Welsh Development Agency, *Annual Report and Accounts 1983-84*, p15.
[3] Lonsdale, C, 'Reassessing the role of government in bridging the equity gap', *UK Venture Capital Journal*, November/December 1995, p19.
[4] Lorenz, T, *Venture Capital Today*, Cambridge, Woodhead-Faulkner, 1985, p16.
[5] Harrison, R and Mason, C, 'Developing the Informal Venture Capital Market: A Review of the Department of Trade and Industry's Informal Investment Demonstration Projects', *Regional Studies*, Vol 30, No 8, 1996, p778.
[6] *Ibid.*
[7] *Ibid.*, pp779-780.
[8] *Ibid.*, p779.
[9] *Ibid.*, p780.

[10] *Ibid.*, p781.
[11] *Ibid.*
[12] *Ibid.*, p782.
[13] *Ibid.*
[14] *Ibid.*, pp781-782.
[15] MacErlean, N, 'EIS plans face a tax minefield', *The Observer*, 16 January 1994, pB10.
[16] MacErlean, N, 'Unhappy birthday for son of BES', *The Observer*, 8 May 1994, pB12.
[17] Gourlay, R, 'A second chance', *Financial Times*, 2 August 1994, p9.
[18] *Financial Times*, 'VCTs wait for flood', 16 January 1996, p12.
[19] Watts, C, 'Putting the bite on venture capital trusts', *Small Business Investor*, March 1996, p23.

PART III

CONCLUSION

7 Conclusion

This chapter concludes the study by fulfilling two objectives. Firstly, the relative effectiveness of the alternative approaches to bridging the equity gap are analysed. This reveals that while none of the individual policies has made a significant impact on the equity gap, certain policy approaches, if properly implemented, have a greater potential to do so. Secondly, and in the light of this analysis, recommendations are made for a government policy to assist in bridging the gap. It is argued that government should pursue a policy agenda which develops the current adherence to direct state intervention, fiscal intervention, and non-financial intervention. In the case of fiscal intervention, there is a need for a scheme which, while restricting investment to specific areas of the economy, is more attractive to investors in terms of tax-relief and less complicated to participate in. In the cases of direct state intervention and non-financial intervention, there is a need for a controlled expansion of their use.

The Existence of an Equity Gap for Small Business in the UK

It is impossible to prove conclusively that an equity gap exists in the UK, or anywhere else for that matter. In the case of any unfunded company, it is not possible to know for certain what growth would or would not have occurred should finance have been available. In most cases, of course, the directors of such companies argue that a huge opportunity for growth has been lost. Many surveys have investigated the issue but they are never likely to settle the argument; indeed, the results of many of these surveys are influenced by the nature of the questions asked, which in turn are often influenced by the pre-conceived views of the survey's author. A survey of small businesses in Birmingham was, in fact, undertaken by this author in early 1994. It was found that 31.7% of the directors questioned felt that an inability to acquire finance affected their business adversely. A much larger number, 56.2%, felt there was a problem in general, even if it did not affect their company personally. The figures also showed that the problem was more serious for the smallest category of companies in the survey - those employing between 5 and 20 people. The finance problem was also benchmarked against other business problems. This approach revealed that while acquiring finance was substantially less of a problem than difficulties encountered in recovering payment from debtors, it was only slightly less serious than problems with skills shortages - a much celebrated issue in the political arena - and was deemed to be an equally serious problem as the difficulties encountered with government bureaucracy - again, a prominent political issue.

The Relative Effectiveness of Alternative Government Policy Approaches to the Equity Gap

From the evidence presented in this study, it is possible to make a number of judgements about the relative effectiveness of alternative government approaches attempted over the past twenty years. These will be made by using the three criteria adopted in this study: effectiveness in raising finance; effectiveness in targeting that finance; and the financial performance of the investments made/promoted.

Raising finance

The findings of this study reveal that the raising of finance is not the main problem for the four policy approaches, although it must be commented that it is too early to be certain in the case of non-financial intervention. In the case of *direct state intervention* the outcome in this respect is political. For this type of policy it is a merely a question of the amount of finance *provided for* the policy rather than the amount raised. In the case of the NEB, the initial allocation was £700 million, with further provision made in January 1979. In both cases these provisions were made through the passing of an Industry Act. The same was the case for the WDA and the SDA. SE, the organisation which replaced the SDA, has been active in 1996 in raising a joint public-private fund, but the public element of that finance is still provided from the public purse. In terms of the potential of this policy approach in the future, there is no doubt that an increased political will to use the state to finance small firms would lead to an increase in resources.

With the other three policy approaches the level of finance raised is primarily determined by the market. In the case of the institutional venture capital industry, which the government has allowed to function without interference (*laissez-faire*), its development has been dramatic. In 1979 the industry only invested about £20 million; this has risen in the 1990s to an annual figure of about £2 billion, a figure which makes it a recognisable player in the financial sector. It has also been shown in this study that a policy of *fiscal intervention* can raise a significant amount of finance. Over the ten years of its operation, the BES promoted over £4 billion of investment, a significant amount of finance to be raised from private investors who have a myriad of other investment options before them. Evidence is also emerging that BIS, a product of a policy of *non-financial intervention*, can also be effective at raising finance. The client bases built up by the five government-sponsored BIS suggests that there is a possibility for the services to establish themselves within their local business community as a major source of finance.

Targeting finance at the equity gap

With the second of the three performance criteria, the effectiveness of policy in targeting finance at the equity gap, a major factor in the failure of government policy is identified. Most of the policies featured in this study have performed poorly in this respect. The reasons for the failure, however, are different in each case, a fact which holds significance for the prospects of their functioning successfully in the future. With *direct state intervention* again the outcome is determined by the policy-maker. This can be illustrated once more in the case of the NEB, although the same has been true of the WDA and the SDA. The NEB invested well over £2 billion during its ten years of active life, yet only £300 million was directed at new investments, the vast majority having been used to finance the transferred holdings from the Department of Industry. Furthermore, only about £30 million of this reduced figure could be described as having been invested in companies which were suffering from the existence of an equity gap. This targeting of resources, which largely took place during the Labour years, reflected the industrial policy goals of the Labour Government. The Government was primarily concerned to prop up a number of very large employers, rather than look to promote promising small firms; there was no convincing policy plan in this respect. The key problem, therefore, as far as the NEB bridging the equity gap was concerned, was the fact that its objectives were wide-reaching. This was also the case with the WDA and the SDA. These two bodies had responsibility for all of industry in their regions, not just those companies suffering from the existence of an equity gap. This does not have to be so with policies of direct state intervention, however, and, ironically, the Conservative policy of reducing the operations of the NEB after 1979 had the effect of reshaping the organisation into a form which was actually what a state institution to bridge the equity gap should look like. The post-1979 NEB primarily concerned itself with start-ups and small firms in high-risk and often high-technology areas. This form was only a staging-post in a gradual wind down of the NEB, yet it demonstrates that government can make the state institutions invest in any way it wishes; the policy-makers are not relying on the acquiescence of the market. It also shows that it is difficult for the small firm role to flourish if it has to share an institution's attention with other roles.

In the case of policies of *fiscal intervention,* the targeting of finance is largely determined by the rules of the particular policy concerned. Investors will, in general, look for investments that promise the lowest level of risk whilst still remaining within the rules. Consequently, it is important that the qualifying rules of a scheme restrict investment to within its objectives; something the BES so obviously failed to do. The first five years of the BES were characterised by endless unsuccessful attempts at closing loopholes; the second five years were simply the result of the Government giving up on this task. It was never truly in control of the BES at any stage of its ten year life, but in the period after the 1988 decision to permit investments under the assured tenancy scheme, any ability the scheme may have possessed to have an impact on the equity gap was completely lost. Between 1988 and 1993 between most of the overall finance raised under the scheme went to assured tenancy deals. This was clearly and inevitably to the detriment of small, high-risk businesses, whose ventures the scheme had been created to finance.

Yet, as was seen in the case of direct state intervention, there are a number of ways a policy of fiscal intervention can be operated; the EIS has demonstrated this. The rules on which it is based are more specific than was the case with the BES, especially in its latter form and this has resulted in an absence of the more extreme features from which the BES suffered. The absence of this problem, however, has been replaced by a new problem: the changing of the qualifying rules has simply led to a low amount of finance being raised, only £42 million in the first two years of the scheme. The squeeze on the funds raised by the EIS has also been caused by a reduction in the up-front tax relief on offer from 40% to 20%. The Government has still not demonstrated that it is capable of creating a scheme which balances the raising of a substantial amount of equity finance with the need for it to be targeted at the equity gap. In theoretical terms the possibility does exist, as will be discussed later.

As far as policies of *non-financial intervention* are concerned, insufficient data is available to comment on its performance in this respect. The early evidence, however, compiled by Mason and Harrison suggests that the investments promoted by BIS will be very much within the range of the equity gap. The average investment for the five BIS they studied was about £60,000, very much a problem area for small firms. The final method of government intervention to assess in this respect is *laissez-faire*, the approach the Government has adopted towards the institutional venture capital industry since its election in 1979. There can be no doubt that the industry has, since 1979, failed to target a significant amount of finance towards the equity gap. Furthermore, with a policy of laissez-faire necessarily involving government having no influence over the actions of economic players, the trend away from investing in the range of the equity gap, which still continues, is unlikely to be significantly reversed in the near future, if ever. The industry turned its back on small and early-stage investments very early in its development, mainly because such investments were considered to be high-risk. The industry soon came to the realisation that it was easier and safer to invest in later-stage businesses and that the returns they could make on such investments were acceptable to their own masters.

In 1994 the proportion of finance the industry allocated towards start-up and early stage investments - often within the financial range of the equity gap - fell to 5%, a reduction from 27% in 1984. In absolute terms (taking into account inflation) the amount of finance channelled to start-up and early stage businesses between 1984 and 1994 barely increased, whereas the amount of finance invested by the industry as a whole multiplied by more than ten-fold. Consequently, it would seem that as far as bridging the equity gap is concerned, laissez-faire policies are inappropriate. Quite simply, the problem of the equity gap comes about due to the perceived unattractiveness of small firms by financiers operating in a free market. Investment decision-makers (usually) act rationally, and only after a thorough analysis of the potential of a particular investment. The outcome of a policy of laissez-faire was only ever going to reflect the incentives in the market which were widely believed to favour larger and later-stage firms. Indeed, it is surprising that anyone imagined that any other outcome was possible, except perhaps in the short-term when the industry was maturing and settling into its patterns of preference and expectations.

In summary, it can be seen that the NEB, the BES, and the institutional venture capital industry all performed poorly in this respect. However, the different reasons for the relative failure indicate there is a difference in the prospects of the *policy approaches* they represent performing better in the future; indeed there is already evidence of more recent attempts at direct state intervention and fiscal intervention having an improved level of success. With the EIS it will remain to be seen whether the more stringent qualifying rules will still allow it to remain a significant policy instrument; the initial evidence is not promising. With direct state intervention it has been seen with the recent SE investment activity that it is within the powers of government to make bodies invest within the range of the equity gap; it is merely a question of political priorities. The non-financial intervention policy of the BIS also gives grounds for optimism in this respect. It would appear, from the limited evidence available, that equity gap investments are the natural type these bodies promote. The least promising policy stance is that of laissez-faire. Leaving the market to operate freely would not appear to be an approach which suits this particular economic problem, simply because it is a problem *caused* by the free operation of markets.

Performance of investments

The performance of the investments made or promoted under each of the approaches is important for a number of reasons. Firstly, it is important for the success of the economy that small firms thrive. Secondly, it is important for investors to make a return on their investment. If they do, there is a good chance they will continue to invest; if they do not then they will be discouraged from doing so. Thirdly, it is important for the policy itself. If a policy is unsuccessful in making or promoting profitable investments, then its impact is undermined. The aim of a policy to bridge the equity gap is to facilitate an expansion of small firms which would otherwise not have taken place. If a majority of the investments made under a policy fail, then it will not have succeeded in this. This situation, if it should be perpetuated, would result in the policy approach becoming seriously discredited. The performance of investments promoted under the various policy approaches in the study has been mixed, with none of them achieving unqualified success.

In judging the performance of *direct state intervention,* evidence from two institutions can be utilised (not sufficient being known about the specific small venture capital investment record of the WDA). Firstly, a good deal of evidence is available on the record of the NEB. Its profit record was mixed to say the least, but that fact does at least refute the accusation of the right that the policy was an ignominious failure. Amongst the investments the Board made under £200,000, there were many failures. Only 9 out of the 41 investments *recorded* at this level were realised at a profit, and a number of these were only marginally profitable with a very low IRR. A few were more successful, and the jewel in the crown was the investment in Aqualisa Products Ltd, which made the NEB £5.3 million. So large was the profit on this investment that it balanced all the *recorded* losses on other investments under £200,000. It may be argued that a high-risk venture capital fund is all about high returns and high levels of failure and, indeed, this may be true. The 80% failure rate of the NEB, however, was too high and it would be foolish not to attempt to understand why the rate was so high; about 50% would have been more acceptable. Part of the reason was certainly the economic climate that was present at the time when the Board undertook a large number of its investments. The early 1980s recession was horrendous, especially for vulnerable early-stage firms, and this was undoubtedly a significant factor in the high failure rate. There is also evidence that the Board was under political pressure to invest, especially in parts of the country where there was high unemployment. As a consequence, some investments were made in small firms which, surely not just in retrospect, had poor prospects for profitability. It may also be the case that if a state body invests as part of a syndicate with private sector investors it attracts a higher standard of company. It was known with the NEB that many companies were unwilling to become involved with it as they feared being involved with a 'socialist' institution, and also did not wish to be labelled as a 'lame duck'. In short, the Board had an image problem.

The validity of these factors can to some extent be tested by looking at the further example of SE. SE have pursued a policy whereby they are not seen as a 'political' organisation, something emphasised by the manner in which they mix their finance with that of their private sector co-investors. They would also appear to have a stricter commercial discipline than was the case with the NEB, enforced in part by heavy private sector involvement. Partly as a result of these two factors, SE have been very successful in their investment since 1991. Their IRR of 25% is about twice that achieved, on average, by the private sector, and demonstrates that there is nothing about the public sector which *necessarily* means that it cannot invest successfully -

as many on the right of the political spectrum have always maintained. SE's example would suggest there is justification in a government pursuing this type of policy as a way of alleviating the problem of the equity gap, as there would appear to be no reason why the success achieved in Scotland should not be replicated throughout the whole of the UK. Indeed, funds like that of SE, particularly when they act as the lead investor of a syndicate, are exactly what is required in the UK. Furthermore, with their new fund, SE have also demonstrated their ability to raise large amounts of finance on the basis that they are a successful investor upon which financial and governmental institutions can rely. The £25 million fund raised in 1996 is a significant development in the realm of state venture capital in the UK, and indeed in that of UK venture capital in general. The example of SE shows that the public sector can invest successfully and that this role of government is not a relic of the 1970s.

Many who argue that the public sector has no role to play in providing venture capital are those who believe that only private sector financiers, operating free from interference by government, can be successful investors. Yet from the recent BVCA performance surveys, it can be seen that private sector venture capitalists are struggling to make returns from start-up and early stage investments - often those in the range of the equity gap. Despite the 1995 results being an improvement on the first results compiled a year before, the rate of return on start-up and early-stage investments was only 4.3%. The return on development capital was also poor at 6.9%, and this despite the fact that the definition of development capital used by the BVCA included all investments in expansion, development, and MBO capital under £2 million. Such a definition would include many relatively mature businesses which one would expect investors to profit highly from. It is clear, therefore, that the returns to the private sector in this respect have been very modest. It is also the case that the modest returns achieved in this section of the market (everybody knew they were poor long before the BVCA's official confirmation) have been a major factor in causing the low levels of finance targeted at the gap, commented upon in the previous section.

The important, not to say contentious, question that arises is whether this indicates a poor investment performance on the part of the industry, or instead reflects the quality of small firms in the UK, or those at least which pursue the avenue of equity capital. One would have to say, given the details of SE's investment, that not all the blame for the poor IRR of the industry can be blamed on the quality of small firms in the UK. The disparity in the performance of private sector venture capitalists also suggests this. A number of private sector operators have done well from this type of investment, but not enough, with the worst quarter of the funds in the BVCA survey achieving -2.3% and -4.8% on their investment in start-up and development capital investments respectively; not an impressive return. The free operation of market forces in this area of the economy has not delivered the results many in the Conservative Government of 1979 expected.

The level of investor satisfaction with the performance of investments made under policies of *fiscal intervention* to some extent depends on the level of tax relief offered. If, say, the investor is receiving 60% tax relief on the money invested in a small firm, he/she can afford to be relatively sanguine about the firm not making huge profits. Even if the investor only receives back the original stake, he/she will probably not have achieved too bad a rate of return. Where tax relief is lower, the investor will depend much more on the performance of the firm. When judging the performance of a policy, however, such notions have to be put to one side; fiscal intervention schemes have to be judged on their ability to promote profitable investments. The performance of investments made under the BES was disappointing for there was not a single year in which BES investments retained their original value. This has led many BES fund managers to warn their clients that they will not get back all of their capital. The irony is that much of the reason for the poor performance of BES investment is the fact that investors took the 'safe' option of investing in property. Unfortunately, it is too early to tell whether this poor performance was the result of the specific nature of the BES or whether it is likely to be a feature of all policies of fiscal intervention. The EIS and the VCT have only been in operation since 1994 and so investments are still in the early stages of their cycle.

Whilst it must be stated again that the evidence on BIS is limited, what is available is worth commenting upon. The information presented by Harrison and Mason shows that *from their sample* no investor has made any significant amount of money. Indeed, on the contrary, the evidence suggests that a large proportion of them have lost a substantial amount of their original stake. They hope that a factor in this is inexperience, which in the long-term will be replaced by better judgement. It is to be hoped this is true as the performance of BIS in this respect overshadows the potential the services appeared to show in terms of targeting finance. BIS seemed to be the ideal, low transaction cost approach to investment in this area, which was developing a growing presence in the UK; time will tell.

The findings on this criteria support two conclusions. Firstly, venture capitalists often comment that it is more difficult to pick winners amongst early-stage firms than it is to pick them amongst firms which are more mature. Early-stage companies are often quite unstable and although they may give a promising appearance, it is very difficult to be sure that they will fulfil that promise, with any number of factors being able to affect their development adversely. It may be that their product develops technical problems, that the market turns out to be smaller than expected, or that a number of competitors emerge. Alternatively, it may be that management makes a number of serious mistakes, from which the company cannot recover. This is not to say that it is not possible to make money from such investments, as a section of the institutional venture capital industry and SE has shown, but there is no doubt the challenge is greater.

Whilst this first point is essentially practical, the second is more political. The evidence shows that problems over picking winners is by no means confined to public sector actors; the problem also affects those in the private sector who are trying to make similar investments. This is largely because of the practical problems outlined above, yet it contradicts the free market assessment which claimed that the NEB's failures were a function of its public sector status. Indeed, the performance of SE and that of many institutional venture capital funds turns the free market contention on its head. Clearly, if a method is to be found which can promote consistently profitable small and early-stage equity investments, a more sophisticated approach must inform the policy than simplistic free market ideas. The laissez-faire policy the Government has pursued in relation to the institutional venture capital industry could scarcely have had a better chance to prove its worth than has been the case over the past 15 years or so, yet it has failed to do so.

Summary of findings

Whilst it can be recognised that none of the policies highlighted in this study has provided a solution to the problem of the equity gap, there have been features which encourage a belief that the state can yet make a significant impact. This has been particularly so due to the success of SE's investment in the 1990s and the emergence of a network of BIS. For the state to be able to make such a contribution, though, it is necessary to throw aside political pre-occupations, whether they be a hostility towards public sector venture capital or a resistance to giving private investors tax relief. The final task of this study, therefore, is to develop a revised policy programme for the bridging of the equity gap in the future.

Recommendations for Future State Policy to Bridge the Equity Gap

The failure of government policy since 1945 has often been more to do with the poor design of policies than an ignorance of the way in which the state can facilitate investment in small firms; the BES is a prime example. Indeed, the recommendations made in this section are far from radical as they look to build on the successful elements of the policy approaches which have been tried over the past twenty years or so. The recommendations include the redesigning of the current policies of fiscal intervention, and the expansion of the current policies of non-financial intervention and direct state intervention. There is also a call for the abandonment of the laissez-faire policy towards the institutional venture capital industry. Although not discussed in detail in this section, mainly because it already exists, it is also necessary to note how important the success of the AIM is, as a means of enabling investors to exit their investment.

Before this section proceeds two statements must be made. Firstly, that the private market will continue to provide for most of the financing needs of the small business sector is not questioned in this section. Any other interpretation of these recommendations would be mistaken; the policies are for the bridging of a perceived specific gap which is being left by the private sector. Secondly, it must also be said that no government measure in this area can be a substitute for a consistently successful macro-economic policy. It is the argument of this study that the recommendations made will alleviate the problem of the equity gap, but this argument is based upon the assumption that the UK will continue to enjoy, if that is the right word, the rate of growth it has experienced for most of the post-war period, that is, about 2.3% per annum. It has been argued in this study that a successful macro-economic policy (not that 2.3% represents notable success) is a *necessary* but not *sufficient* factor in bridging the equity gap. The fact that it is not sufficient, illustrated by the fortunes of the institutional venture capital industry in the second half of the 1980s, brings forward the need for specific micro-economic policies.

Fiscal intervention - fourth time lucky ?

The first recommendation is for the reform of the policies of fiscal intervention currently operating. It has been conclusively demonstrated (and it is, anyway, widely understood) that the BES had little impact on the equity gap. This was not, however, necessarily caused by the principle behind the scheme: the offering of tax relief for chosen types of investment. The main reason for its failure was the framing of the qualifying rules, which did not encourage investors to put their capital into small high-risk ventures, and indeed after 1988 they did precisely the opposite (or so it was thought at the time). The two new schemes, the EIS and the VCT, have gone some way towards addressing the errors of the past, yet their early performances do not suggest that they will end the search for a policy which promotes a high level of investment finance predominantly targeted at the equity gap. The following two reforms could achieve such an ambition.

Table 7.1 Alternative Fiscal Intervention Schemes and their Effects

Rules of the Scheme	Tax Relief on Offer	Result of the Scheme
1. Tightly defined rules. Investment raised aimed at the equity gap.	Low tax relief. i.e. Ineffective in changing an investor's view of the risk-reward ratio.	Very low amount of finance raised under the scheme. Where finance is invested the project will often be of a low risk nature. As low risk as the rules permit.
2. Loosely defined rules. Investment raised has no preferred area. Equity gap considered but not focused upon.	High tax relief. i.e. Effective at changing an investor's view of the risk-reward ratio.	A high amount of finance raised, but very little of it targeted at the equity gap. Much exploitation of the scheme as a tax shelter.
3. Tightly defined rules. Investment raised aimed at the equity gap.	High tax relief. i.e. Effective at changing an investor's view of the risk-reward ratio.	A moderate amount of finance raised, but highly targeted at the equity gap.

Balancing the incentives and restrictions

The starting point for a policy of fiscal intervention is a clear understanding of the specific problem that it is being created to address, in this case the bridging of an equity gap. In this study it has been argued that a gap exists for start-up and early-stage investments and for investments of up to £400,000. The rules, therefore, should be tailored to target that requirement. The lessons of the BES and the early signs of the EIS provide a guide to the correct approach. The BES demonstrated that if the rules are not tight, then finance will go in all directions except to investments that are relevant to the equity gap. The EIS, on the other hand, has shown in the first three years of operation that the up-front tax relief of 20% is insufficient to entice many into the scheme at all.

The scheme proposed here tries to avoid these situations since what is, in fact, required is a combination of high tax-relief and tight rules. The tax-relief needs to be high because investments in the range of the equity gap normally involve a higher than average risk. The relief must change the investor's perception of the risks involved. At the same time the rules must be very tightly framed to ensure that the finance raised is targeted towards the gap, and that the scheme is not hi-jacked by opportunists. Table 7.1 shows the consequences of three different versions of fiscal intervention. The first row illustrates what is happening with the EIS (and will happen with any other similarly framed policy); the second row illustrates what happened with the BES (and will happen with any other similarly framed policy). The final row is a prediction of what would be achieved by the version of fiscal intervention suggested in this section.

- *Tightly defined rules / low tax relief*

Under this version of the rules there is no significant impact on the gap because the tax relief is too low for the risk/reward profile to be substantially tilted in the investor's favour. This is particularly so because the tightly-framed qualifying rules only allow relatively high-risk investments to be made. It has to be borne in mind that the individual investor has a range of investment options before him, many with favourable tax treatment; the scheme is competing for investor attention. Furthermore, the finance raised is likely to be invested in the lowest-risk ventures permissible under the rules;

few would be willing to take substantial risks. Overall, a scheme framed this way is unlikely to fulfil its objectives.

- *Loosely defined rules / high tax relief*

Here the scheme has very loose rules, at least as far as targeting the equity gap is concerned. As a result, the problem is not that the scheme does not raise acceptable levels of finance; indeed, as the tax relief is generous it raises a great deal. It is instead that, as the restrictions on investment are so loose, very little of it goes towards bridging the equity gap. If the rules are as loose as they were under the BES after 1988, three things will happen. Firstly, a certain area will tend to be targeted, particularly by the institutions running funds. They will be the areas in which the investors or the investment managers believe there is the least risk; in the case of the BES it was rented property. The impact on the gap, therefore, will be minimal. This is exacerbated by a second point. It may be thought that in amongst all the finance raised under the scheme, a large amount because of the rules and the generous tax relief, some must, almost by the law of averages, be directed towards the equity gap. Many would argue that the general buoyancy of the scheme would lead to all round benefits. This is not what happens in practice, however, as the allowance of low-risk investments crowds out higher-risk investments (higher-risk investments being defined as non-asset backed small and early-stage companies). Thirdly, even if the amount of high risk finance did increase in proportion with the increase of overall investment raised under the scheme, it would still be indefensible in terms of cost-efficiency. The majority of tax relief would still be subsidising low-risk investments, investments which may well have been made in the absence of the scheme. The only defence for a scheme with these rules would be if a government decided that it was to fulfil a different policy goal. In the case of the BES this is effectively what happened, with the scheme becoming a way of reviving the rented property market. That does not alter the fact that the scheme has little impact on the equity gap.

- *Tightly defined rules / high tax relief*

The final setting of the rules is the recommendation of this study. The policy-maker should decide where and at what level he feels an increase of finance is required, and then provide the tax relief that will see such finance raised.

Obviously the fine details of such a scheme would have to be worked out by experts in the tax field; nevertheless, the principles of the scheme can be outlined. The scheme should be tightly targeted at the equity gap, and for this study that means no business should be able to raise more than £400,000. There should also be asset backing rules. Those of the EIS seem reasonable: 'A qualifying company cannot have more than half its net assets in land and buildings. This is because the purpose of the EIS is to encourage investment in trading companies which are not in the position to obtain loans on the security of their assets.'[1]

With the tightness of the criterion for qualification limiting the scope of the investments that can be made under the scheme, the level of tax relief can be high. Indeed, given that the criterion allows only medium-to-high risk investments to be made, it will need to be high for it to attract investors. This will mean that the up-front tax relief will have to be higher than the 20% offered under the EIS. Despite this increased level of tax relief, however, the scheme would still cost the Treasury less lost revenue than the BES, as the scope of the investments would be much narrower. There would not be anywhere near the level of 'wasted' tax relief as there was with the BES. The rules could be manipulated after the policy is launched, perhaps to increase the financial limits slightly; judgements would have to be made according to how the scheme progressed. Indeed, it was probably somewhat harsh to criticise the Government for having made a number of changes to the BES in its early years, as they faced a financial community searching desperately for loopholes, determined destroy the spirit of the scheme. The initial policy should not be the final word, if unintended consequences are caused.

Simplifying the scheme

It has been argued that a further reason why the EIS has been relatively unpopular with investors, is that the scheme is very complicated. Warnings were given at the very beginning of its life that many firms and their intended investors would find, at a late stage, that their project had fallen foul of an obscure element of the rules. It has also been said that the scheme has been hindered by the reluctance of accountants to become acquainted with its complexities; they are not sending their small business clients down to the DTI. The Inland Revenue's position is that the complexity of the rules is necessary to avoid the scheme being abused by those seeking to contravene its spirit. A simple solution, however, would surely be the appointment of a panel of adjudicators who would have power of veto over any proposal which was put before it. If such a panel were created, there would be a reduced need for all of the safeguards in the scheme's rules, thus making it more 'user-friendly'.

A fiscal intervention scheme offering high tax relief and uncomplicated rules, whilst operating within boundaries drawn up in line with the perceived nature of the equity gap, and under the auspices of an all-powerful panel of adjudicators would appear to address the shortcomings of the three previous attempts to make this type of policy work. If it did not, then it may have to be accepted that this policy approach is simply not appropriate as a response to the problem of the gap.

Direct state intervention - time once again for the state to pick winners ?

The second element in a policy to alleviate the problem of the equity gap, is the extension of the practice of SE to the rest of the UK. The example of SE suggests there is no reason why public sector venture capitalists cannot invest profitably (even the example of the NEB was not disastrous) and, given the existence of a gap, there is no reason why this approach to the problem should not be pursued, except for the fact that many people in the political arena, and most of those in the financial arena consider such a development a threat to market forces, etcetera. Beyond such concerns, the keys to the success of this policy approach would appear to be flexibility and an adherence to commercial investment criteria. The policy, therefore, should follow the following broad outline:

- Government should set up agencies to act as public sector venture capital funds to serve small firms suffering from the existence of an equity gap. The institutions would have an investment limit of £500,000 (the perceived level of the equity gap plus some leeway). There would be no bias in the stage at which the funds were invested, although they would be mindful not to neglect the crucial need for finance to be available to start-up and early-stage firms. The agency would be free to invest in all sectors of the economy, except perhaps for media, property and retail. Although primarily a source of equity, the agencies would also have powers to include loans and preference shares in their investment packages. A standard investment procedure could also help keep down the transaction costs.

- The policy would cover the whole of the UK in broad geographical regions. These regions would be Wales (through the WDA); the South-east; the South-west; the Midlands; the North-east; and the North-west. The agencies should seek to become closely identified with the region.

- Each of the agencies would be provided with an amount of state finance, but would be expected to create a fund which also contained private finance. The European Union could also be a target for the agencies. Each of the six agencies should be provided with £5 million in the first instance, with further finance provided on the basis of performance and need. Further finance would, of course, be required to operate the agencies, not least through the need to take on investment executives. Given that the larger SDF organisation employs six executives, the new agencies should be able to run with two, especially if a standardised investment process was developed. Overall, so long as the agencies were run efficiently, the costs need not be prohibitive.

Private finance is included in the funds for a number of reasons. Firstly, the involvement of private finance with a public sector venture capital fund provides it with credibility in the eyes of the business community which it has been placed to serve. Business people are suspicious of government at the best of times, and various political actors have encouraged the view that the state is a disastrous 'picker of winners'. In many cases, of course, this view has been justified. The Labour Government of 1974-1979, for example, did back a number of 'lame ducks', yet the point to be made is that it is wrong to suggest that the public sector will necessarily fail if it becomes involved in financing industry. Indeed, evidence to the contrary has been presented in this study.

The second reason for the inclusion of private finance is that it simply makes the fund go further. The involvement of a public agency (if it has gained the respect of the financial community as it would have appeared to have done in Scotland) can be a crucial factor in private financiers becoming interested in an investment. It will often not be necessary for the public agency to invest all of the capital in a deal, and taking lesser stakes enables a greater number of firms to benefit from its resources. Thirdly, the use of the state finance in conjunction with private finance reduces the exposure of the agency to financial risk; the agency is not forced to put too much of its finance into one firm. Finally, the agency will also be able to take advantage of the knowledge and experience of the co-investors. No single venture capital fund has a monopoly on investment wisdom. However, the agency would need to be flexible and not frightened to invest a greater proportion of the finance, or indeed all of it, if it feels it has an excellent opportunity to make a high return. The record of the UK institutional venture capital industry in this area has been very moderate, both in terms of investment levels and investment performance; the agencies should not worry unduly about occasionally treading on its toes.

- The agencies should be put under no pressure, political or otherwise, to invest their funds within a particular time-frame. The judgements made by the investment executives should be based upon sound commercial criteria. The example of SE has shown that such standards are not necessarily incompatible with imagination and substantial risk-taking, as is often assumed to be the case.

- The agencies should be put under no pressure, political or otherwise, to return their investments to the private sector. They should be allowed to choose the time when they believe they can realise the maximum worth for their risk-taking. Opportunities should be taken, however, as the finance can then be re-cycled for use in other deals. It should not be the aim of the agency to build up a large portfolio for vanity's sake.

- The agency should liase with other sources of small-firm risk-finance in the region it serves, whether this be banks, private sector venture capitalists, or business introduction services. The idea is to provide clients with their most suitable type and source of finance.

Business Introduction Services - ensuring national coverage and adequate resources

One of the most interesting of venture capital in the 1990s has been the development of the informal venture capital market and the emergence of a network of BIS. Whilst Harrison and Mason's early research suggests that by no means all investors will make a profit from their involvement as business angels, the potential of this source of finance for bridging the equity gap is enormous. Firstly, the average size of an angel investment lies comfortably within the range of the equity gap. Secondly, there is said to be a huge pool of investment finance waiting for suitable business opportunities; the figure of £2 billion has been mentioned. Thirdly, this method of investment does not involve the huge transaction costs which are incurred when institutions finance companies. The problem that had hitherto affected informal venture capital had been the absence of an established link between potential investors and small firms. There has been much progress during the 1990s with BIS emerging with ever-increasing frequency. In the BVCA directory published in 1995, 37 services are listed. Three concerns persist, however. Firstly, it has been questioned whether in the long-term it is economic for BIS to operate as private businesses. Secondly, there are doubts as to whether the currently operating BIS are promoting sufficient matches. Many of the BIS report a great deal of activity, but admit they have only promoted a handful of deals, or in some cases fewer (it might be suggested that this second point is related to the first). Thirdly, there are still parts of the UK which do not enjoy the presence of a service, which is important because usually BIS are very much local organisations.

The development of a network of BIS, therefore, (whether or not they co-operate with each other) covering all corners of the UK, and operating at a level where they become a very visible feature of the local business community and a valuable source of funding, would appear to be an end government should be keen to promote. Government might be able to act to speed up the development which is already taking place, as it did in the early part of the decade. A number of policy options appear to be feasible. Firstly, government could offer to sponsor BIS in areas where there is currently no service, this could be done in the same way in which the five BIS were selected in the early 1990s. Secondly, government could set up a fund to which currently operating BIS could apply for funds to extend their operations. This could be through either the expansion of their investment base, or the number of business opportunities they were offering, or indeed both. The finance could also fund ways to increase the visibility of BIS within the local business community, or even increase the number of staff dedicated to the service. The BIS would have to prepare a case, as any business does, when it is applying for finance from either government or private sector financiers. Thirdly, government could play a non-financial role by encouraging co-operation between the various BIS; this would already appear to be happening between neighbouring services which suggests mutual benefits.

Institutional venture capital initiatives - policies to reverse the trend

This study has confirmed the poor performance of the institutional venture capital industry in undertaking and producing significant returns from small and early-stage investments. As matters stand, there would appear to be no grounds for expecting the situation to change radically; there is a need for government to intervene so that the large UK industry can be better utilised. An option would be for Government to offer venture capitalists guarantees to underwrite certain types of investment. To avoid blatant exploitation, these guarantees would have to be limited to certain discrete areas, for example, start-up investments in certain high-technology industries which had been singled out as sectors with considerable potential for the economy as a whole. There are bodies within the public sector which could advise on such matters, including the Council for Science and Technology which was set up as a result of the 1993 science White Paper *Realising Our Potential*. The Council's role is to 'ensure that the Government benefits from independent and expert advice when deciding its own research spending priorities.'[2] An alternative to this would be for government to underwrite the costs of *making* certain types of investment. As has been discussed, the transaction costs are a serious disincentive to the making of investments under £400,000 as they are disproportionately large. Venture capitalists may be encouraged to make more of these investments, if a way could be found for these costs to be offset against tax. The venture capitalist would still have to incur the investigation costs of those investments it decided not to invest in, but, given that most proposals fall by the wayside after the initial assessment, this factor should not undermine the initiative too seriously. Such a scheme might at least prevent venture capitalists rejecting sound proposals merely on the grounds of the transaction costs being too onerous. Again, safeguards would have to be built in to avoid the scheme being exploited.

Devising policies to make more of the substantial UK institutional venture capital industry is by far the most problematic task. The two suggestions in this section are as much an attempt to put the need to intervene in the industry on the agenda, as they are specific policy proposals. It is an unsatisfactory situation that in all the discussions about bridging the equity gap, the institutional industry is never mentioned. Nothing has been attempted, as yet, to influence their activities in respect of the equity gap; it is time to at least try.

Some Concluding Comments on Government and the UK Equity Gap

The policy agenda presented here is not particularly radical; it merely consists of the expansion and amendment of previously implemented policy approaches. Nevertheless, there is reason to believe it would improve the financial options available to small and early-stage firms and thus make a contribution towards bridging the equity gap in the UK. The 1997 report delivered by the Institute for Public Policy Research into the UK's economic position as it enters the new millennium, confirmed again the existence of a long tail of underperforming businesses. Providing small and early-stage firms with easier access to equity finance will help in ensuring that some of these firms will fulfil their potential and develop into the innovative medium-sized firms the economy requires to remain a leading industrialised nation in the 21st century.

Notes

[1] Department of Trade and Industry, *A Guide to the Enterprise Investment Scheme*, London, HMSO, 1994, p6.

[2] Cmnd 2250, *Realising Our Potential: A Strategy for Science, Engineering and Technology*, London, HMSO, 1993, p6.

Appendices

In this section the comprehensive details of the investment activity of the NEB and Scottish Enterprise are recorded. In the case of the NEB the details reveal just how many loss-making investments they made. There is also a full list of the BVCA recorded BIS and their activities during 1994 and 1995.

Appendix A
NEB: Full Investment Disposal Record 1977 to 1990
The following is a full record of the known disposals of the NEB.

	Profit / (Loss) (£m)
ASR Servotron Ltd *Industrial Servo Controls*	(0.32)
Agemaspark Ltd *Spark Erosion Machines*	(2.00)
Allen Thornton and Sons Ltd *Textile Piece Dyeing and Finishing*	(0.03)
Anglo-American Venture Fund Ltd *Consultancy and Management Services*	(0.37)
Aqualisa Products Ltd *Domestic Showers*	5.34
Aregon Group Ltd *Viewdata Software Products*	1.17
Automation and Technical Services Ltd *Communications Equipment*	0.75
BTB (Engineering) Ltd *Specialised Vehicles*	(0.03)
Barlin Consumer Products Ltd *Electrical Convector Heaters*	(0.05)

Barrow Hepburn Group Ltd (0.18)
Chemicals, Engineering, Merchanting
British EKG Monitors Ltd (0.05)
Medical Electronics
British Robotic Systems Ltd (0.96)
Vision Sensing Systems
British Tanners Products Ltd (5.56)
Leather and Tanning Chemicals
British Underwater Engineering Ltd (8.33)
Underwater Engineering Equipment
Britton-Lee Inc 2.76
Database Machines
Brown Boveri Kent (Holdings) Ltd * (0.70)
Industrial Instruments
Bull Motors Ltd (2.06)
Variable Speed Rotating Machines
CAP Group Ltd 3.90
Software Services
CIC Investment Holdings Ltd * (12.05)
Scientific and Medical Instruments
Caltec Insulations Ltd (0.15)
Phenolic Foams
Celltech Ltd 8.40
Bio-Engineering
Centre for Software Engineering Ltd (0.05)
Industrial Software Safety Consultants
RR Chapman (Sub-Sea Surveys) Ltd 0.30
Unmanned Submersibles
Computer and Systems Engineering Ltd 1.22
Communications Equipment
Consine International Ltd (1.10)
Test Technology
Data Recording Instrument Co Ltd /
    DRI Holdings Ltd (7.44)
Computer Peripherals
Dunford and Elliott Ltd * 0.16
Steel
Dytes Ltd 0.12
Biotechnology

EIS plc	(0.10)
Process Machinery	
Edward G Herbert Ltd	0.05
Engineering	
The Energy Equipment Co Ltd	(0.43)
Combustion Engineers and Contractors	
Epichem Ltd	0.07
Manufacturer of Silane Gas	
Euromatic Machinery and Oil Co Ltd	(0.02)
Turbine Flowmeters Manufacturer	
Excelarc Engineering Co Ltd	(0.08)
Stainless Steel Engineering	
Fairey Holdings Ltd	3.81
Engineering	
Ferranti Ltd *	49.80
Mechanical Electrical and Electronic Engineering	
Ferranti Resin Ltd	(0.29)
GRP Tanks and Insulation	
Focom Systems Ltd	0.68
Fibre Optics and Video Communication	
Francis Shaw plc	(0.27)
Process Machinery	
Gemspar Ltd	(0.25)
Computerised Monitoring Systems	
George P Brown	0.09
Welding and Metal Forming Equipment	
Grosvenor Development Capital Ltd	(0.53)
Investment Holding Company	
Hemmings Plastics Ltd	(0.20)
Pharmaceutical Plastics	
Herbert Ltd *	(57.36)
Machine Tools	
Hilton Products Ltd	(0.24)
DIY Products	
Hivent Ltd	(0.11)
Air Pollution Control Equipment	
ICL Ltd *	24.21
Computers	

Imtec Group plc *Microfilmers and Readers Manufacturers*	(0.13)
Information Systems Investment Corp. Inc *Computer Bureaux*	(2.42)
Inmos International Ltd *Integrated Circuits*	29.60
INSAC Group Ltd *Software Marketing*	(7.18)
J & P Engineering *Electronic and Medical Engineering*	(0.20)
Keland Electrics Ltd *Electrical Transformers*	(0.26)
Kongsberg Systems Technology Ltd *Integrated Control Systems for Machine Tool Manufacturers*	(0.48)
Logica Group of Companies *Computer Software*	(0.56)
Mayflower Packaging Ltd *Packaging Machinery*	(0.17)
Merseyside Enterprise Fund Ltd *Investment Company*	(0.04)
Microform Communications International Ltd *Micrographics*	(0.57)
Microsell Systems Ltd *Electric Point of Sale Equipment*	(0.04)
Mikro Industrial Instruments Ltd *Microelectronics*	(0.02)
Modular Office Systems Ltd *Network Computer Systems*	(0.27)
The Mollart Engineering Co Ltd *Precision Engineering*	(0.99)
Momex (UK) Ltd *Export Promotion*	(0.05)
The Monotype Corporation Ltd *Typesetting Equipment*	2.63
Monotype Holdings Ltd *Typesetting Equipment*	(6.56)
Muirhead Office Systems Ltd *Facsimile Equipment*	0.01

Multi-Arc Vacuum Systems Ltd	0.02
Coating for High Speed Tools	
Negretti & Zambra Ltd	(0.67)
Process Control Equipment	
NEXOS Office Systems Ltd	(33.11)
Electronic Office Systems	
North East Audio Ltd	(0.44)
Audio Equipment	
P Shapira Ltd	(0.20)
Clothing Manufacturer	
Pakmet International Ltd	(0.36)
Packaging Machinery	
Pitcraft Ltd	0.08
Coalface Mining Machinery	
Polyfoam Ltd	(0.18)
Insulation Materials	
Power Dynamics Ltd	(0.03)
Hydraulic Machinery	
Preformed Road Markings Ltd	(0.13)
Road Markings Manufacturer	
Program Products Ltd	0.00
Software Marketing	
Protel Ltd	(0.46)
Television Computer Systems	
Q1 (Europe) Ltd	(5.01)
Micro-computer Systems	
Quest Automation plc	(1.32)
Computer Products	
Reed and Smith Holdings Ltd	0.76
Paper	
Rigby Electronics Ltd	(0.07)
Electro High Vacuum Equipment	
St. Modwen Properties plc	0.40
Property	
Sandiacre Electrics Ltd	(0.51)
Control Systems Engineering	
Shelton Instruments Ltd	(0.12)
Microcomputing Systems	

Sinclair Radionics Ltd	(7.92)
Microelectronics	
Speywood Laboratories Ltd	(0.18)
Blood Products	
Solglo Ltd	0.00
Road Reflectors	
Systems Designers International Ltd	1.00
Computer Software Systems	
Systime plc	(2.28)
EDP Systems Marketing	
Technalogics Computing Ltd	(0.04)
High Technology Microcomputers	
Technical Resources (Equipment) Ltd	(0.33)
LPG Cylinders and Pressure Vessels	
Thwaites and Reed Ltd	(0.45)
Clocks	
Twinlock plc	2.88
Office Filing Systems and Furniture	
United Medical Enterprises Ltd	11.48
Hospital Management Services	
VS Technology Group plc	(0.84)
Welding and Metal Forming Equipment	
Vicort of London Ltd	(0.12)
Sports Equipment	
Western Enterprise Fund Ltd	(0.38)
Investment Company	
White Cross Rubber Products Ltd	0.01
Rubber Products	
Wholesale Vehicle Finance Ltd	2.56
Motor Distributor Finance	
Yates Duxbury and Sons Ltd	(2.50)
Paper Manufacturer	

* Transferred from the Department of Industry 1975-6

Transfers to other bodies
In the year 1985/86 17 investments were transferred to Oakwood Loan Finance Ltd, an NEB subsidiary. These investments were:

Blue Ridge Care Ltd
Disposable Nappies
Bradford Microfirms Ltd
Microfirm Workshop Unit
Britpharm Ltd
Healthcare Products
Designworkshop (Shelley) Ltd
Furniture Manufacturer
Durascreen Ltd
Electroplated Rotary Printing Screens
James Howorth and Co (Holdings) Ltd
Advanced Air Engineering
Inmar Contracting Equipment
Shot Blasting Equipment
JJ Electronic Components Ltd
Thick-film Technology
Lancashire and Mersey Investment Fund Ltd
Investment Company
Mather Machinery Co Ltd
Machinery for Textile Finishing and General Engineering
Neolith Chemicals Ltd
High Pressure Water Pumps and Liquid Cleaning Chemicals
Northern Software Consultants Ltd
Software House
RV Partitions Ltd
Manufacturer of Partitions, Ceiling Components and Fittings
Silicon Microsystems Ltd
Design of Custom and Semi-Custom Integrated Circuits
Tantoward Ltd
Specialist Fittings for Petrochemical and Nuclear Products
Textile Computer Systems (TCS) Ltd
Computer Aided Design
Towniprene (UK) Ltd
Urethane Resin Product

Individual disposal details of these companies are not available. The disposal of the 17 investments to Oakwood caused the NEB a loss of £1.98 million in 1985-6 (NEB Annual Report 1985/86, p14).

216 *The UK Equity Gap*

In 1985-6 10 investments were transferred to the National Research Development Corporation. These investments were:

BIT Business Information Techniques Ltd
Expert System Software
BVT Ltd
Vacuum Chambers for Roll Coating of Substrate Materials
Bradford University Software Services Ltd
Computer Software
C Squared Co Ltd
Computer Communications and Consultants
Cawdor Ltd
Microcomputer Sales and Manufacturer
IQ (Bio) Ltd
Immunoassay
Orange Medical Instruments Ltd
Manufacturer of Medical Sensors
Percom Ltd
Software House
Tangram Computer Aided Engineering Ltd
Computer Aided Engineering
Venture Technology Ltd
Special Battery Systems

Individual disposal details of these companies are not available. The disposal of the 10 investments to the National Research Development Corporation led to the NEB showing a profit of £60,000 (NEB AR 1985/86, p14).

Appendix B
Business Introduction Services in the UK: Activity 1995-1996

1. Number of investment opportunities from July 1 1994 to June 30 1995
2. Number of current investors
3. Number of successful matches from July 1 1994 to June 30 1995

	Status	Year of Formation	1	2	3
Albermarle Group plc	Private	1992	50	50	3
Anglia Business Angels	Private	1995	61	46	9
Bedfordshire Investment Exchange	TEC	1992	20	35	4
Blackstone Franks & Co	Private	1976	30	750	10
The Business Angels Bureau Ltd	Private	1994	10	40	1
Business Link Gloucestershire	Bus. Link	1992	52	60	8
Capital Access	n/k	1993	40	35	1
Capital Connections	TEC	1992	42	40	3
The Capital Market	Bus. Link	1994	40	96	8
Capital Match	TEC	1994	24	25	1
Cavendish Management Resources	Private	1984	250	200+	10
Cheshire Contacts	Public	1994	13	22	6
Company Broking Consultants Ltd	Private	1993	12	15	3
Daily Telegraph Bus. Angel Netw'k	Private	1992	270	n/a	n/a
Dunstable Management Group	Private	1992	60	130	5
Entrust	n/k	1982	30	32	5
Equity Link	Bus. Link	1994	63	62	8
Great Eastern Investment Forum	Private	1995	10	36	1
Haines Watts Corporate Finance	Private	1994	c90	c300	c20
Halo Ltd	Private	1994	31	40	6
Hilling Wall Corporate Finance	Private	1989	40	70	12

IDJ Ltd	Private	1972	50	200	3
Informal Register of Inv. Services	Bus. Link	1992	32	56	4
LINC	Private	1987	345	340+	36
LINC Scotland	Private	1993	see	above	
Mercantile 100	Private	1992	160	55	3
Milestone Services Ltd	Private	1989	2	53	2
NatWest Angels Service	Private	1994	n/a	n/a	n/a
Oxfordshire Inv Opportunity Netwk	Private	1994	15	90	3
Principality Financial Management	Private	1990	30	265	7
Solutions for Scotland	Private	1992	20	2000	1
South West Investment Group	Pub/Pri	1992	36	69	10
Talisman Ventures Ltd	Private	1990	1	300	1
TEChINVEST	TEC	1993	32	102	9
VentureNet	Private	1994	75	1000	n/a
Venture Capital Report	Private	1978	99	635	19
Winsec Corporate Exchange	Private	1992	120	170	1

Source: BVCA, *Sources of Business Angel Capital*, London, BVCA, 1995.

Author's note: Any unusual figures may well have been caused by the respondents misunderstanding of the BVCA's questions. The BVCA would appear to have printed the responses without amendment.

Bibliography

Adeney, M, *The Motor Makers: The Turbulent History of Britain's Car Industry,* London, Fontana-Collins, 1989.

Aldous, H, 'Backing the winners: the climate for the risk investor is improving, aided by the Chancellor', *Venture Capital Report*, May 1984.

Anslow, M, 'Performance data shows wide spread of IRRs for UK independent funds', *UK Venture Capital Journal*, November-December 1995, p12.

Arthur Andersen, *UK Biotech '94*, London, Arthur Andersen, 1994.

Artis, M and Cobham, D, (ed), *Labour's Economic Policies*, Manchester, Manchester University Press, 1991.

Ashdown, P, *Citizen's Britain*, London, Fourth Estate, 1989.

Baldwin, A, 'Budget business - I think we'd better think it out again !', *Venture Capital Report*, May 1985.

Ball, Sir J, 'Short-termism: Myth or reality', *National Westminster Quarterly Review*, August 1991, pp20-30.

Bank of England, 'Financing British Industry', *Bank of England Quarterly Bulletin*, September 1980, pp319-323.

Bank of England, 'Takeover activity in the 1980s', *Bank of England Quarterly Bulletin*, February 1989, pp78-85.

Bank of England, 'Venture Capital in the United Kingdom', *Bank of England Quarterly Bulletin*, February 1990, pp78-83.

Bannock, G, 'The Clearing Banks and Small Firms', *Lloyds Bank Review*, October 1981, pp15-25.

Bannock, G, *The Economics of Small Firms*, Oxford, Blackwell, 1981.

Bannock, G, *Britain in the 1990s: Enterprise Under Threat ?*, London, 3i, 1990.

Bannock, G, *The Economic Impact of Management Buy-outs*, London, 3i, 1990.

Bannock, G and Peacock, A, *Corporate Takeovers and the Public Interest*, Aberdeen, Aberdeen University Press, 1991.

Becket, M, 'Venture funding at record £2 billion', *The Daily Telegraph*, 12 April 1995, p21.

Benn, T, *Against the Tide: Diaries 1973-1976*, London, Hutchinson, 1989.

Bethell, J, 'Clarke struggles to solve BES riddle', *The Sunday Times*, 28 November 1993, p3.7.
Bethell, J, 'Clarke looks to Angels to revive Britain's spirit of enterprise', *The Sunday Times*, 5 December 1993, p3.2.
Bethell, J, 'Grosvenor deal a sign of the times', *The Sunday Times*, 27 February 1994, p3.10.
Bethell, J 'Capital ventures to replace BES sparks argument', *The Sunday Times*, 22 May 1994, p3.13.
Bolton Committee, *Report of the Committee of Inquiry on Small Firms*, Comd 4811, London, HMSO, 1971.
Bose, M, 'A Cautionary Tale for Investors', *Investors Chronicle*, 24 July 1992, p14.
Bradford, J. 'Banks and Small Firms: An Insight', *National Westminster Bank Quarterly Review*, May 1993, pp13-16.
British Business, 'NRDC sets up small business fund with initial £2 million', 26 September 1980.
British Business, News, 25 December 1981, p12.
British Business, 'New role for BTG announced', 7 October 1983, p303.
British Venture Capital Association, *Report on Investment Activity*, London, BVCA, 1984 to 1993.
British Venture Capital Association, *Business Plans and Financing Proposals*, London, Arthur Andersen, 1992.
British Venture Capital Association, *Guide to Venture Capital*, London, BVCA, 1992.
British Venture Capital Association, *Directory*, London, BVCA, 1992-1993 to 1996-1997.
British Venture Capital Association, *The BVCA Sensor: A survey of venture-backed companies*, London, BVCA, 1993.
British Venture Capital Association, *Directory of Business Introduction Services*, London, BVCA, 1993.
British Venture Capital Association, *Tax Submission,* London, BVCA, 1993.
British Venture Capital Association, *Performance Measurement Survey 1995*, London, BVCA, 1995.
Brown, G, *Where There is Greed ... Margaret Thatcher and the Betrayal of Britain's Future*, Edinburgh, Mainstream, 1989.
Buckingham, L and Whitebloom, S, 'Tories preach capital heresy', *The Guardian*, 12 March 1994, p40.

Budd, A, 'Do we need a national investment bank ?', *National Westminster Bank Quarterly Review*, August 1986, pp36-48.
Business in the Community, *Report of the Working Party on Loan Capital / Equity Support for Small Businesses*, London, Business in the Community, 1986.
Buxton, J, 'Sights focused on expansion', *Financial Times*, 29 August 1995, p8.
Bygrave, W and Timmons, J, *Venture Capital at the Crossroads*, Boston, Harvard Business School Press, 1992.
Cary, L, *The Venture Capital Report Guide to Venture Capital in the UK (5th edition)*, London, Pitman, 1991.
Cary, L, *The Venture Capital Report Guide to Venture Capital in the UK (7th edition)*, London, Pitman, 1995.
Channel 4, *The Thatcher Audit*, Channel 4 Television, 1990.
Channel 4, *Greed and Glory*, Channel 4 Television, 1992.
Clements, S, *The Relationship between German SMEs and their Banks*, Cranfield, 3i European Enterprise Centre, 1992.
Clutterbuck, D and Crainer, S, *The Decline and Rise of British Industry*, London, WH Allen, 1988.
Coates, D, *Labour in Power ?*, London, Longman, 1980.
Cohen, N, 'Banks to sell 21 per cent of 3i', Financial Times, 9 June 1995.
Cohen, R, 'Venture capital is crucial to recovery', *The Observer*, 18 October 1992, B2.
Collins, M, *Banks and Industrial Finance 1839-1914*, Basingstoke, Macmillan, 1991.
Coopers and Lybrand, *Made in the UK: The Middle Market Survey - Executive Summary*, London, Coopers and Lybrand, 1994.
Coopey, R and Clarke, D, *3i: Fifty Years of Investing in Industry*, Oxford, Oxford University Press, 1995.
Coventry, Liverpool, Newcastle, North Tyneside Trades Councils, *State Intervention in Industry: A Workers' Inquiry*, Newcastle, Coventry, Liverpool, Newcastle, North Tyneside Trades Councils, 1980.
Cowe, R, 'Business lament on slow payers', *The Guardian*, 25 May 1994, p14.
Cowe, R, '3i sets float price despite sinking feeling', *The Guardian*, 23 June 1994, p20.
Cox, A, *Adversary Politics and Land*, Cambridge, Cambridge University Press, 1984.

Curry, A, 'NEB - the risk taker', *New Statesman*, 26 February 1982, p4.

Department of Trade and Industry, *Finance Without Debt: A Guide to Sources of Venture Capital Under £250,000*, London, DTI, 1993.

Department of Trade and Industry, *A Guide to the Enterprise Investment Scheme*, London, DTI, 1994.

Department of Trade and Industry, *Increasing the Supply of Informal Equity Capital: A Guide to Setting Up a Business Introduction Service*, London, DTI, 1994.

Department of Trade and Industry, *Sources of Finance for Small Business: A West Midlands Guide*, London, DTI, 1994.

Dodgson, M, *The Management of Technological Learning: Lessons from a Biotechnology Company*, Berlin, Walter de Gruyter, 1991.

Drummond, R, 'Overcoming an image problem', *Investors Chronicle, Survey: Venture Capital and Europe*, 9 October 1992, p15.

Dutton, D, *British Politics Since 1945*, Oxford, Basil Blackwell, 1991.

Eadie, A, 'A venture to close the equity gap', *The Independent on Sunday*, 19 March 1995, p12.

The Economist, 'The NEB's guidelines favour the bosses', 28 February 1976, p75.

The Economist, 'Curate's NEB', 6 March 1976, p71.

The Economist, 'Uncalculated error', 27 November 1976, p100.

The Economist, 'Tanning for Ryder ?', 23 April 1977, p116.

The Economist, 'State enterprise: year one', 7 May 1977, p77.

The Economist, 'Ryder rides out', 9 July 1977, p102.

The Economist, 'How wicked, public enterprise', 10 December 1977, p92.

The Economist, 'NEB short-circuits the electronics industry', 3 June 1978, p121.

The Economist, 'Joseph tether the NEB', 21 July 1979, p83.

The Economist, 'BL's last battle ?', 15 September 1979, p75.

The Economist, 'Rolls under Whitehall's wing', 24 November 1979, p83.

The Economist, 'Venture capitalists ride again', 11 October 1980, pp110-111.

The Economist, 'Taxpayers' British Technology', 25 July 1981, p18.

The Economist, 'Venture forth and multiply', 26 March 1983, pp86-90.

The Economist, 'How to cultivate companies', 24 December 1983, pp61-62.

The Economist, 'Scorched by dragons breath', 13 July 1985, pp66-67.

The Economist, 'Nothing ventured', 27 July 1985, pp86-88.

The Economist, 'Venture capital drought', 24 June 1989, pp95-96.

The Economist, 'Local heroes', 30 September 1989, p132.
The Economist, 'Win without risk, triumph without glory', 13 October 1990, p108.
The Economist, 'Of birth and businesses', 5 October 1991, p93.
The Economist, 'Plenty to gain ?', 7 December 1991, p126.
Edwards, G, 'British banks do not give credit where it is due', *The Guardian*, 10 February 1992, p11.
Elkin, S, 'Small Firms Investment Companies: Plugging the equity gap in small firm financing', *Venture Capital Report*, March 1983.
Fairtlough, G, 'Exploitation of biotechnology in a smaller company', Royal Society of London Philosophical Transactions: Series B, Vol 324, 1989.
Financial Times, *Biotechnology: Survey*, 9 May 1994.
Financial Times, *Venture and Development Capital: Survey*, 23 September 1994.
Financial Times, 'VCTs wait for flood', 16 January 1996, p12.
Fildes, C, 'Time to break the badge fairy's spell on 3i', *The Daily Telegraph*, 24 May 1993, p23.
Gamble, A, *Britain in Decline*, London, MacMillan, 1994.
Geroski, P, 'Meaning of market failure', *Financial Times Mastering Management 18*, 8 March 1996, p13.
Glyn, A and Sutcliffe, B, 'The Rivalry of Financial and Industrial Capital', in D. Coates and J. Hillard (ed), *The Economic Decline of Modern Britain: the debate between left and right*, Brighton, Wheatsheaf, 1986, pp 245-246.
Gourlay, R 'The shape of things to come', *Financial Times*, 18 January 1994, p12.
Gourlay, R, 'Suppliers under threat', *Financial Times*, 15 February 1994, p12.
Gourlay, R, 'European adventure', *Financial Times*, 15 February 1994, p12.
Gourlay, R, 'UK banks aim to sell off a third of their 3i stake', *Financial Times*, 24 February 1994, p27.
Gourlay, R, 'Government as venture capitalist', *Financial Times*, 30 August 1994, p8.
Gourlay, R, 'EC's venture seedling', *Financial Times*, 4 April 1995, p12.
Gourlay, R, 'Blossoming of an unwanted child', *Financial Times*, 6 June 1995, p14.
Gourlay, R, 'Banks reap profit of £176 million with sale of 3i shares', *Financial Times*, 23 June 1995, p22.

Government response to the House of Lords Select Committee Report on Innovation in Manufacturing Industry, *Hansard*, June 1991.
Grant, W, *Business and Politics in Britain*, Basingstoke, Macmillan, 1987.
Green, D, 'Merck - Celltech deal on asthma drug', *Financial Times*, 21 July 1994, p23.
Green, M, (ed), *Venture Capital: International Comparisons*, London, Routledge, 1991.
Griffiths, A, 'Business angels in all of a flutter over match maker rival', *The Daily Telegraph*, 14 November 1994, p33.
Grosvenor Venture Managers, *Grosvenor - The First Five Years*, Slough, Grosvenor, 1987.
Grylls, M and Redwood, J, *The National Enterprise Board: A Case for Euthanasia*, London, Centre for Policy Studies, 1980.
H.M. Government, *Realising Our Potential: A Strategy for Science, Engineering and Technology*, London, HMSO, Cmnd 2250, 1993.
Halcrow, M, *Keith Joseph: A Single Mind*, London, Macmillan, 1989.
Hall, G, 'Government bank could fill a gap', *The Guardian*, 24 April 1995, p11.
Hamilton, K, '3i prepares for summer plunge into the market', *The Sunday Times*, 27 February 1994, p3.10.
Hamilton, K, 'Stock Exchange hits its new market target with AIM', *The Sunday Times*, 11 September 1994, p3.13.
Hamilton-Fazey, I, 'Award takes first prize', *Financial Times: Survey - Venture and Development Capital*, 20 September 1996, p5.
Harrison, R and Mason, C, *The Roles of Investors in Entrepreneurial Companies: A Comparison of Informal Investors and Venture Capitalists*, University of Southampton, Department of Geography and Ulster Business School, Working Paper No 5, August 1992.
Harrison, R and Mason, C, 'The Regional Impact of National Policy Initiatives: Small Firms Policy in the United Kingdom', in R. Harrison and M. Hart, *Spatial Policy in a Divided Nation*, London, Jessica Kingsley, 1993, pp193-215.
Harrison, R and Mason, C, 'Developing the informal venture capital market: a review of the Department of Trade and Industry's informal investment demonstration projects', *Regional Studies*, Vol 30, No8,1996, p777-783.
Hawkins, I, 'No way out ?', *Investors Chronicle*, Survey: Venture Capital and Europe, 9 October 1992, p8.

Hindley, B, (ed), *State Investment Companies in Western Europe*, London, Macmillan, 1983.

Hird, C and Wintour, P, 'Last days at the NEB', *New Statesman*, 30 November 1979, p838.

Holland, S, *The Market Economy*, London, Weidenfield and Nicholson, 1987.

Holmes, M, *The Labour Government 1974-1979: Political Aims and Economic Reality*, London, Macmillan, 1985.

Howard, M, 'A major package of measures to help small firms', *Venture Capital Report*, December 1991.

Hughes, A, *The "Problems" of Finance for Smaller Businesses*, Working Paper No15, Cambridge, Small Business Research Centre: University of Cambridge, 1992.

Hughes, A, 'The "Problems" of Finance for Small Businesses', in N. Dimsdale and M Prevezer (ed), *Capital Markets and Corporate Governance*, Oxford, Clarendon Press, 1994.

Hutton, W, 'Short changed by short-termism...', *The Guardian*, 20 June 1990, p11.

Hutton, W, 'Takeover legacy has touched us all at great cost', *The Guardian*, 3 September 1990, p10.

Hutton, W, 'Could it just be that the system of investing in British industry has been wrong for the last century ?', *The Guardian*, 10 December 1990, p13.

Hutton, W, 'Britain's overblown financial services sector', *The Guardian*, 24 December 1990, p10.

Hutton, W, 'Counting the cost of financial deregulation', *The Guardian*, 4 February 1991, p12.

Hutton, W, 'No credit to their system', *The Guardian*, 8 June 1991, p14.

Hutton, H, 'The Treasury wakes up to our real problems', *The Guardian*, 10 March 1994, p17.

Industrial Reorganisation Corporation, *Annual Report and Accounts*, London, HMSO, 1971.

3i, *Company Facts Guide*, London, 3i, 1992 & 1993.

3i, *Guide to Investment Capital for Professional Advisers*, London, 3i, 1993.

3i, *Guide to Investment Capital for Senior Directors*, London, 3i, 1993.

3i, *Mini Prospectus*, London, 3i, 1994.

The John Bull Business, BBC Television, 1992.

Ingham, G, *Capitalism Divided: The City and Industry in British Social Development,* Basingstoke, Macmillan, 1984.
Initiative Europe, *UK Venture Industry Review*, London, Initiative Europe, 1994.
Institute of Directors, *Short-termism and The State We're In*, London, IoD, 1996.
Investors Chronicle, *Management Buy-Outs: Survey,* 10 March 1995.
Johnson, C, *The Economy Under Mrs Thatcher 1979-1990*, London, Penguin, 1991.
Johnson Fry, BES Bulletin, London, Johnson Fry, 1993-1994.
Joseph, K, *Stranded on the Middle Ground ?: Reflections on Circumstances and Policies,* London, Centre for Policy Studies, 1976.
Keasey, K and Watson, R, 'Banks and Small Firms: Is Conflict Inevitable', in *National Westminster Bank Quarterly Review*, May 1993, pp30-40.
Keegan, W, *Mrs Thatcher's Economic Experiment*, Harmondsworth, Penguin, 1984.
Keith, Lord 'Industry, the City of London and Our Economic Future', in D. Coates and J. Hillard (ed), *The economic Decline of Modern Britain: The Debate Between Left and Right*, Brighton, Wheatsheaf, 1986, pp67-76.
Kompass, *Company Information 1993/4*, East Grinstead, Reed Information Services, 1993.
Kramer, D, *State Capital and Private Enterprise: The Case of the UK National Enterprise Board*, London, Routledge, 1988.
Labour Party, The, *The National Investment Bank*, London, Labour Party, 1985.
Labour Party, The, *Going for Growth: Helping Small Businesses to Succeed*, London, Labour Party, 1994.
Labour Party Study Group, *The National Enterprise Board: Labour's State Holding Company*, Opposition Green Paper, London, The Labour Party, 1973.
Langston, P, 'No start-ups please, we're British', *Venture Capital Report*, July 1993.
Leigh-Pemberton, R, 'Don't blame the banks', *The Sunday Times*, 16 November 1980, p18.
Lever, H, and Edwards, G, 'Why Germany Beats Britain', *The Sunday Times*, 2 November 1980, pp16-17.
Lever, H and Edwards, G, 'How to Bank on Britain', *The Sunday Times*, 9 November 1980, p16.

Lindblom, C, *Politics and Markets*, New York, Basic Books, 1977.
Lisle-Williams, M, 'The State, Finance and Industry in Britain', in A.Cox (ed), *The State, Finance and Industry*, Brighton, Wheatsheaf, 1986, pp231-273.
London Business School, *Management Buy-Outs and the Economic Cycle*, London, LBS, 1992.
Longstreth, F, 'The City, Industry and the State', in C. Crouch (ed), *The State and Economy in Contemporary Capitalism*, London, Croom Helm, 1979, pp157-190.
Lonsdale, C, 'Re-assessing the role of government in bridging the UK equity gap', *UK Venture Capital Journal*, November-December 1995, pp17-20.
Lorenz, T, *Venture Capital Today: A Guide to the Venture Capital Market in the UK*, Cambridge, Woodhead-Faulkner, 1985.
Lukes, S, *Power: A Radical View*, London, Macmillan, 1974.
Lynn, M, 'Government switches to "picking winners"', *The Sunday Times*, 6 March 1994, p3.10.
MacErlean, N, 'EIS plan faces a tax minefield', *The Observer*, 16 January 1994, pB10.
MacErlean, N, 'BES firms seek market rescue', *The Observer*, 5 June 1994, pB2.
MacKinnon, R, *Small Firms and their Problems*, London, Aim of Industry, 1972.
Macpherson, E, 'Will the bait be tasty enough ?', *Financial Times*, 10 May 1994, p12.
Macmillan, H, *The Middle Way*, London, Macmillan, 1938.
McLoughlin, J, 'Minister decides new role for NEB', in *The Guardian*, 1 October 1983, p18.
McNally, K, *Bridging the Equity Gap ? The Role of Corporate Venture Capital*, Department of Geography, University of Southampton, Venture Finance Working Paper No 10, October 1994.
McNally, K, *External Equity Finance for Technology-Based Firms in the United Kingdom: The Role of Corporate Venture Capital*, Department of Geography, University of Southampton, Venture Finance Working Paper No 13, April 1995.
Marsh, D and Lockesley, G, 'Capital in Britain: It Structural Power and Influence Over Policy', *West European Politics*, Vol 6, No 2, 1983, pp36-60.

Mason, C, *Informal Venture Capital: A New Form of Financing Small and Medium Sized Enterprises*, Conference Paper, Confederation of Finnish Industry and Employers, October 1993.

Mason, C, Harrison, J and Harrison, R, *An Assessment of the Business Expansion Scheme*, London, Small Business Research Trust, 1988, Executive Summary.

Mason, C and Harrison, R, 'The role of the Business Expansion Scheme in the United Kingdom', *Omega International Journal of Management Science*, Vol 17, No 2, 1989, pp147-157.

Mason, C and Harrison, R, 'The informal supply of venture capital in the UK', *Venture Capital Report*, November 1991.

Mason, C and Harrison, R, *Promoting Informal Venture Capital: Some Operational Considerations for Business Introduction Services*, University of Southampton, Department of Geography and Ulster Business School, Working Paper No 4, July 1992.

Mason, C and Harrison, R, 'Finance for the growing business: The role of informal investment', *National Westminster Bank Quarterly Review*, May 1993, pp17-28.

Mason, C and Harrison, R, 'Strategies for Expanding the Informal Venture Capital Market', *International Small Business Journal*, Vol 2, No 4, 1993, pp23-38.

Mason, C and Harrison, R, *Why "Business Angels" Say No: A Case Study of Opportunities Rejected by an Informal Investor Syndicate*, University of Southampton, Department of Geography and Ulster Business School, Working Paper No 7, May 1994.

Mason, C, Harrison, R and Allen, P, *Informal Venture Capital: A Study of the Investment Process, the Post-investment Experience and Investment Performance*, University of Southampton, Department of Geography and Ulster Business School, Working Paper No12, February 1995.

Miller, R, 'Private investors may be cool to BES successor', *The Times*, 4 December 1993, p23.

Moran, M, 'Power, Policy and the City of London', in R. King (ed), *Capital and Politics*, London, Routledge, 1983, pp49-68.

Murray, G, 'The second equity gap', *UK Venture Capital Journal*, January 1993, pp23-29.

National Enterprise Board Annual Report, 1976 to 1991.

National Enterprise Board, *NEB's Report on British Leyland's Corporate Plan and 1978 Business Plan*, London, NEB, 1978.

National Research Development Corporation, *25 Years of Service to Innovation: Bulletin of the National Research Development Corporation*, Autumn 1974.

Oakland Loan Finance Ltd, *Financial Statement*, 1985-1993.

Peat Marwick, *Report on the Business Expansion Scheme*, London, Inland Revenue, 1986.

Pollard, S, 'The Treasury's Contempt for Production', in D. Coates and J. Hillard (ed), *The Economic Decline of Modern Britain: The Debate Between Left and Right*, Brighton, Wheatsheaf, 1986, pp196-204.

Ramesh, R, 'Successor to USM set for lift-off', in *The Sunday Times*, 26 February 1995, p2.9.

Redwood, J, *Going for Broke: Gambling With Taxpayers' Money*, Oxford, Basil Blackwell, 1984.

Reece, D, 'BES bosses under fire from 'rebel' investors', *The Sunday Telegraph*, 23 April 1995, pB8.

Rigby, M, 'Risk aversion - Are UK venture capitalists prepared to back up high technology start-ups ?', *Venture Capital Report*, February 1989.

Rigby, M, 'Risk and return: small scale venture capital revisted', *Venture Capital Report*, November 1992.

Rose, H, 'Britain's Financial System and Economic Performance: Old Charges Renewed', *Barclay's Review*, May 1982, pp28-34.

Ruddock, A, 'Shares' bull run pushes start-ups to sidelines', *The Sunday Times*, 6 February 1994, p3.9.

Scottish Development Agency, *Annual Report and Accounts*, 1976-1991.

Scottish Enterprise, *Annual Report and Accounts*, 1992-1996.

Smith, D, *Mrs Thatcher's Economics*, Oxford, Heinemann, 1988.

Smith, D, 'Treasury ponders funding boost', *The Sunday Times*, 13 November 1994, p3.11.

Spiers, J, 'Full circle for the BES ?', *Venture Capital Report*, June 1989.

Stanworth, J and Gray, C, *Bolton 20 Years On: The Small Firm in the 1990s*, London, Paul Chapman, 1991.

Stoy Hayward, *Guide to Venture and Buy-out Capital 1994*, London, Stoy Hayward, 1994.

Tate, M, '3i flotation set to top £1.5bn', *The Observer*, 3 April 1994, pB2.

Taylor, P, 'The Business Expansion Scheme: Is it filling the equity gap', *Venture Capital Report*, June 1984.

Thapar, N, 'BTG heads for early flotation', *The Independent on Sunday*, 3 March 1994, pB1.

Thompson, G, 'The relationship between the financial and industrial sector in the United Kingdom economy', *Economy and Society*, Vol 6, 1977, pp235-283.

Tighe, C, 'Tec launches fund for venture capital', *Financial Times*, 12 June 1993, p8.

Tobin, J, 'On the efficiency of the financial system', *Lloyds Bank Review*, July 1984, pp1-15.

UK Venture Capital Journal, 'Pension funds are still dominant source of capital', January 1987, p4.

UK Venture Capital Journal, 'Current issues facing the venture capital industry', March 1987, pp10-17.

UK Venture Capital Journal, 'Budget favours small business', March 1987, p2.

UK Venture Capital Journal, 'Venture capital after the crash', November 1987, p2.

UK Venture Capital Journal, 'Budget moves the goal posts for venture capitalists', March 1988, pp2.

UK Venture Capital Journal, 'The changing face of the UK venture capital industry', September 1988, p9-14.

UK Venture Capital Journal, 'Special Report: Two gaps in the UK Venture Capital Market', in Venture Capital Journal, November 1988, p8-12.

UK Venture Capital Journal, 'Pension funds and venture capital', March 1989, pp10-18.

UK Venture Capital Journal, 'Neutral budget for the venture capital industry', March 1989, p2.

UK Venture Capital Journal, 'Review of 1988 investment activity', May 1989, pp9-16.

UK Venture Capital Journal, 'An industry on the brink of the 1990's', November 1989, p7-12.

UK Venture Capital Journal, 'Venture investment and the economic downturn', November 1990, pp8-19.

UK Venture Capital Journal, 'The place of factoring in venture capital projects', November 1990, p20.

UK Venture Capital Journal, 'Warwick study highlights changes in UK venture capital industry', January 1991, p3.

UK Venture Capital Journal, 'BVCA reaches agreement on valuation guidelines', January 1991, pp4-5.

UK Venture Capital Journal, 'Recession fuels growth in UK buy-outs', January 1991, p5.
UK Venture Capital Journal, 'Hard times on the USM', March 1991, p5.
UK Venture Capital Journal, 'Greater London Enterprise', March 1991, pp22-23.
UK Venture Capital Journal, '3i stresses "growth capital" investment', May 1991, p6.
UK Venture Capital Journal, '3i floatation will spur institutional interest in venture capital', November 1991, p3.
UK Venture Capital Journal, 'BES gets the bullet', March 1992, pp5-6.
UK Venture Capital Journal, 'Management consortium wins the battle for BTG', March 1992, p6.
UK Venture Capital Journal, 'Who sees the early stage technology deals', March 1992, p6.
UK Venture Capital Journal, 'Ten years on - the Enterprise Board experience', May 1992, pp18-21.
UK Venture Capital Journal, 'Growth companies - are there enough ?', September 1992, pp22-24.
UK Venture Capital Journal, 'Bank shake-up strengthens ventures division', January 1993, p9.
UK Venture Capital Journal, 'Venture capital and the early stage deal', January 1993.
UK Venture Capital Journal, 'Venture capitalists explore options for their own stock exchange', January 1993, pp4-5.
Upcott-Gill, V, 'TEChINVEST: The Cheshire approach to informal investment', *Venture Capital Report*, June 1993.
Vasey, C, 'Comment on the Budget for venture capitalists', *Venture Capital Report*, May 1991.
Vincent, L, 'Keen eye on the prize at 3i', *The Observer*, 26 June 1994, pB9.
Vittas, D, 'Banks Relations with Industry: An International Survey', *National Westminster Bank Quarterly Review*, February 1986, pp2-13.
Wallace, J, 'Seedcorn capital and investment in small businesses', *Venture Capital Report*, February 1992.
Watts, C, 'Putting the bite on venture capital trusts', *Small Business Investor*, March 1996, pp23-25.
Welsh Development Agency, *Annual Report and Accounts*, 1976-1990.
White, M, 'Labour woos small firms', *The Guardian*, 26 March 1994, p38.

Whitebloom, S et al, 'City faces scrutiny of willingness to invest in British industry', *The Guardian*, 10 March 1994, p1.
Whitson, K, 'How banks could come to appear positively angelic', *The Guardian*, 27 June 1994, p13.
Widlake, B, *In the City*, London, Faber and Faber, 1986.
Williams, P, 'Short-Termism in the UK: Myth or Reality?', *National Westminster Bank Quarterly Review*, August 1991, pp31-38.
Wilson, H, *Final Term: The Labour Government 1974-1976*, London, Weidenfeld and Nicolson and Michael Joseph, 1979.
Woodcock, C, 'Investment opportunities slip through the networks', *The Guardian*, 23 August 1993, p12.
Woodcock, C, 'Going where even angels fear to tread', *The Guardian*, 20 September 1993, p12.
Woodcock, C, 'Small companies welcome plan for enterprise investment', *The Guardian*, 4 December 1993.
Woodcock, C, 'Department eases paths where angels fear to tread', *The Guardian*, 17 January 1994, p10.
Woodcock, C, 'Spreading data networks could prevent fall into funding gap', *The Guardian*, 27 June 1994, p14.
Woodcock, C, 'Survey finds that taking soft option can provide a solid financial boost', *The Guardian*, 5 September 1994, p12.
Woodcock, C, 'Chance for state-funded show of long-termism', *The Guardian*, 19 September 1994, p14.
Woodcock, C, 'Europe must rescue second-tier markets', *The Guardian*, 30 September 1994, p12.
Young, S and Lowe, A, *Intervention in the Mixed Economy*, London, Croom Helm, 1974.
Zagor, K, 'Son of BES could prove wayward', *The Guardian*, 4 December 1993, p34.
Zysman, J, *Politics and Markets*, Oxford, Martin Robertson, 1983.

House of Commons Committee Reports:
House of Commons Committee to Review the Functioning of Financial Institutions, *Interim Report: The Financing of Small Firms*, London, HMSO, 1979.
House of Commons Committee to Review the Functioning of Financial Institutions, Report, London, HMSO, 1980.

House of Commons Committee of Public Accounts, *Department of Industry: The National Enterprise Board*, 14 February 1980.
House of Commons Industry and Trade Committee, *National Enterprise Board*, 18 June 1980.
House of Commons Committee of Public Accounts, *Department of Industry: National Enterprise Board; Rolls Royce Limited*, 7 August 1980.
House of Commons Public Accounts Committee, *Department of Trade and Industry: Monitoring of British Technology Group*, 30 November 1983.
House of Commons Committee of Public Accounts, *Department of Trade and Industry: Nexos*, 15 July 1985.
House of Commons Trade and Industry Committee, *Competitiveness of UK Manufacturing Industry*, 20 April 1994.

House of Lords Committee Reports

House of Lords Select Committee on Finance and Industry, *Report*, London, HMSO, Cmnd 3897, 1931.
House of Lords Select Committee on Innovation in Manufacturing, *Report*, London, HMSO, 1991.
House of Lords Select Committee on Overseas Trade, *Report*, London, HMSO, 1985.

House of Commons Debates

House of Commons Debate, Industry Bill: 2nd Reading, *Hansard*, 17 February 1975.
House of Commons Debate, National Enterprise Board, *Hansard*, 10 April 1978.
House of Commons Debate, Industry Bill: 2nd Reading, *Hansard*, 18 January 1979.
House of Commons Debate, National Enterprise Board, *Hansard*, 19 July 1979.
House of Commons Debate, Industry Bill: 2nd Reading, *Hansard*, 6 November 1979.
House of Commons Debate, National Enterprise Board and Rolls Royce, *Hansard*, 21 November 1979.
House of Commons Debate, National Enterprise Board, *Hansard*, 26 November 1979.

House of Commons Debate, Industry Bill: 2nd Reading, *Hansard,* 1 December 1980.
House of Commons Debate, Finance Bill, *Hansard,* 30 April 1987.
House of Commons Debate, Finance (No.2) Bill, *Hansard,* 9 May 1988.

Venture Capital Annual Reports and Statements
Abingworth plc, *Issue to the Public* (1983)
Electra Risk Capital (1987 to 1993)
Electra Kingsway (1992)
Equity Capital for Industry (1977)
ECI Ventures (1992)
Legal and General Ventures, Company Statement, 9 March 1995.
Murray Ventures (1992)
Yorkshire Enterprise, Internal Company Statement.

Index

Abingworth plc, 141-2
Agemaspark Ltd, 105-6, 107, 108
Allen, Peter, 147-8
Alternative Investment Market (AIM), 5, 197
Anysz, Barry, 180
Aqualisa Products Ltd, 99-101, 119, 193
Ashdown, Paddy, 13-4
Association of Metropolitan Authorities (AMA), 75
Automation and Technical Services, 97
Avon Enterprise Fund, The, 140
Award Ltd, 116-7

Bank of England, 6, 17, 20, 35, 38-44
Benn, Tony, 46-8
Berglund, Jan, 143-4
Board of Trade, The, 39-40, 44
British Leyland (BL), 50-1, 87-90, 119
British Robotic Systems Ltd (BRSL), 106, 108
British Tanners Products (BTP), 49-50
British Technology Group (BTG), (ch 3) 45, 54-58, 116
British Venture Capital Association (BVCA), 5, 59, 62, 125, 134-5, 145, 151, 152, 153

British Venture Capital Association (BVCA) Performance Measurement Survey, 135-40
Brown, Gordon, 74-5
Brownlow, Claude, 146, 149, 150
Bull Motors Ltd, 104
Business Angel Network for Wales, 68
Business Expansion Scheme (BES), (ch 5) 27, 71-5, 123, 188-197, 198-9, 200-1
Business Introduction Services (BIS), 28, 76-7, 145-50, 175-9, 189, 191, 195, 196, 204-5
Business Start-up Scheme (BSS), 27, 69, 70-1, 123, 175

Carey, Dr Norman, 110, 111-2
Carey, Sir Peter, 54
Cary, Lucius (see also VCR), 28, 145, 146
Celltech Ltd, 55, 96, 109-16, 121
Charterhouse Industrial Development Co., 37
Clark, Rodney, 24
Clarke, Donald, 39-43
Clements, Stephen, 21-22
Cohen, Ronald, 5
Confederation of British Industry (CBI), 17, 20
Coopey, Richard, 38, 39-43

235

Council for Science and
    Technology, 205
Credit for Industry, 37-8

Dodgson, Mark, 55, 110-1
Dorrell, Stephen, 34-5
Doyce Electronics Ltd, 106
Dragon Data Ltd, 67, 141
Drummond, Robert, 23
Dytes Ltd, 56, 113

ECI Ventures, 142-3
Edwards, George, 11, 12
Edwards, Jeremy, 22
Edwardes, Michael, 50
Electra Investment Trust, 143
Electra Risk Capital (ERC), 70-1, 141
Emtage, Dr Spencer, 110
Energy Equipment Co Ltd, 104-5
Enterprise Investment Scheme
    (EIS), 27, 75, 77-8, 123, 179-81, 190, 192, 195, 198-9, 201
Epichem Ltd, 57, 102

Fairey Group, 50, 56, 91
Fairtlough, Gerard, 55, 109, 110
Fisher, Klaus, 22
Forth, Eric, 76
France (performance of financial system), 12

Gallagher, Steve, 146
Genentech, 124

Germany (performance of financial system), 7, 12, 13, 21-2, 43
Glyn, Andrew, 16
Gourlay, Richard, 180
Grosvenor Development Capital, 56, 96, 98, 119
Grylls, Michael, 51-2

HM Treasury, 6, 38-44
Hafren Investment Finance Ltd, 64-5
Hale, Hamish, 110, 111, 112
Hamilton, Ronald, 116-7
Hanson, Lord, 35
Harris, Derek, 144
Harrison, John, 162, 164-5
Harrison, Richard, 147-8, 152, 162, 164-5, 167, 175-9
Hay, Roger, 114
Hemmings Plastics Ltd, 103-4, 108-9
Hodgson, Chris, 146
Howe, Sir Geoffrey, 69-70
Hutton, Will, 9, 12, 14, 36

Industrial and Commercial
    Finance Corporation (ICFC), 6, 34, 38-44
Industrial Reorganisation
    Corporation (IRC), 26, 46, 49
Ingham, Geoffrey, 14-6
Inland Revenue, 157, 180
Inmos, 50, 109
Insac, 50, 109

Inmos, 50, 109
Insac, 50, 109
Institute for Public Policy
    Research (IPPR), 9, 207
Institute of Directors (IoD), 17, 21
International Monetary Fund
    (IMF), 7
Investors in Industry (3i), 39
IQ (Bio) Ltd, 56, 114

JJ Electric Components, 118
J and P Engineering Ltd, 107
Japan (performance of financial
    system), 12
Johnson Fry, 167, 168, 179
Johnston, Edmund, 144
Joseph, Sir Keith, 50-1, 53-4, 55, 69, 110, 125

Kaufman, Gerald, 52
Keith, Sir Kenneth, 54
King, John, 54
Knight, Arthur, 54, 113
Kramer, Daniel, 120, 121

Lawson, Nigel, 159
Leadenhall Securities
    Incorporation, 37
Legal and General Ventures, 143
Leigh-Pemberton, Robin, 35
Lever, Harold, 11
Lidbury, Charles, 41
Lisle-Williams, Michael, 37

Loan Guarantee Scheme (LGS), 70
Lockesley, Gareth, 30
Longstreth, Frank, 35-7

MacDonald, Oonagh, 73
Macmillan Committee on Finance
    and Industry (1931), 3, 6, 33-4, 124
Macmillan, Harold, 13
Macpherson, Ewen, 23
Marsh, David, 30
Marxist ideas, 16, 30
Mason, Colin, 145, 147-8, 150, 152, 162, 164-5, 167, 175-9
Mayflower Packaging Ltd, 107
Moore, John, 72
Murphy, Sir Leslie, 52, 54
Murray, Gordon, 5
Murray Ventures, 143

National Enterprise Board (NEB),
    (ch 3) 26, 30, 45, 46-58, 188-97, 202
National Enterprise Board, Green
    Paper (1973), 47, 88
National Research Development
    Corporation (NRDC), 44-5, 54-6, 98
National Westminster Bank, 35
Nexos Office Systems, 50, 109
Norman, Montagu, 40

O'Brien, Leslie, 35

Oakwood Loan Finance Ltd, 53, 57, 87, 96, 98, 102, 119

Peat Marwick report on the BES (1986), 162, 165, 168
Precision Systems Ltd, 102-3
Prutec, 67, 113, 141

Q1 (Europe), 109

Radcliffe Committee (1959), 45-6
Redwood, John, 52
Rolls Royce, 46, 53-4, 87-90
Rose, Harold, 17-20, 23
Ryder, Lord, 48-9, 89

Scottish Development Agency (SDA), 58-62, 171-3, 188-9
Scottish Development Finance (SDF), 62, 171-3
Scottish Enterprise (SE), 59, 62, 116, 171-3, 188-9, 192, 193-4, 196, 202, 204
Securities Management Trust, 38
Seymour, Don, 112, 114, 116
Speywood Laboratories Ltd, 56, 113
Sutcliffe, Bob, 16

Taylor, Patrick, 73-4, 161
Tebbitt, Norman, 72
Thatcher, Margaret, 8
Thompson, Michael, 146, 149

Training and Enterprise Councils (TEC), 28
Trippier, David, 72

United States (performance of financial system), 7, 123-4
Unlisted Securities Market (USM), 5, 124

Varley, Eric, 48, 52, 88
Vaughan, Caroline, 55
Venture Capital Report (VCR), 28, 140, 145
Venture Capital Trusts (VCT), 27, 75, 78, 123, 195, 198
Venture Economics, 132
VentureList, 150
Vittas, Dimitri, 22-3

Ward, David, 146, 149
Welsh Development Agency (WDA), 26, 62-8, 174, 188-9, 192-3, 203
Welsh Venture Capital Fund, 65-6
Williams, Keith, 144
Wilson, Harold, 44-5, 47-8
Wood, Frederick, 54, 55

Yorkshire Enterprise Ltd, 142

DATE DUE			

Demco, Inc. 38-293